T5-DGG-570

PROBLEMS AND PLANNING IN THIRD WORLD CITIES

PROBLEMS AND PLANNING IN THIRD WORLD CITIES

EDITED BY MICHAEL PACIONE

ST. MARTIN'S PRESS NEW YORK

Library of Congress Cataloging in Publication Data

Problems and planning in Third World cities.
    Includes index.
    1. Underdeveloped areas—City planning—Addresses,
essays, lectures. 2. Underdeveloped areas—Urbanization—Addresses, essays, lectures. I. Pacione,
Michael.
HT169.5.P76   1981   307.7'6'091724   81-5334   AACR2

ISBN 0-312-64737-9

CONTENTS

TO EVELYN AND EMILIO

LIST OF FIGURES

LIST OF TABLES

PREFACE

Growing concern for the future of cities and for the wellbeing of city dwellers, stimulated by trends in world urbanisation, the increasing number and size of cities, and the deterioration of many urban environments, has led in recent years to much emphasis being placed upon the applied or problem-solving approach to the study of the city. The importance of this viewpoint has been widely recognised. The consequent scale and pace of developments in applied urban geography and related fields has inevitably diminished the relevance and usefulness of many standard urban texts. Much of the material that is available on urban problems and planning is now outdated or is restricted in its geographical coverage. These deficiencies were highlighted during the preparation of a series of undergraduate lectures on urban geography and planning. It soon became evident that lecturers, students and others interested in urban problems and planning in the modern world must be prepared to expend considerable time and energy scouring less accessible reports and numerous academic journals across several disciplines in order to obtain satisfactory detailed information. This book, together with the companion volume on *Urban Problems and Planning in the Developed World*, attempts to offset some of these deficiencies by providing a collection of discussions on the problems and planning activities in a number of cities selected to reflect the differing economic, cultural and political regimes of the modern world.

Michael Pacione
Milton of Campsie

INTRODUCTION

The problems of cities and the efforts directed towards their alleviation command global attention because of the increasing proportion of the world's population being affected by such issues. Urbanisation and its consequences are world-wide phenomena and the increasing size and scale of urban settlements is a characteristic of the contemporary era. Four out of every ten of the world's population now live in an urban setting and the expectation is that by the year 2000 AD half of the world's inhabitants will be urban dwellers.

In North America 54 per cent of the population was urban in 1925, while 50 years later this proportion had increased to 77 per cent (Table I.1). Even more dramatic increases in urbanisation have been

Table I.1: Percentage of Total Population in Urban Localities in the World and Eight Major Areas, 1925-2025

Major area	1925	1950	1975	2000	2025
World total	21	28	39	50	63
Northern America	54	64	77	86	93
Europe	48	55	67	79	88
USSR	18	39	61	76	87
East Asia	10	15	30	46	63
Latin America	25	41	60	74	85
Africa	8	13	24	37	54
South Asia	9	15	23	35	51
Oceania	54	65	71	77	87

Source: United Nations (1974).

experienced in the USSR, where the urban population rose from 18 per cent in 1925 to 61 per cent in 1975, and in Latin America, where the corresponding figures were 25 and 60 per cent. The rate of world urbanisation in general has shown no slackening since 1800 and in all regions the trend is towards increased urbanisation and city growth.

The pronounced rate of growth in the world's total urban population over the period 1925-75 is clearly shown in Table I.2. While the growth rate between 1925 and 1950 was 73 per cent, this figure more than

Table I.2: Urban Population in the World and Eight Major Areas, 1925-2025 (millions)

Major area	1925	1950	1975	2000	2025
World total	405	701	1548	3191	5713
Northern America	68	106	181	256	308
Europe	162	215	318	425	510
USSR	30	71	154	245	318
East Asia	58	99	299	638	1044
Latin America	25	67	196	464	819
Africa	12	28	96	312	803
South Asia	45	108	288	825	1873
Oceania	5	8	15	26	38

Source: United Nations (1974).

doubled over the next 25 years. In some areas the growth of urban population was even more spectacular. In Oceania the number of city dwellers trebled over the half century from 1925 to 1975; in the USSR and East Asia it grew fivefold; in South Asia sixfold; and in Latin America and Africa nearly eightfold. United Nations estimates for the next 50 years call for most of these trends to continue. The distribution of the world's population is also changing. Whereas in 1925 two-fifths was in Europe, by 1975 this proportion had fallen by half. Meanwhile, East and South Asia, which together had about one-quarter of the urban population in 1925, had increased their joint share to 38 per cent by 1975. A continuation of present trends would mean that these two areas together will contain about one-half of the world's urban population by 2025. By the same date the urban populations of both Africa and Latin America will also exceed those of Europe. These trends in urbanisation and city growth are reflected in the distribution and different growth rates of metropolitan areas (Table I.3) and 'million cities' (Table I.4). In both cases, while the number and relative importance of such cities remains greatest in the developed realm, the fastest rates of growth are occurring in the developing world. Greater Mexico City is already nearing 18 millions and is of almost megalopoli-

Table I.3: Number of Metropolitan Areas and Average Annual Growth Rate, by World Region

World region	Number of Metropolitan Areas[a]	Average Annual Growth Rate of Metropolitan Areas (%)	Proportion of Regional Population in Metropolitan Areas (%)
World	1387	2.4	–
North America	169	2.4	51.0
Europe	308	1.5	27.0
USSR	220	2.3	27.0
Latin America	125	3.8	30.0
Africa	59	4.5	13.5
East Asia ⎫ South Asia ⎭	481	⎧ 3.4 ⎫ ⎩ 2.6 ⎭	14.0
Oceania	12	2.4	50.0

a. Defined as a single functional unit with a population of at least 100,000.
Source: R.M. Northam (1979).

tan proportions in itself. Several others are only slightly less vast. Bogota quadrupled in population between 1950 and 1970, while Bombay and Singapore doubled. The reality of these soaring rates of growth and the effect on social and economic conditions is of immediate concern, since the impact of urbanisation will press most heavily upon those societies which at present are most deficient in the economic, technological and managerial resources required to maintain and improve a complex urban environment (Ford Foundation, 1972).

The major trends in world urbanisation and city growth seem clear, but there are difficulties in predicting future levels of urban population; this is illustrated by the classic S-shaped urbanisation curve (Figure I.1). Different countries reach different points on the curve at different times. Britain was the first country to experience large-scale urbanisation, and England and Wales reached the upper portion of the curve shortly after 1900, whereas the USA did not reach the same point until approximately 1950. The initial stage of the urbanisation process is characterised by a 'traditional' economic structure (Rostow, 1960).

Table I.4: Million Cities, 1950-85

Region	Number of cities			Million-city population as a percentage of total population		
	1950	1970	1985	1950	1970	1985
World total	75	162	273	7	12	16
More-developed realm	51	83	126	15	20	27
Less-developed realm	24	79	147	3	8	13
Europe	28	36	45	15	19	22
North America	14	27	39	23	32	38
USSR	2	10	28	4	9	17
Oceania	2	2	4	24	27	37
East Asia	13	36	54	5	11	17
South Asia	8	27	53	2	6	10
Latin America	6	16	31	9	19	28
Africa	2	8	19	2	5	9

Source: United Nations Population Division (1972).

Figure I.1: The Urbanisation Curve

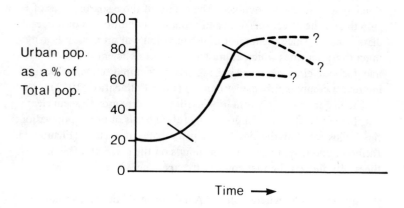

The emphasis is on the agrarian sector of the economy, characteristically accompanied by a dispersed population with a relatively small proportion resident in cities. During the acceleration stage there is a pronounced redistribution of the population, such that from less than 25 per cent the urban component rises to around 70 per cent of the total. This is a phase of concentration of people and economic activity, during which the secondary and tertiary sectors of the economy assume increased importance. As the urbanisation curve approaches 100 per cent, it will tend to flatten, as has occurred in England and Wales since 1900. In this terminal stage the urban population is typically in excess of 70 per cent, with the remainder being rural farm and non-farm inhabitants.

Speculation on the future form of the urbanisation curve must include the possible flattening of the upper portion at a lower level, or even a reversal of the curve, as has occurred in some parts of the developed world (Hall *et al.*, 1973; Berry, 1976; Bourne and Logan, 1976; Falk, 1978). In the developing world most states are moving into the middle section of the curve, although a distinct minority are still in the initial stage of urbanisation (McGee, 1971; Breese, 1972; Abu-Lughod and Hay, 1977). For the foreseeable future the cities in developing countries will continue to grow even if national policy biases favouring urbanisation are eliminated and rigorous decentralisation measures are deployed. Modern industrial and service activities benefit from the economies of agglomeration and, to the extent that industrialisation and structural change are a necessary adjunct of economic development, the impetus for urban growth is well-nigh inexorable (World Bank, 1979).

Study of the magnitude of the urbanisation process should not be confused with an analysis of its underlying dynamics. The urbanisation process denotes a complex interplay of social, economic, political, technological, geographical and cultural factors. Acknowledgement of the utility of the urbanisation curve as a normative model does not carry with it acceptance of the similar-path or convergence theory of development. As Berry (1973) points out, we must disavow the view that urbanisation is a universal process, a consequence of modernisation that involves the same sequence of events in different countries and that produces progressive convergence of forms. Neither can we accept the view that there may be several culturally specific processes but that they are producing convergent results because of underlying technological imperatives of modernisation and industrialisation. Not only are we dealing with several fundamentally different processes that have arisen out of differences in culture and time, but these processes are producing different results in different world regions, transcending any superficial similarities.

Urbanisation in the Third World exhibits a number of key contrasts with the earlier process in the developed world (Berry and Kasarda, 1977).

(1) It is taking place in countries with the lowest levels of economic development, rather than the highest, as was the case when accelerated urbanisation began in Western Europe and North America.

(2) It involves countries in which people have the lowest levels of life expectancy at birth, the poorest nutritional levels, the lowest energy-consumption levels and the lowest levels of education.

(3) It involves greater numbers of people than it did in the developed world.

(4) Migration is greater in volume and more rapid.

(5) Industrialisation lags far behind the rate of urbanisation, so that most of the migrants find at best marginal employment in cities.

(6) The environment in cities of the Third World is usually more healthy than in their rural hinterlands, in contrast to the industrial cities of the West. Urban fertility is greater in Third World cities and net reproduction rates are higher than they ever were in most of the industrial countries.

(7) Massive slum areas of spontaneous or transitional settlements characterise most large cities of the developing world.

(8) Rising expectations mean that pressures for rapid social change are greater than they were in the West.

(9) Political circumstances conducive to revolutionary take-overs of government are present as a result of the recent colonial or neo-colonial status of most of the Third World nations.

(10) Most of the developing countries have inherited an intentionally centralised administration, with the result that government involvement in urban development is more likely in these countries today than it was in the nineteenth-century West.

Clearly, therefore, in examining urban problems and planning in the modern world some disaggregation of the global view is essential. In applying the conventional distinction between the developing world (the focus of this volume) and the developed world (the concern of a companion volume), we are acutely aware of the problems of defining development, and of the great variations within these broad realms, as well as within individual countries, and within cities. Nevertheless, the distinction is a useful and valid classificatory base. Within each of these broad areas, individual cities were selected as representative of the main socio-political and geographic regions. In the context of the study of urban problems and planning, the USA, UK, Australia, Japan, USSR, Poland, Spain and South Africa are regarded as developed countries; and Singapore, Iran, Mexico, Colombia, China, Tunisia, Nigeria and India as part of the developing world. Some basic characteristics of the nations from which cities have been selected for inclusion in this volume are presented in Table I.5.

Rodwin (1970) has remarked on how, prior to World War II, almost no one wanted the central govenment to determine how cities should grow, and yet today, only a generation later, national governments throughout the world are adopting or being implored to adopt urban-growth strategies. These comments highlight the fact that large-scale urban planning is essentially a post-war phenomenon, and that the planning method and political process are inextricably linked. As Webber (1969) puts it, planning is inside the political system. Within the developing world some countries have conservative authoritarian military regimes, while others have reformist and left-wing military regimes; there are also civilian governments with widely differing degrees of popular support. The extent to which the state intervenes also varies (Roberts, 1978). The selection of cities aimed to provide representatives of the range of socio-political ideologies that directly determine the nature of the planning response to urban problems. Subsidiary aims were to provide a reasonable geographic coverage of the modern world and to include important cities which have previously been neglected or which merit attention as a result of changing world circumstances.

This book, together with its companion volume, *Urban Problems and Planning in the Developed World*, is a direct response to the increasing importance that is attached to the problems of cities by governments, international organisations and independent researchers. The book does not set out to provide an account of urbanisation, or a history of planning in the different countries. This book is concerned with the major product of the urbanisation process – the city. The method of analysis favoured is the in-depth case study.

Contents Overview

Mexico may be regarded as a relatively high-income developing country

Table I.5: National Characteristics: Selected, Urban, Economic and Demographic Indices

Country	Per capita GNP ($) 1977	Per capita GNP ($) 1978	Population (millions) 1977	Population (millions) 1978	Urban/total population ratio (%) 1960	Urban/total population ratio (%) 1975	Urban/total population ratio (%) 1980	Proportion (%) of urban population — In largest city 1975	In largest city 1980	In cities of >500,000 1975	In cities of >500,000 1980	Number of cities of >500,000 1960	1975	1980
Singapore	1666	3290	2	2	100	100	100	100	100	100	100	1	1	1
Iran	1242	2160	35	36	34	45	50	29	28	41	47	1	4	6
Mexico	684	1290	63	65	51	63	67	32	32	47	48	3	6	7
Tunisia	596	950	6	6	36	48	52	32	31	32	31	1	1	1
Colombia	399	850	25	26	48	66	70	24	26	48	53	3	4	5
Nigeria	211	560	79	81	13	18	20	17	17	33	57	2	5	9
China	270	230	886	952	19	23	25	6	6	43	44	38	56	65
India	103	108	632	644	18	21	22	6	6	35	47	11	28	36

Sources: World Bank (1979, 1980); International Bank for Reconstruction and Development (1976).

(Table I.5) and since the recent discovery of the enormous extent of its oil reserves the nation seems destined to play an increasingly influential role in the world. One of the biggest problems facing the country is the burgeoning size of the capital city. If the current unregulated rate of growth continues, it will be the world's largest metropolis, with over 35 million inhabitants, by the year 2000. Peter Ward describes the growth of this megalopolis and its problems, and examines the policies that have attempted to resolve major difficulties. He demonstrates how *ad hoc* measures rather than comprehensive physical planning have been the rule, and illustrates the impotence of planning laws through a detailed examination of irregular settlements in the city. He concludes that planning in Mexico is weakened by the fact that so many facets of the political system act against it, and that, unless traditionally sacrosanct elements in the distribution of power are altered, prospects are bleak for the current citizens of Mexico City and for their children.

The interrelationship between political ideology and planning also underlies Alan Gilbert's analysis of urban problems and planning in Bogota. Based on the view that governmental reactions must be seen not simply as technocratic responses to politically neutral issues but as the outcome of political and class conflict, he investigates why particular responses to the problems of the city have gained precedence. He focuses on the issue of power and the subsequent allocation of resources, giving particular attention to the question of land acquisition for the urban poor. He concludes that since, in Bogota as elsewhere, control is maintained through the budget, and budget-allocation decisions are taken at national government level, a choice between better services for the poor and higher taxes on land and incomes is normally resolved in favour of higher-income groups. Improvements occur when there is a threat to the legitimacy of the regime, but such electoral threats are rare in Bogota and, as a consequence, the political system responds to the poor in *ad hoc* fashion rather than through a well-planned offensive to remove the problems.

In a world context, North Africa is only moderately urbanised but, like other parts of the developing world, it is changing rapidly, and North African cities are experiencing high growth rates. In Chapter 3, Richard Lawless and Allan Findlay identify housing and unemployment as the most critical problems facing Tunis, and present a detailed examination of conditions in the Medina, an area which has been transformed from a citadel of urbanity to a central ghetto for migrants to the city. They suggest that urban-planning proposals are no longer characterised by romantic idealism, disregard of socio-economic realities and an obsession with international norms, and that some moves towards advocacy planning are underway, but conclude that planning policies for Tunis cannot hope to be more than cosmetic in character if constructed in isolation from the broader strategies of regional development and the more equitable distribution of human and physical resources.

The initial structure of the urban system in West African states was established to pursue colonial objectives. The rapid growth of urban populations in the decades since World War II is presently straining the capacity of these colonial systems and creating massive problems for the now independent governments. Nigeria has one of the largest urban populations in Africa, and Lagos, its major urban agglomeration, has in recent years exhibited growth rates of over eleven per cent per annum. The problems arising from rapid urbanisation and urban growth are starkly apparent in Lagos. The failure to ensure adequate provision of basic services such as housing, health-care facilities, educational institutions, recreational facilities, water, electricity and sewerage systems remains the greatest challenge to the metropolis. Bola Ayeni examines these problems and points to the lack of effective urban management, serious functional and jurisdictional fragmentation between authorities, and financial insolvency due to the inability of the administration to tap all available revenue-yielding resources, as major contributory factors. The traditional system of land holding in the city also hampers corporate action. He concludes that, while some of the city's problems can be resolved by more effective town planning, others will have to be tackled within a regional-planning perspective, with serious attention given to the decentralisation of activities from Lagos.

Many of Tehran's problems stem from the speed with which the city has grown, its present size and its likely rapid growth in the future. In Chapter 5, Vincent Costello provides a detailed account of the development of the city, its problems and the planning responses. Particular attention is given to planning activities under the monarchist-capitalism system of the Shah. Overcrowding and its concomitant effects resulting from an acute shortage of housing is recognised as the single most important problem in Tehran. As in other Third World cities, the construction of public housing for the credit-worthy does little to ameliorate the position of the majority of the urban poor. Since the Islamic Revolution of 1979, Iran has seemingly moved away from the capitalist philosophy of the Imperial era, which wholeheartedly embraced Western technology and institutions, towards a form of Islamic fundamentalism. Whether that will lead towards socially redistributive policies and alleviation of Tehran's problems remains an open question.

There are more people living in cities, and more cities, in Asia than in any other continent. Part of the phenomenal demographic expansion in India during the last three decades finds expression in the vast urban sprawl that is Greater Bombay, where one person in five lives in slum conditions. Chandrashekar Deshpande and Balsubramania Arunachalam trace the functional and spatial changes in the city's urban fabric since independence in 1947. They discuss the major issues of housing, traffic management, service provision and environmental problems such as flooding, sewage disposal and pollution. The major planning objectives for the city include a comprehensive programme of slum clearance, and the dispersal of population and decentralisation of commerce and industry, in combination with the development of a new urban area on the mainland. Doubts are expressed as to whether the planned decentralisation of urban functions will be accomplished in practice, and lack of finance is identified as a major obstacle to the development of New Bombay. It is suggested that a major problem for Greater Bombay is the inability of different local planning organisations to agree on strategy, and the authors conclude that the establishment of a single metropolitan regional development authority with adequate powers and finances is essential if future urban development is to avoid chaos and disorder.

Singapore is widely regarded as a model of successful urban development. The city state provides a unique example of a former colonial foundation that has emerged from the Third World to the threshold of the developed world, with all the concomitant urban problems such a transition entails. In Chapter 7, Liang Huew Wang and Teck Min Tan examine the activities of the state in the fields of public housing, urban renewal, environmental improvement, population control, transportation and economic development. Most of the changes on the island have taken place in the last twenty years, following the election of the current government in 1959. Planning philosophy is based on an interesting combination of free-market economics together with strong centralised control of land development. It is the legislative power of land acquisition held by the statutory agencies that enables the smooth implementation of large-scale 'space-reorganisation' projects. The government has favoured a pragmatic approach to planning in its determination to create a prosperous urban society. Development decisions are based on a master plan embodied with statutory powers of enforcement and a more flexible concept plan which provides general guidelines. Most of the major housing and employment objectives have been achieved by now, and future problems will be related to the upgrading of older housing and industrial estates, further improvement of the transportation system, diversification of the economic base, reclamation of the sea floor and, perhaps most challenging of all, how to satisfy the rising expectations of urban dwellers as society becomes more affluent.

In China, soon after the communist party came to power in 1949, transformation of the economic role of cities became an integral part of the nation's development policy, under which existing consumer cities were to be converted into producer cities assuming a new role as growth centres of the nation's planned economic development. National industrial-development policy, including the decision to build small and medium-sized cities and to disperse population and industry away from large cities, the emphasis on developing industries in the interior and the classification of cities for investment allocation purposes, has directly affected the growth and development of Shanghai. Ka-iu Fung and Michael Freeberne examine the relationship between national policy decisions and urban planning in the city. They pay special attention to the nature and development of satellite towns and to the various regulatory measures deployed to curtail the growth of Shanghai, since the policy of urban decentralisation represents part of an overall scheme to achieve the ideological goal of creating a classless society by breaking down the distinction between city and countryside, industry and agriculture, and mental and manual workers. They conclude that the Chinese accomplishment in large-scale urban transformation and their success in containing the spatial growth of large industrial centres is a remarkable achievement in urban and regional planning, which should be studied closely by planners in both the developed and the developing countries.

Many of the key problems identified independently in these studies are common to several cities, despite often wide differences in socio-political ideologies. Furthermore, similar solutions have been attempted in many instances. Nevertheless it must be accepted that no one country and no one city has developed techniques, models, plans or policies which can serve as a guide to all. The disparities in political, administrative, economic, social and cultural conditions preclude the formation or adoption of rules capable of universal application. Provided these qualifications are borne in mind, however, there are valuable lessons of experience to be learned from the study of selected cities which, *mutatis mutandis*, may be applied elsewhere.

Bibliography

Abu-Lughold, J. and Hay, R., *Third World Urbanisation* (London, 1977).

Berry, B.J.L., *The Human Consequences of Urbanisation* (London, 1973).

—— (ed.), *Urbanisation and Counterurbanisation* (London, 1976).

Berry, B.J.L. and Kasarda, J., *Contemporary Urban Ecology* (London, 1977).

Bourne, L.S. and Logan, M.I., 'Changing Urbanization Patterns at the Margin: The Examples of Australia and Canada' in B.J.L. Berry (ed.), *Urbanisation and Counterurbanisation* (London, 1976), pp. 111–43.

Breese, G., *The City in Newly Developing Countries* (New Jersey, 1972).

Falk, T., 'Urban Development in Sweden 1966-1975: Population Dispersal in Progress' in N.M. Hansen, *Human Settlement Systems: International Perspectives on Structure Change and Public Policy* (1978).

Ford Foundation, *International Urbanization Survey: Findings and Recommendations* (New York, 1972).

Hall, P., Gracey, H., Drewett, R. and Thomas, R., *The Containment of Urban England*, vol. 1, *Urban and Metropolitan Growth Processes* (London, 1973).

International Bank for Reconstruction and Development, *World Tables* (Baltimore, 1976).

McGee, T.G., *The Urbanization Process in the Third World* (London, 1971).

Northam, R.M., *Urban Geography*, 2nd edn (New York, 1979).

Roberts, B., *Cities of Peasants* (London, 1978).

Rodwin, L., *Nations and Cities* (Boston, 1970).

Rostow, W.W., *The Stages of Economic Growth* (Cambridge, 1960).

United Nations Population Division, 'The World's Million Cities' ESA/P/WP 45 (1972).

United Nations, *Concise Report on the World Population Situation in 1970-75 and Its Long Range Implications* (New York, 1974).

Webber, M.M., 'Planning in an Environment of Change', *Town Plan Rev.*, vol. 39, no. 4 (1969).

World Bank, *World Development Report* (Washington DC, 1979, 1980).

1   MEXICO CITY

Peter M. Ward

Mexico has been referred to as a 'relatively high income developing country' (Grimes, 1976) and since the recent discovery of the enormous extent of its oil reserves (an estimated 50 billion barrels: LBI, 1980), it has become ever more likely that the nation will play an increasingly influential role in the future. In other respects, too, people will look to Mexico for a lead. It will be instructive to evaluate whether Mexico, embarking upon a formal population programme relatively late in 1973, manages to reduce the rate of natural increase from 3.2 per cent per annum to one per cent per annum by the year 2000 (CONAPO, 1978). Similarly, eyes will be focused upon the way in which Mexico attempts to grapple with its unevenly distributed national population, concentrated at two extremities. On the one hand, Mexico City contains around 20 per cent of the national population, and on the other there are over 95,000 settlements with less than 2500 people living in them (SAHOP, 1978). Somehow an integrated urban-development plan has to accommodate these extremes. However, perhaps one of the biggest question marks of all falls over Mexico City itself. Contemporary estimates are that the city contains over 14 million people and, if it continues to grow at an unregulated rate of 5.6 per cent per annum, it would be over 35 millions by the year 2000 (SAHOP, 1978). Assuming that the current strategies are successful and that the rate of population were reduced to 2.5 per cent by 1982 (the medium hypothesis of CONAPO, 1978) and thereafter reduced to one per cent by the end of this century, then the position would be less drastic – an estimated 23,400,000 by the year 2000. The numbers game is just one small facet of the problem. In addition, questions arise about an appropriate administrative structure to achieve developmental goals, about how controls can be enforced and about how opportunities for the bulk of the population – the poor – can be generated without further accelerating the shift from the countryside to the towns.

1.1 The Growth of Mexico City: Emergent Problems and Ad Hoc Planning

Political Boundaries of Mexico City

Throughout this chapter the term Mexico City refers to the urban area or the continuous built-up area of the city. It includes, therefore, most of the *Federal District* (Figure 1.1), which is subdivided into 16 subunits called *delegaciones*, three of which (Milpa Alta, Tlahuac, Cuajimalpa) may be excluded as they comprise, for the most part, rural communities dedicated to agricultural activities. Since the 1950s, urban development has spread over into the adjacent *municipios* of the State of Mexico. The 'metropolitan area' goes somewhat beyond the actual built-up area, and includes two of the three aforementioned delegations and a total of eleven *municipios* of the State of Mexico (Unikel, 1972). The conurbation zone was created in 1976 and comprises some 85 *municipios* of five states. In this chapter little reference will be made to the wider conurbation though, inevitably, it is an area that will gain increasing importance over the next 20 years — an importance that has already been recognised in the creation of a special commission to coordinate its development.

Mexico City: An Overview of Post-war Expansion and Economic Activity

'Fuera de Mexico: todo es Cuatitlán' (metaphorically — outside Mexico City everything is like Cuatitlán, i.e., barren and devoid of enticements). This popular idiom of the 1950s, while exaggerated, reflects the image that then existed that everything was to be found in the capital city. Already by 1940, commercial and industrial consolidation over the two preceding decades, as the nation emerged from the Revolution, had given rise to a city of 1.76 millions (Bataillon and D'Arc, 1973). At this time the city, then on the eve of Mexico's rapid economic development, provided residence for eight per cent of the total population. The Federal District adequately held the population within its political boundary and the entity held 32 per cent of the total national industrial product (Unikel and Lavell, 1979), most of the plant being located in the north around the railway heads. Discussion in this chapter will address the impact of city growth that has been sustained after that date.

The years 1936 to 1940 represent a critical turning-point, both in the nation's history and, more specifically, in that of the capital city. The rapid economic expansion that occurred from 1940 onwards took advantage of the disruption to international trade that resulted from World War II and which stimulated the development of an import-substituting industrialisation programme financed at first by largely

Figure 1.1: Administrative and Political Boundaries of Mexico City, 1970

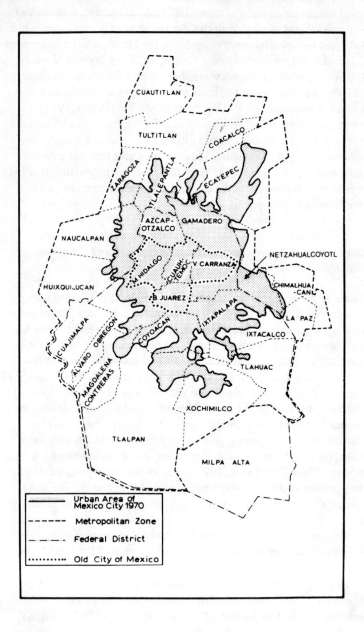

indigenous capital, and increasingly by foreign investment from the 1950s onwards (Eckstein, 1977; Wionczek, 1971). In the first few years of the 1940s the national product achieved annual growth rates of up to 13 per cent and averaged 6.7 per cent per annum for the decade and 5.8 per cent during the 1950s (Connolly, 1980). In large part this dynamism was the result of the expanding industrial sector, which had annual growth rates of 8.9 per cent, 7.3 per cent and 8.2 per cent, respectively, over the three decades after 1940 (Hansen, 1971). The state intervened to encourage this development, providing fiscal supports and heavy-investment infrastructural improvements that would be attractive to industry. However, the impact of industrialisation and concomitant urban growth was highly concentrated upon three centres: Mexico City, Guadalajara and Monterrey, all of which enjoyed the relative advantages of sizeable populations and ready supply of labour, an infrastructure already oriented toward industry and capable of extension, easy access to major financial and credit-authorising institutions, as well as to Federal agency offices necessary to acquire import permissions, etc. In addition, the agglomeration economies that accrue to industries, together with the cultural and social facilities offered by these cities, all further encouraged the location of enterprises in these three centres. Mexico City in particular had outstanding advantages, being the national capital, being situated in the centre of the country and being the seat of decision-making of what was already a highly centralised Federal bureaucracy.

The result was a concentration of enterprises in these three cities, so that by 1965 about two-thirds of the largest private national companies were located in or around these three metropolitan centres, 48 per cent of which pertained to Mexico City. In 1955 this excessive concentration was already causing concern to the government, which abolished the fiscal advantages that had operated previously in favour of establishment of industry in the Federal District. However, the impact of this law was spurious, insofar as it simply shifted the location of new industrial developments to the adjacent state of Mexico where the advantages still applied. This enormous industrial expansion fuelled the demand for labour, which, accompanied by a declining productivity of the agricultural sector (Hansen, 1971), led to a shift of population from the countryside to the towns. Some 60 per cent of all migrants ended up in the capital; of these, 70 per cent came from eleven of the 31 states, and in particular from those states in which traditional subsistence agriculture had predominated (Unikel and Lavell, 1979; Munoz *et al.*, 1977).

The growth of the city was dramatic: 3.05 millions in 1950; 5.17 in 1960 and 8.7 in 1970 (Bataillon and D'Arc, 1973), with annual growth rates of six per cent, 5.7 per cent and five per cent in the three decades after 1940 (Suarez-Contreras, 1972). Today the urban area continues to grow at around 5.4 per cent per annum (COPEVI, 1977a) with a total population of over 14 millions, making it one of the largest in the world. Of course, a considerable proportion of this growth reflects the very high rates of matural increase experienced nationally (3.5 per cent per annum), and in particular its rise from 1.7 per cent in 1940 as a result of the massive reduction in the death rate (CONAPO, 1978). In Mexico City, the birth rate has closely reflected that of the country as a whole (Bataillon, 1964), largely because of its youthful age structure, though we may expect a reduction in the fertility rate in future, as the impact of the Population Council's programme begins to take effect.

While natural increase of the city's residential population is today the most important contributor to the 5.4 per cent rate of growth (it accounts for over 60 per cent of the decennial increase), this was not always the case. During the earlier phase of urbanisation, when the city had less inhabitants and a less youthful age structure, the direct impact of migration accounted for 73 per cent and 65 per cent of decennial growth (1930-40, 1940-50; Suarez-Contreras, 1972). However, once these young migrants had arrived, and they themselves had entered the family-building stage, so the importance of natural increase became accentuated. In some studies the children of migrants are sometimes differentiated in demographic analysis and are referred to as 'indirect' migrants (Munoz *et al.*, 1977).

The economic dominance of Mexico City is apparent from Table 1.1, which indicates that the city's share of the gross internal product was 30.6 per cent in 1940, when the proportion of population was 7.9 per cent, growing to 37.4 per cent though the share of the total population also increased to 18.2 per cent by 1970. It is particularly instructive to observe changes that have occurred within sectors over that period. Between 1950 and 1960 one sees a massive increase in the relative proportion of industrial output that the city provided (from 27.2 to 42.7 per cent of the national total) and within the city the industrial sector provided 39 per cent of the total output. Since 1960, however, this proportion has declined, while services have increased dramatically (to 66.6 per cent). Garza and Schteingart suggest that part of this increase may be explained in that many firms have decentralised their manufacturing operations to outlying cities but retained their administrative headquarters in the capital, taking advantage of the commercial, banking and political structures alluded to earlier (Garza and Schteingart, 1978a).

Table 1.1: Mexico City and the Nation: Gross Internal Product by Sectors of Economic Activity, 1940-70 (millions of pesos of 1950)

Sectors	1940		1950		1960		1970	
	Nation	UAMC[d]	Nation	UAMC	Nation	UAMC	Nation	UAMC
Total	22,889	7010	41,060	12,427	74,215	26,858	151,760	56,731
Agriculture[a]	5170	30	9242	28	13,917	37	17,643	54
Industry[b]	6789	2286	12,466	3378	24,603	10,509	52,009	16,086
Transportation	865	576	1988	1038	3638	2184	4778	2775
Services[c]	10,065	4118	17,364	7983	32,057	14,128	77,330	37,816
			(Vertical percentages)					
Total	100.0	100.0	100.0	100.0	100.0	100.0	100.0	100.0
Agriculture	22.6	0.4	22.5	0.2	18.7	0.1	11.6	0.1
Industry	29.6	32.6	30.4	27.2	33.2	39.1	34.3	28.4
Transportation	3.8	8.2	4.8	8.4	4.9	8.1	3.1	4.9
Services	44.0	58.8	42.3	64.2	43.2	52.7	51.0	66.6

a. Includes agriculture, livestock, forestry, hunting and fishing. b. Includes extractive, petroleum, transformation, construction and electricity industries. c. Includes services, commerce and government. d. Urban area of Mexico City.

Source: Garza and Schteingart (1978a).

Levels of Employment

An overriding problem facing Mexico today is that of achieving an efficient use of its labour resources. Nationally, an estimated 44.8 per cent of the total labour force is underemployed (CNSM, 1974; Cornelius, 1975), with particularly high figures in the agricultural sector (60 per cent), services (31 per cent) and commerce (22 per cent) (Lomnitz, 1975). Nationally, economic expansion is creating only 60 per cent of the jobs that are required to absorb the yearly increase in the workforce (CNSM, 1974).

In Mexico City, the rapid expansion of employment in the industrial sector that occurred during the 1940s and 1950s has declined since the 1960s, so that today an increasing proportion of the workforce looks to the service sector for employment. Between 1960 and 1970 the economically active population in transformation industries in the city declined from 35.7 to 33.6 per cent, while the service sector increased concomitantly from 22.2 to 28.8 per cent (Munoz *et al.*, 1973).

Unemployment and underemployment are particularly selective of certain groups of the population, so that Munoz *et al.* (1973) found, in a stratified sample, that occupational marginality is greater for migrants than for the city-born, and that this is particularly pronounced for recent migrants. One observes the effect of reduced opportunities in productive sectors of employment by certain responses. 'Credentialism' (Balan, 1969), or the requirement of formal qualifications for access to work, is on the increase (Ward, 1976a) and it appears that some migrants who maintain close links with their areas of origin have increased their levels of intra-ethnic consciousness and adherence to traditional customs, as a direct response to the declining employment opportunities during the 1960s and 1970s (Arizpe, 1975). In addition, the problem of unemployment and underemployment appears to affect certain areas of the city in particular. In 1974 an estimated 5.7 per cent of Mexico City's economically active population were classified as unemployed, but rates were particularly high in Ciudad Netzahualcóyotl (6.3 per cent). Estimates for underemployment for Mexico City give figures of 35.3 per cent (Cornelius, 1975). An additional problem is the use of minors in the workforce, which is estimated to include something like 100,000 underage children. These children work largely in the service sector – either in supermarkets, where they work as checkout packers (*cerillos*), and are often wholly dependent upon tips, or on the streets, working as boot-blacks, selling chewing gum, comics, etc.

Nevertheless, a large proportion of the population is gainfully employed and, in various studies of irregular settlements, something like 60 per cent of heads of household were reported as having secure employment – indicated by their coverage and social-security affiliation, which is automatic for all blue-collar employees. However, while many have guaranteed employment, wages are low. In 1974, 70 per cent of the economically active population in the metropolitan area earned around the minimum wage or less. Today the proportion remains the same, and the 1979 minimum wage equalled approximately US $ 170 per month, which would just be adequate for a family to subsist. The problem is that Mexico's development does not appear to be resulting in any improvement in income distributions (Eckstein, 1977). Navarrete (1972) found that a projection to 1980 of trends operating between 1958 and 1963 would result in an overall decline of the percentage total income in the lowest-paid 40 per cent of the population, with a corresponding increase in the coefficient of income concentration. She demonstrated that, even allowing for modest swings in favour of the most disadvantaged income groups, the situation would change very little.

Physical Expansion

The pattern of Mexico City's physical expansion was one of initial concentration in the four central *delegaciones* up until 1950, which then contained around 70 per cent of the urban area (DDF, 1976). Table 1.2 shows the rapid process of suburbanisation that took place thereafter, first affecting the *delegaciones* surrounding the central four (between 1950 and 1960) and then, from 1960 onwards, spilling over into the adjacent state of Mexico. Netzahualcóyotl, formally established in 1964 (but populated from 1959 onwards), had a total population of over 600,000 by 1970. Today it accommodates something in the order of two millions.

City expansion has meant the absorption into the built-up area of many previously outlying towns such as Tacubaya, San Angel, Coyoacán, Tlalpan, Coapa, etc. Also, as we shall see below in greater detail, much of this development comprises irregular settlements established on agricultural lands or, more commonly, on lands unsuited to urbanisation (such as the desiccated lake bed of Texcoco in the east, and the ravine and disused open-cast mines in western districts). This largely uncontrolled development has led to serious problems of large urban sprawl and low levels of open spaces. Today, data for the Federal District only show that 54 per cent of the built-up area is allocated to housing, five per cent to industry, five per cent to services and only six per cent to open spaces and 28 per cent to transport networks. The level of 'green spaces' of 0.5 m^2 per person is very low compared with current recommended norms of 12.5 m^2 per person (DDF, 1980).

Industrial sites are overly concentrated in the north, with heavy industry particularly concentrated around the railheads. Industrial development in the east of the city (in Ixtapalapa), where there are lower levels of infrastructure and lower densities, largely comprises light industry. The *delegacion* of Alvaro Obregon in the west provides a locus for cement and associated manufacturing industries. Significantly, while zoning laws — on the statute since 1936 and 1941 — have been virtually irrelevant in controlling and directing Mexico City's growth, the early zoning of industrial sites (1941) did set the direction of what would become industrial and, by default, low-income residential areas (despite the prohibition of mixed land usage). Once heavy and noxious

Table 1.2: Population Growth in the Metropolitan Area of Mexico City, 1940-75

	Population					1940-50 Annual growth rate (%)	1950-60 Annual growth rate (%)	1960-70 Annual growth rate (%)
	1940	1950	1960	1970	1975			
Metropolitan area	1,670,314	2,960,686	5,144,462	8,889,100	11,550,075	5.9	5.2	5.4
Federal District	1,670,314	2,931,542	4,833,102	6,963,286	8,157,558	5.8	4.8	3.7
Delegations:								
Bénito Juarez	⎱1,448,422	336,649	521,415	577,004	577,004	⎱3.9	⎱4.4	1.2
Cuauhtemoc		990,572	966,888	925,752	858,949		-0.4	-0.4
M. Hidalgo	⎰	420,716	612,428	604,623	608,149	⎰	3.8	-0.1
V. Carranza		375,848	570,194	747,513	767,972		4.3	2.7
Atzcapotzalco	63,000	188,596	372,244	542,994	543,400	11.6	7.0	3.9
G. Madero	41,567	290,826	701,333	1,224,536	1,386,776	21.5	9.2	5.7
Ixtacalco	11,212	37,328	200,066	480,412	517,999	12.8	18.3	9.2
Ixtapalapa	25,393	74,240	264,876	555,980	844,194	11.3	13.6	7.7
Coyoacán	35,248	68,952	156,603	319,794	468,815	6.9	8.5	7.4
A. Obregon	32,313	125,771	274,923	501,856	766,332	14.6	8.1	6.2
M. Contreras	13,159	22,044	40,873	99,881	148,349	5.3	6.4	9.4
Caujimalpa			19,278	37,212	99,173		7.1	6.8

Table 1.2 (Continued)

Tlalpan		61,426	149,335	233,588		6.5	9.3
Xochimilco		70,552	119,079	231,129		4.1	5.4
Tlahuac			64,454	105,729			17.8
State of Mexico	29,144	233,764	1,907,003		7.2	12.1	
Municipalities:							
Tlalnepantla	29,144	106,301	387,378	n.d.	7.2	13.8	13.8
Ecatepec		41,067	232,687	n.d.		10.4	18.9
Naucalpan		86,396	407,826	n.d.		11.1	16.8
Netzahualcóyotl			651,000	n.d.			26.0
Chimalhuacan			18,811	n.d.			n.d.
La Paz			34,297	n.d.			15.8
Zaragoza			47,729	n.d.			19.4
Tultitlán			55,162	n.d.			13.5
Coacalco			13,902	n.d.			13.3
Cuautitlán			42,421	n.d.			7.5
Huixquilucan			34,601	n.d.			7.8

Source: Garza and Schteingart (1978a).

industrial locations had been zoned, the future land-use pattern of
Mexico City was established.

Current population densities in Mexico compared with other world
cities is high and relatively homogenous (except for the downtown area,
where it is over 600 persons per hectare). This is a result of the city's
restricted location in a broad central valley, the lack of adequate suburban transport systems and the small proportion of the city dedicated to
open spaces. Data for the Federal District show that densities in the
peripheral areas have increased steadily between 1960 and 1970 (from
140.6 to 160.35 persons per hectare). This relates to densification processes in the older irregular settlements as land is occupied, family size
increases and lots are subdivided between kin, or frequently sold and
made over for cheap high-density rental tenements (Brown, 1972;
Ward, 1976b, 1978). Many settlements that began as squatter invasions
at the fringe of the city during the 1950s now form part of the intermediate ring, and may achieve very high densities (see the settlement
Sector Popular, with 753 per hectare, in Ward, 1976c). Recent estimates
for the *municipios* of Netzahualcóyotl, Ecatepec, Naucalpan and
Tlalnepantla give crude densities of 217, 137, 154 and 156 persons per
hectare, respectively (SAHOP, 1978). As opportunities for further
expansion are reduced, densities are certain to increase substantially
over the next decade and, in particular, attention will be directed
towards a high proportion of small, scattered vacant lots that exist
within the Federal District (estimated to be around 18 per cent of the
total built-up area; DDF, 1980).

Today the areas that are most liable to change their land use — often
by illegal sale or land captures — are the agricultural and wooded mountain slopes of the south of the city and the *ejido* lands[1] located to the
west of the city in Naucalpan, Zaragoza, Huixquilucan. It is likely too
that low-income residential developments will also extend in a 'corona'
from Ecatepec around the mountain of Guadaloupe into the *municipio*
of Coacalco, eventually linking it up with Tlalnepantla in the northwest.

Housing and Services

Given the large part of the built-up areas taken up by housing, and that
the development of Mexico City, like that of most other Third World
cities, has been irregular via squatting or, more usually, by illegal sale to
low-income households, the housing and servicing problems are two of
the most immediate for the authorities. In Mexico City the *colonias
populares*, as they are called, have increased from 23.48 per cent of the
built-up area and 14 per cent of the total population in 1952 to some-

thing on the order of 40 per cent or more of the total population today (Ward, 1976b; a much higher figure, around 60 per cent, is given by COPEVI, 1977a) and 40-50 per cent of the total built-up area (Figure 1.2). Detailed discussion of the methods of land alienation will be developed later in this chapter, but the period of accelerated expansion of irregular settlements accompanied industrialisation during the 1940s, 1950s and 1960s, and in the latter two decades their growth rate has been estimated at 10-15 per cent per annum (Turner *et al.*, 1971-2). These areas are not the only type of housing alternative available to low-income residents, however. Many of the poor — particularly recently arrived migrants or young unmarried individuals — begin their city residential trajectories in rental accommodation. Different types of rental opportunity present themselves. In the past, the old colonial buildings of the downtown area provided tenement accommodation, but demand for these *vecindades* long ago exceeded supply and today's migrants have to make do with single rooms in new *vecindades* located in the older *colonias populares* of the intermediate ring and, more recently still, in the outer suburbs (Brown, 1972; Ward, 1976b). Another type of rental accommodation is provided by shanties (*ciudades perdidas* — lost cities), which were developed during the 1940s and 1950s alongside railway lines or on vacant lots around the city centre (Ward, 1976c). These areas, unlike the *colonias populares*, show none of the characteristics of upgrading or improvement, largely because rents and insecurity of tenure are both high, factors which combine to reduce the individual's incentive or ability to improve his dwelling structure. It is important to recognise that low-income housing opportunities in Mexico City are not homogeneous, but rather their characteristics vary considerably such that different policy solutions must be developed to deal with each.

For *colonias populares* the principal problems are those of land regularisation (legalisation), and in the Federal District alone it is estimated that something in the order of 700,000 lots required legalisation in 1976. In addition, there is an equivalent, if not greater, number outside the Federal District boundary. (*Plan Sagitario*, an agency dedicated to land regularisation in the State of Mexico, claims to have regularised over 100,000 lots in the period 1978-9.) In addition, most of these areas lack one or more of the essential services. Most settlements begin with no services whatsoever, even those in which the lot was purchased from a subdivider who defaults on service installation. Until 1972, most residents of Netzahualcóyotl and Ecatepec lacked water and drainage; a massive investment programme from 1973 onwards means that today

Figure 1.2: Distribution of Irregular (self-build) Settlements in Mexico City, 1978

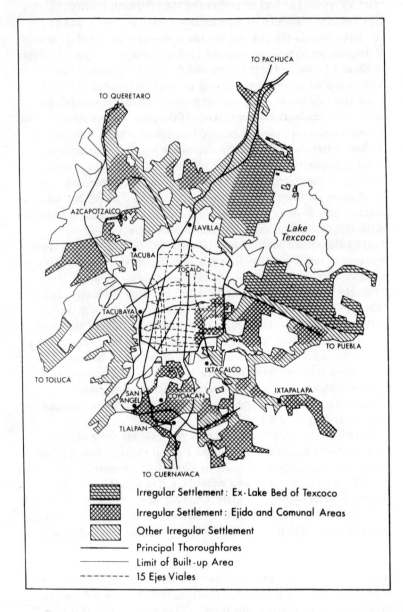

TO PACHUCA

TO QUERETARO

AZCAPOTZALCO

LAVILLA

Lake Texcoco

TACUBA

ZOCALO

TACUBAYA

TO PUEBLA

TO TOLUCA

IXTACALCO

SAN ANGEL

COYOACAN

IXTAPALAPA

TLALPAN

TO CUERNAVACA

Irregular Settlement: Ex-Lake Bed of Texcoco

Irregular Settlement: Ejido and Comunal Areas

Other Irregular Settlement

Principal Thoroughfares

Limit of Built-up Area

15 Ejes Viales

most lots are served with water and drainage facilities, though the cost is being paid for by the residents rather than by the land developers. Moreover, the service is inadequate, with widespread complaints that the water is only on line for short periods of the day and is undrinkable due to unclean piping systems. In many cases, the household drainage networks have fallen into disrepair. In the Federal District today, major water and drainage extension programmes are being undertaken, in conjunction with local residents who put up much of the labour required and, later, will be expected to defray the costs. The official target is to reach the 1.2 million who lack an installed water service (DDF, 1980) and the two million who are not linked to a system of mains drainage.

The problem is not simply to provide an adequate delivery network but also to get adequate water into the city to supply the population. In 1973 the total water supplied to the city was 35 m³/s, (according to the newspaper *El Dia*, 15 August 1973); which was to be raised to 60 m³/s by 1980. The additional 25 m³/s was to be obtained over two stages, the first (15.5 m³/s), coming from wells at a radius of 15-70 km distant and costing US \$ 80 million, half of which was to be assisted out of a World Bank loan. Today 56 m³/s are utilised in the central valley (38.2 m³/s in the Federal District, of which 10.1 m³/s have to be bought from the Central Valley Water Commission). Increasingly, water has to be acquired from more distant locations, and today works are contemplated to go as far as Rio Alto Balsas and Rio Tecolutla — over 200 km away. Pumping from local aquifers has produced severe problems of subsidence, particularly in the central city area, and the Grand Canal drainage system, originally built to operate under gravity flow, now depends upon pumping where subsidence has inverted the gradients.

Mexico City in 1970 had a formal housing deficit of 577,000 units (44.6 per cent of the dwelling units in existence), and this includes 242,000 units for those without homes, 148,000 in need of renovation due to deterioration and 187,000 needed to eliminate overcrowding (Garza and Schteingart, 1978a). The formal response of the private and public sectors to the enormity of the problem has not been impressive. Three broad phases may be outlined. Prior to 1964, public-sector housing was financed by the Federal Government, and the emphasis was upon rental accommodation. However, the total number of units (121,000) that were constructed nationally between 1947 and 1964 was negligible relative to the increased demand. The period from 1964 to 1970 saw a considerable increase in the yearly rate (from 6734 to

Table 1.3: Public-housing Production: Total and Metropolitan Area, 1963-75

	Total	Average per annum	Metropolitan area
1963-70			
BNOSPSA	28,291	3535	23,880
FOVI	92,051	11,501	33,953
DDF	13,000[a]	1625	13,000
INV	5929[b]	741	3996
ISSSTE	27,245[b]	3405	17,790
Total	166,480	20,810	92,619
1970-5			
BNOSPSA	14,954	2991	13,603
FOVI	78,030	19,507	28,793
DGHP	39,461	7892	39,461
INDECO	30,785	6157	20,749
FOVISSSTE	14,721	4907	8212
INFONAVIT[c]	59,965	19,988	22,932
Total	237,916	47,583	136,860

a. Includes housing projects 1962-3. b. Estimates. c. Total to October 1976 = 101,000. The average is calculated for 1973-6.

Source: Garza and Schteingart (1978b).

to 20,810 nationally; Table 1.3) as a result of the establishment of a housing fund, the PFV, which was created to administer funds for 'social-interest' housing and which was guaranteed by the Alliance for Progress. A total of 74.4 per cent of the public sector production during the period was financed by the PFV and, as Table 1.3 indicates, the Mexico City urban area received a lion's share of the total production. It should be noted, however, that much of this housing, albeit social-interest, often fell outside the rate of repayments that could be afforded by minimum-wage earners (Evans, 1974). Under the 1971-6 administration, there was a marked increase in state intervention in housing, in particular as a result of the creation of an agency (INFONAVIT) whose funds were generated by a five per cent levy on the wage bill of employers. As a result it was able to offer low-interest, no-deposit mortgages at favourable repayment rates (representing about 14-18 per cent of

monthly incomes). The impact of INFONAVIT over the first two years
was formidable — exceeding that constructed by the PFV between
1964 and 1970. It also managed to shift coverage to the lower end of
the spectrum, and the majority of credit went to workers earning less
than 1.5 times the minimum wage. In addition, another agency that
operated within the Federal District (*Habitación Popular*) experimented
with a wide variety of cheap housing units, largely to reaccommodate
residents from the *ciudades perdidas* that were then being eradicated
(Ward, 1976c). Considerable though these joint achievements were
between 1970 and 1976, it is again apparent that the Mexico City
urban area received beneficial treatment compared with the rest of the
nation (Table 1.3).

More recently, in an attempt to reduce the attraction of migrants to
Mexico City, the government has reduced its commitment to the construction of public housing and the urban plan, approved in 1980, only
allows for 29,000 new homes to be constructed in the Federal District
through to 1982 (although it anticipates developing some 43,500 self-
build lots; DDF, 1980). However, interviews with heads of all agencies
that are given responsibility for housing lead me to believe that it is
unlikely that either of these two goals will be pursued vigorously. In
addition, INFONAVIT has lapsed into relative quiescence, and today
finances private worker promotions rather than directly building
programmes of its own.

Segregation

Figure 1.3 describes the highly segregated distribution of different
income groups throughout the city, which is a product of the differen-
tial attractiveness of land for speculation and real-estate development,
industrial zoning laws and the existence of rapid transit routes. The
high-income residential districts of the west are located on elevated
land with ready access to the downtown districts. Poor neighbourhoods
are located throughout the city, but the major areas tend to be a large
suburban arc from the southeast to the northwest, corresponding
broadly with the low-lying, saline, ex-lake bed of Texcoco. It is difficult
to ascertain whether this segregation is increasing or decreasing. Evidence of the former would occur if there is significant further development of rented housing for the very poor in the existing *colonias
populares*. However, against this is the fact that lands in the northeast
and east today are moving up-market in price, thereby breaking down
the homogeneity of income groups in these areas. Added to this one
must take account of the upgrading process found in consolidating

Figure 1.3: Distribution of Socio-economic Groups and Family-income Levels in 1978

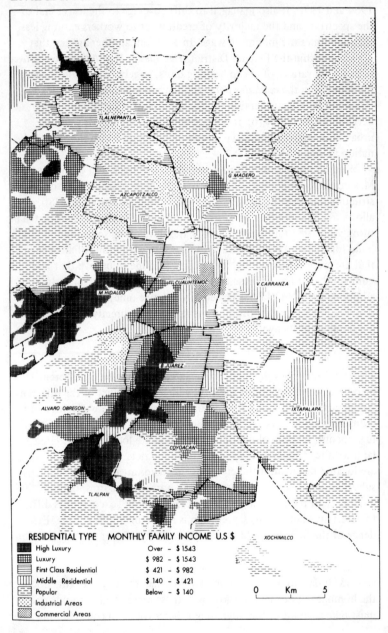

RESIDENTIAL TYPE   MONTHLY FAMILY INCOME U.S $

High Luxury	Over – $1543	
Luxury	$982 – $1543	
First Class Residential	$421 – $982	
Middle Residential	$140 – $421	
Popular	Below – $140	
Industrial Areas		
Commercial Areas		

0   Km   5

settlements, which also leads to increased heterogeneity. Moreover, as outlined earlier, the lands that today are most liable to illegal developments are to be found on the western margins of the cities which, if allowed to develop, will lead to massive expansion of *colonias populares* in the northwest and west.

Pollution

The location of Mexico City in an interior upland basin surrounded by mountains, together with frequent temperature inversions, means inevitably that it is liable to experience difficulties in the dispersion of any pollution that is created. However, the absence of firm pollution controls (or more accurately, the absence of their enforcement) means that this particular problem has reached serious levels. Altogether, 60 per cent of pollution is emitted by cars and buses; this amounts to 5850 tons of pollutants falling on the city daily (Bravo Alvarez, quoted in Sudra and Turner, 1973), and 35 per cent emanates from over 300,000 factories, of which only 12.5 per cent comply with the anti-pollution laws. The remaining five per cent results from dust blows (*tolvaneras*) from the desiccated lake bed in the east, which are now especially frequent during the hot dry season (the average expectancy in March is 13 days; Jauregui, 1971).

The degree of atmospheric pollution has become apparent over the period from 1937 to 1960, during which time average visibility has declined from 15 km to between 4 and 6 km. The photochemical smog produced from car emissions can cause headaches, as well as considerable irritation to the eyes. In November 1973 the *New York Times* estimated that living in downtown Mexico City was equivalent to smoking 40 cigarettes a day. Fox (1972) describes the distribution of mortality and morbidity rates for large districts of the city, and notes that death in children from bronchial disorders in the east of the city was twice that of the overall average.

Transportation

The city has a wide range of transportation systems, which, together, make up a rather chaotic whole. Bus transportation traditionally has been the most important (7.5 million journeys daily) and is cheap, as diesel fuel is subsidised and fare prices have been held down. The effect has been to cause a deterioration in the standard and often a reduction in the length of journey offered for a flat fare, so that changes between systems are necessary. Collective taxis run along specific routes and offer a reasonably cheap method of transport, though most Mexicans cannot afford to make constant use of them. Trams are being phased out, but the electrical trolley-bus system is being extended, particularly in conjunction with the *ejes viales* rapid internal roadway system. The metro system is one of the most modern in the world, but until 1978 had one of the smallest networks (47 km), carrying 1.5 million people daily. Extensions and additions are being carried out today, with the aim of an 85-km network by 1982 to carry 4.5 million people daily (DDF, 1980). The metro continues to operate at a flat fare of one peso, which is the same as when it opened in 1968. This represents a subsidy of approximately four pesos for every journey made.

The principal problems are the time taken to get to work, since many have to travel across the city from peripheral locations, and the congestion created on the roads. The average vehicular speed in the city centre is 12 km/h (4 km/h at rush hours); this compares unfavourably with London and Paris, which average between 20 and 25 km/h with something like three times as many vehicles (Bataillon and D'Arc, 1973). Private cars account for only 23 per cent of total journeys, but ownership is growing, with about 400 new registrations daily.

Development of the road system has taken place in association with different presidential periods. Avila Camacho (1941-6) developed the Boulevard out towards Queretaro in the northwest; Miguel Aleman (1946-52) developed the extensions southwards (Calsada Tlalpan) and part of the internal circuit, which was extended by President Echeverria in 1970-6. President Lopez Mateos (1958-64) gave his name to much of the ring motorway in the west of the city, part of which was extended by his successor, Diaz Ordaz, in the south ready for the 1968 Olympics. Today, true to form, the major project is a system of 15 *ejes viales*; this network of urban freeways resulted from a massive investment programme to open up what had previously been two- or three-lane roads, many of them residential. These were converted into one-way and two-way three- to four-lane highways, sometimes through compulsory purchase and the wholesale demolition of streets. It runs on a computerised traffic-control system. In addition, major construction programmes are in hand to extend the metro, to complete the outer ring motorway and to extend the *ejes* beyond the interior circuit. The total cost of these works has been estimated at an additional 150,000 million Mexican pesos.[2] The philosophy appears to be one of generating a more rapid system, which will improve or at least preserve the *status quo* as far as travel is concerned, rather than a total rethink about how economic opportunities might be better distributed throughout the metropolitan area, thereby reducing the need to make long journeys.

These problems, growing in intensity, read something like a catalogue of horrors. State intervention to predict, control and regulate growth has either been nonexistent or, where there has been a policy, it has been promoted by an individual president or mayor and abandoned once his term of office came to an end. This is clear on transportation policy, and the network has developed in fits and starts as different individuals have sponsored the development of different elements within it. Political and economic interests often lie behind such projects. President Echeverria (1971-6) was opposed to massive investment in the development of the metro, both as a result of his familial ties with the groups who run the bus networks, and because the original system was a product of his predecessor. The *ejes viales* programme has facilitated a vast extension of patronage from the mayor to major construction firms. Elsewhere, highway development has often been designed to inflate the value of lands held by major decision-makers. There has been a total lack of an integrated programme that transcends presidential periods. Solutions have been reactive to problems as they have been perceived by the National Executive.

Housing and settlement policy emerged only after the problems had evolved. In 1964 Freiden argued for the need to take over lands in the east of the city so as to achieve a regulated expansion of settlement in that area in future years. The opportunity was lost, partly, as we shall see below, because of the complicity between government authorities and real estate developers. Only when massive protest arose over the irregularity of land title and the lack of services in Netzahualcóyotl and Ecatepec in the early 1970s did the government react, installing services and creating various agencies responsible for land regularisation CoRett in 1973; FIDEURBE in 1973; INDECO in 1971; etc.). Formal programmes of housing projects evolved from representations that were made by the construction industry in the early 1960s (COPEVI, 1977a), and the housing funds created in 1964 arose from internationally promoted seed capital and guarantees. President Echeverria's housing policy — regularisation and some servicing of irregular settlements and the creation of INFONAVIT — was a response to the social unrest of the period rather than the basis of an integrated programme (Tello, 1978).

Land-use planning has been insignificant. Despite its existence since 1936, it has had little overall effect. The zoning of industrial sites did set the direction for future low-income residential development, though it would almost certainly have gone to those areas anyway. The withdrawal of fiscal advantages for new industry in the Federal District had the immediate effect of shifting developments into the adjacent State of Mexico. Likewise, the prohibition on the development of low-income subdivisions in the Federal District at the beginning of the 1950s had little effect, because permissions for large areas between the east of the then built-up area and the Federal District boundary had already been granted, even though they were only developed subsequently. Elsewhere lands were 'invaded' often with the landlord's tacit approval. Also, the legislation enhanced the value of real-estate developments then incipient in the adjacent State of Mexico, which were to become preponderant during the 1960s.

Zoning policy, if effective at all, has tended to ratify developments once they have taken place, rather than providing an instrument against which decisions may be taken. Today, attempts are being made to create an effective zoning plan, as well as an agreed procedure that will allow requests for development permissions to be judged according to technical ground rules. However, it remains to be seen whether this will be successful or not.

Below we describe in detail the contemporary strategies that have been proposed for Mexico City by planning officers. Perhaps we can conclude this section, however, by saying that until 1976 the influence that planners had upon policy formulation was fundamentally weak and their role, to the extent that they had one, was to validate decisions that had already been taken by the National Executive or by executive officers of the Federal District.

1.2 The Impotence of Planning Laws: Irregular Settlements in Mexico City

This section aims to demonstrate the complexity of each of the problems outlined above with reference to one specific sector. It attempts to show how outcomes have been a product of the intervention of different actors in the housing market, negating the impact that planning legislation might otherwise have had. The low-income land market is selected for specific attention since it, more than any other, has had the greatest influence on the physical structure of Mexico City.

Throughout this chapter, I have deliberately eschewed the use of the term 'spontaneous settlement' to describe the self-build-housing phenomenon. This is deliberate, since many authors have described the careful planning that often goes into an invasion strike (Mangin, 1967; Cornelius, 1975), and this fact alone should point to the inadequacy of the

term. However, there is evidence also to suggest that irregular settlements are the outcome of political processes operating at any one point
in time. All too often, research draws attention to periods when invasions or illegal sales were prohibited or opposed, yet the same attention
is not focused upon the periods when they were allowed to blossom; no
one asks how and in whose interest the development occurred, how
different political groups attempted to harness them for their own
purposes, etc. Below I shall briefly relate some of the ways in which
irregular settlements have emerged in Mexico since the 1940s and how
planning regulations were flaunted.

There are three principal ways in which land has been alienated. The
first of these is by illegal land subdivisions, promoted either privately
by individuals or, more commonly in the Mexican case, by real-estate
companies. Lands are subdivided and sold off in plots, usually with
only a minimum level of servicing — electricity, a few standpipes for
communal use and perhaps kerbstones to delineate streets. Contracts
are given which may or may not contain assurances of later service
installation by the subdivider, though these are rarely met. Secondly,
land 'cessions' occur, in which land holders who do not own the land
'cede' it to another user. This has occurred on various *ejidos* in the
Federal District, and is a widespread practice today. *Ejidatarios*, or
their leaders, subdivide lands into lots and make them over to private
individuals, who pay them as though they were in fact purchasing that
plot. The mechanism abuses a provision of the agrarian reform law that
allows for the creation of an urban zone within an *ejido* for the use of
the *ejidatarios* and associated workers (Articles 91 and 93 of the
Agrarian Reform Law). It is not supposed to apply to the creation of
urban residential settlements. Finally, the third means by which land is
alienated is by land invasions, illegal captures of land which tend to
occur when private land holders or *ejidatarios* have refused to subdivide
their holdings, or been prevented from doing so (as in the freeze on low-
income subdivisions in the Federal District between 1953 and 1966).
They may also be politically motivated: functionaries may move against
their political enemies (as happened when President Echeverria prompted an invasion of lands held by a leading newspaper in 1976, and
forced the resignation of its editorial staff who were critical of him) or
political parties or factions may attempt to use the settlement thus
obtained as a power base from which to recruit political support.

These three mechanisms resulted in the massive physical expansion
of Mexico City from the 1950s onwards, yet it is important to recognise that adequate legislation existed to prevent it, or to regulate its

development. In 1941, the Federal District Government increased the
regulations governing land subdivisions, aiming specifically, according
to the *Diario Oficial* (31 December 1941), to 'facilitate the full legal
process and to ensure the efficient installation of public services and to
avoid the creation of sub-divisions without the intervention of the
authorities'. These regulations required the production of full registered
title; the submission of development plans and budgets of the proposed
subdivision; the transfer of funds to a special account as a guarantee
that public works would be carried out, withdrawal being permitted
only once services had been completed; and prohibition on the sale of
lots until services were completed, together with specifications regarding areas set aside for public utilities. In the same year, taxation of
subdivisions was reviewed, reducing the profitability for subdividers.
These two provisions clearly had no impact in preventing the development of low-income settlements in the Federal District, particularly in
the east, largely because many areas, while barely beginning to be populated, had received authorisations earlier. A subsequent total ban in
1953 on any new authorisations was fairly rigidly adhered to by a hard-
line mayor, who held power through until 1966, which meant that most
entirely new developments that appeared thereafter were invasions, or
'pseudo-invasions' with the tacit acceptance of the landlord, whose
hands were tied. Elsewhere, the actual provisions of the 1941 Act were
flaunted with or without the connivance of the authorities.

Therefore, sufficient slack already existed within the Federal District
to allow low-income residential developments to take place relatively
unrestricted during the 1950s. This was complemented by events in the
State of Mexico at that time. Vast areas of land that in the 1920s had
been made over by the government to private landlords for agricultural-
improvement purposes were now being subdivided by a growing number
of large real-estate companies who had since acquired the lands (Guerrero *et al.*, 1974). From 1946 onwards, the state government espoused
the development of subdivisions in the area, and in 1952 regulated the
establishment of moral-improvement boards or *juntas* at settlement
level, ostensibly with a view to assisting community improvements; in
fact, these boards were invariably manipulated by the companies to
drum up buyers for remaining lands. Large blocks of land were priva-
tised during the 1950s, and land speculation was rife, so that between
1946 and 1959 land increased in value by 27,400 per cent (Guerrero
et al., 1974).

In 1958 the state government also provided a detailed law under
which the subdividers were obliged to provide basic services and

infrastructure. Yet government control of the subdivisions was non-existent: no attempts were made to enforce compliance with the regulations, nor were sanctions applied against those who failed to meet them. In several instances, further authorisations were granted to companies for extensions to existing settlements which remained unserviced and were already the source of intense complaints from residents to the authorities (Guerrero, 1974). The reasons for this are complicity between state authorities and the companies (though there is little evidence to suggest direct overlap of personnel), and the large economic interest involved. One study has calculated that an individual accumulated US $ 10 million during the 1970s, from an initial investment of US $ 300,000 (COPEVI, 1977b). The enormity of profits throughout the period gave considerable scope for bribery and manipulation of local and state government. At the local level during the 1950s and 1960s, subdividers controlled the municipal and settlement organisations; independent leaders who opposed them were bought off, imprisoned and sometimes murdered.

It is instructive also to look precisely at the point at which government connivance changed. Subdivisions were authorised until 1969 and no intervention took place until the level of popular protest and mobilisation to get legal recognition and servicing had culminated in a payments strike. The problem then became intensely political, with pressure on the government from mass demonstrations by residents and also from companies who wanted their money. The government embarked upon a major servicing programme under initiatives from the then state governor and incoming President Echeverria, and an eventual solution emerged in a *Fideicomiso* (development trust) in which all actors were represented. The land developers agreed to make over the remaining lands to the *Fideicomiso* administration, and to take only 60 per cent of the amount owing to them. The government agreed to instal services which were to be paid for by residents over a ten-year period, and residents were awarded a 15 per cent discount on any outstanding land repayments that they still had. This 'solution' has been strongly criticised (Guerrero *et al.*, 1974; Ferras, 1978) for its apparent partiality towards the subdividers, who had, it was argued, renegued on their previous agreements and were now not only allowed to get off scot-free, but were able to do so with a large part of their interests intact and a guarantee on further payments. The *Fideicomiso* also reflects the *ad hoc* reflexive approach to problem solving in Mexico City referred to earlier, together with the intensely political nature of an 'appropriate' solution.

This crisis led almost to the cessation of this particular mechanism of land development. Perhaps the most common method today is the illegal sale of lands by *ejidatarios* − a process that is also apparently sanctioned by the public authorities. The sale of the lands by *ejidatarios* by false reference to the creation of a residential *ejido* zone is promoted either by the local *ejido* directorate, or often by an engineer from the Agrarian Reform Ministry, who receives a pay-off for each title (*constancia*) that he authorises. The Agrarian Reform Archives are replete with cases whereby *ejidal* residential zones had been created for hundreds of applicants who patently fulfilled no function to the benefit of the *ejido* community (as prescribed by law). However, these technicalities together with the sale of *ejido* land are overlooked by the Agrarian Reform Ministry, because of the internal graft that it creates and, more importantly, because of the relative political weight of the agricultural workers' sector (the CNC) − one of the three pillars of the ruling PRI (Institutional Revolutionary Party). Support derived from this mass base is critical to the political influence that the ministry holds, as well as to the stability of the overall regime. It is unlikely, therefore, that *campesino* interests will be readily alienated.

This situation becomes particularly clear when one looks at recent proposals for the treatment of illegally occupied *ejido* areas. A Commission for Land Tenancy Regularisation (CoRett) was established in 1973 and charged with the regularisation of *ejido* lands. While its original functions also allowed, according to the *Diaro Oficial* (7 August 1973), for the creation of land reserves (for future rational urban growth) and, indeed, for the creation of settlements, it was only allowed to be actively operative in the field of regularisation − a process that involves expropriation of the areas affected, indemnisation to the *ejidatarios* and resale to lot holders with full title. Again the procedure *sanctions* the illegal promoters of land development. The restructuring of the public administration (1977) and the allocation of responsibility for human settlements to a ministry of the same name has given weight to recent attempts to create land reserves often at the expense of *ejido* lands. This, ironically, further promotes *ejidatarios* to subdivide and sell willy nilly, in order to guarantee an *ex gratia* initial payment and to elevate the value of the second payment that they can expect to receive via indemnisation. Attempts to forestall this or to quicken the takeover of *ejido* lands are met with resistance from the Agrarian Reform Ministry, and the suggestion of incorporating sanctions against *ejidatarios* is not even countenanced, being regarded as politically untenable. Therefore the problem as articulated here is one of finding not so much a technical solution but a way through the political interests and rivalries embodied within Mexican public administration.

Other policies adopted in the Federal District have been to create urban-development trust agencies (FIDEURBE, 1973-6) charged with the regularisation of land in the most conflictive settlements. More recently, the new administration (1977-82) has created a Commission for Urban Development of the Federal District, one of the principal actions of which has been to begin to regularise the illegal lots in the Federal District area. Recently also, firm action has been taken to eradicate new invasions as they occur in the Federal District, which, while effective insofar as land control is concerned, is having two principal effects. The first is to increase densities in existing areas, which is part of the rationale of the urban-development plan. Secondly, it has led to increased pressures for land sales on *ejido* lands, which, as we have seen, form a relatively 'protected' area. Although *ejidos* exist in the south of the city, they comprise for the most part very productive agricultural lands, so that the pressure is growing in the surrounding State of Mexico, principally in Naucalpan, Huixquilucan and Zaragoza. However, as we shall observe below, it is precisely those areas that are *not* covered by the plan that was recently approved (January 1980).

1.3 Contemporary Planning Commitments in Mexico City

While preceding sections have looked specifically at the problems of Mexico City, it is impossible to evaluate current planning objectives without relating them first to the wider national framework.

Mexico City and National Planning

Despite efforts, during the Presidency of Louis Echeverria (1971-6), to redistribute regional incomes in favour of the poorer regions, to decentralise industry and to stimulate growth poles, little effect was felt on Mexico City, whose growth rate continued at a level of 5.4 per cent per annum and whose participation in the number of industrial establishments actually increased from 32.2 to 34.9 per cent between 1970 and 1975 (Unikel and Lavell, 1979), as did its share of manufacturing production (50.6 to 52.1 per cent) and the economically active industrial population (45.6 to 46.7 per cent). The administration of President Lopez Portillo (1977-82) has established major apparent changes. In 1978 the Ministry of Human Settlements and Public Works (SAHOP) published a national urban-development plan (PNDU) which aimed to

confront the current disequilibrium trends of urban growth. The aim
was to keep Mexico City's growth down to 20 millions, while Guadalajara and Monterrey would take between three and five million people
each, and to create an urban hierarchy with eleven centres of one
million, 17 centres of between 500,000 and one million and 74 cities
of between 100,000 and 500,000 (SAHOP, 1978), thereby creating a
system that would approach log normal.

In short, from 1977 onwards Mexico City became the locus of
policies aimed at ordering and regulating the existing structure. Population increase was to be kept to 20 million maximum by the year 2000;
this was to be achieved by an overall reduction in the rate of natural
increase, together with specific policies outlined by the Population
Council's Regional Demographic Policy (1979). The latter addressed
the question of inter-urban migration; by the year 1982, it was hoped
to have achieved a reduction of over half a million in population
growth, as compared with what would have occurred in the absence of
any policy. This was to be achieved by the 'retention' of population in
rural areas (leading to a nonarrival of 143,000); the redirection of a
further 91,000 toward the Mexican Gulf states; and, lastly, by the
removal of 330,000 people via the administrative-decentralisation
programme.

The Administration of Planning in Mexico City

Planning in Mexico City is not the preserve of a single office. This arises
basically from the fact that political authority over decision-making
does not coincide with the physical city limits. During the early 1970s,
for example, the effectiveness of prohibitions on industrial development
in low-income subdivisions in the Federal District was nullified by the
lack of such conditions in the surrounding State of Mexico, which
simply shifted development over the Federal District limit.

Today, two Federal entities are responsible for the city, each of
which further subdivides responsibilities to different offices. First, in
the Federal District the General Directorate of Planning is generally
assumed to have responsibility for the creation and maintenance of the
overall urban-development plan (referred to as the regulatory plan until
1973, and then as the director plan in the period 1974-7). The production and revision of zoning regulations also come under its jurisdiction,
though to date they have been largely inoperable. In the past, each
Delegación also had its own planning office, though these operated in
close coordination with the General Directorate of Planning. Secondly,
the Commission for Urban Development of the Federal District, created

in 1978 to take over the responsibility of two existing agencies, is also responsible for special development projects and for urban-development planning. Its linkages with the General Planning Directorate have not, to date, been close.

While these two departments have *de facto* responsibility for planning, it is important to recognise that many other general directorates (construction and operation of water resources, the commission of highways and transport, the cadastral and land-tax directorate) also have planning resources built into them and have, in the past, tended to operate almost autonomously under the aegis of the mayor. Certainly the Planning Directorate does not command effective control over the actions of those agencies; rather, the mayor and his closest advisors tend to make critical decisions with or without consulting the Planning Directorate. This low level of horizontal contact and lack of integration, combined with a concentrated channel of communications leading directly upwards, is characteristic of the Mexican bureaucratic structure.

Outside the Federal District, the situation is even more diffuse. The State agency AURIS held a wide range of functions for urban development, housing construction, planning, land regularisation, etc. until the new governor was elected in 1975, but since then many of these functions have been curtailed. It continues to have a planning importance, however, though its location a few metres over the Federal District border rather than in the state capital of Toluca means that it is rather divorced from state-wide planning activities, which are shared in part with the Toluca Municipal Planning Office and the Toluca Conurbation Commission. The principal municipalities adjoining the Federal District have their own planning offices, though these are usually advised by AURIS personnel. However, plans tend to be produced for political municipal entities (e.g., the plan for Tlalnepantla, 1977) and rarely relate or interconnect with those adjacent to them.

In addition to this division of planning functions within each of the two Federal entities, two other institutions have a primary interest in the area. First, the Head of Sector Human Settlements Ministry is formally concerned insofar as it is responsible for the national urban-development plan and for state and municipal urban-development plans. Informally, as we shall observe below, it also became the primary element in the Federal District plan as well. Secondly, the Commission of the Conurbation Zone, established in 1976, is responsible for the elaboration and coordination of a plan for the area that falls into its remit. However, given its lack of executive authority, it is rather weak.

Amongst all these offices a plan or planning body for the urban area of Mexico City is notable by its absence. Although this accurately reflects the political reality, insofar as executive authority is paramount and does not exist at a city-wide level, it also reflects the relatively subordinate status that integrated planning has in contemporary Mexico City.

Given that it is only in the Federal District that any concerted attempt has been made to create a master plan, subsequent analysis is focused almost entirely at this level.

Federal District Urban-development Plans

As intimated in the preceding sections, the function of planning has traditionally been relatively unimportant. Until 1970 it comprised the Planning Office, of which a department was responsible for the regulatory plan. This existed on paper only, and never fulfilled a regulatory function; rather it was occasionally updated to keep pace with events and had little impact in shaping them. Under Echeverria however, it was accorded greater weight; it was upgraded, renamed the General Directorate of Planning and charged with the elaboration of a master plan (*Plan Director*). The *Plan Director* was a major master plan based upon studies carried out in part by the Planning Directorate but more usually contracted out to private consultants and institutions. The end product was never actually approved, nor was the primary and secondary zoning that was drawn up late in 1976 and revised in 1977.

The Director of the Planning Office held her post after the new mayor took office, wholly a result of the presidential support that she enjoyed. However, her aim that the *Plan Director* should become the basis for a first stage of the general urban-development plan of the Federal District was thwarted by opposition from the mayor, who, rather surprisingly, looked to SAHOP to produce the plan for him. The fact that he was prepared to put out a major blueprint of his city's development to another ministry can only be explained in political terms, about which we can only speculate. Certainly the mayor had a very close tie with both the Minister and the Underminister of Human Settlements, and he would have been reluctant to delegate, and thereby promote, a department whose head was not his own appointment and whom he did not trust. Also, faced with the danger of mounting opposition to the special rapid-transport system that he was literally and metaphorically bulldozing through during 1978-9, and with the need to go back to the Cabinet for additional funds, the mayor needed a plan that might be used to validate decisions already taken. The plan would be doubly attractive, since it could be drawn up by someone else and thus he would not in fact be responsible for it should it threaten to blow up into his face. For SAHOP, the advantages were prestige and cash, the application of funds to them to carry out the plan over a minimum six-month period being 172 million pesos. However, soon after initiation, this plan was suspended, ostensibly because of its excessive cost.

Some months later, in February 1979, the Federal District Authorities again approached SAHOP, requesting elaboration of the plan within 20 days on a budget of 15 million pesos. Inevitably, an integrated development plan produced in 20 days could only be the result of a paste-and-scissors job. However, even when it was produced, it was instantly locked away in a store, since it was no longer considered 'urgent' and therefore more time could be spent upon it. It seems likely that again the mayor was facing a crisis over the financing of the *ejes viales* programme such that he needed to be able to show that it was contemplated within an overall strategy. In the end, he was assured the finance without recourse to the plan, at which point it became wholly inconvenient for a major informative blueprint to be published for public assessment.

This stop-go approach accurately reflects the nature of planning in contemporary Mexico. All of the heads of planning and associated agencies who were interviewed espoused the view that there were many plans but no *planning*, and that planning was totally subordinated to political criteria, though several felt that the production of plans had led to a more efficient programming and allocation of funds. As far as a system of planning goes, however, Mexico is, as one high-level functionary put it, still in the dark ages. This should not be confused with a *lack* of technical expertise. The following description of the plan that was eventually approved demonstrates perfectly that planners are technically competent, but that their plans are ineffective because they are limited to aspects of physical planning *only*.

The Federal District Urban-development Plan

This was finally approved early in 1980 and was the fruit of the joint labour between the Federal District authorities and SAHOP, though the latter took responsibility for the general coordination. It takes as its starting point the national urban-development plan, the Population Council's projections together with the industrial development plan of SEPAFIN. The plan only addresses the Federal District, and little mention is made of the metropolitan area, except to say that the total population in the year 2000 will not go beyond 21.3 millions, 14 millions of whom will be accommodated within the Federal District (DDF, 1980).

The overall objective aims principally at improving the balanced distribution between centres of economic opportunity and the population, a tighter and more integrated physical structure, better access to the 'benefits of urban development' (i.e., land, housing, infrastructure, public services and utilities) and the conservation and preservation of the environment. The strategy adopted contains four principal actions in the urban area and two in the nonurban areas. First, the plan aims to establish and consolidate nine urban centres (Figure 1.4), which will provide the locus for intensive commercial and industrial activity and, to a lesser extent, housing. Each will be complemented by a hierarchical system of subcentres and *barrio* centres. Secondly, collective transport systems are to be stimulated; principally, these will comprise extensions to the metro, the creation of a great number of east-west transport linkages, greater use of pollution-free vehicles (trolley buses) and the extension of the ring motorway (the *periferico*) and of the *ejes viales*. Thirdly, urban corridors of intensive land use are to be developed. Fourthly, a land-use zoning system will be generated, with control over different population densities. In the nonurban areas the plan revolves around conservation areas (Figure 1.4) which will be subject to severe controls; and 'buffer' zones, envisaged as areas between the city and the land designated for conservation, in which only temporary land uses will be granted to public associations — one assumes for sports fields, zoos, picnic areas, etc. These areas imply a low level of construction, and any servicing or infrastructure networks that will be permitted must be independent of the general network of the city.[3]

Turning to an evaluation of the likely effectiveness of the plan the reader should by now be aware of several limitations. First, this plan, like its predecessors, does not address economic or social development issues. It is purely concerned with physical planning and, one would argue, lacks adequate attention to economic, marketing and employment structures, particularly in regard to how each is to be stimulated and maintained in equilibrium with the population growth. Secondly, the heavy dependence upon intersectoral cooperation is unrealistic in the light of past experience and, if our earlier argument is accepted, because it runs counter to the way in which the bureaucracy behaves. Thirdly, it requires programme continuity through 1988, and ideally until the year 2000, which is subject to the same criticism as the second point. Fourthly, it is entirely unclear how the Federal District plan relates to that part of the city which falls outside the Federal District

Figure 1.4: Proposed Land Use in the Federal-district Urban-development Plan

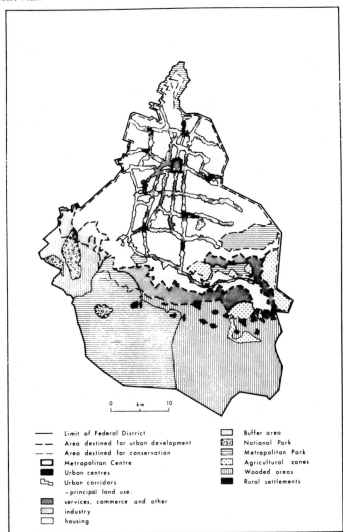

and to possible contingencies that might arise as a result of developments which take place in the area beyond its remit. Fifthly, the proposals are highly centralised and contain no provision for a reconstituted administrative structure within the Federal District, particularly as regards reformed fiscal and tax incomes. Sixthly, many of the programmes are too rigid and unrealistic in their specific aims.

On the positive side, two notable credits stand out. The first is the aim of formally promoting centres which already exist within the urban area and function in a way that the plan desires, albeit inadequately. These centres are, more often than not, the loci of unskilled employment opportunities, cheap markets, cheap social facilities and ready access to public utilities, etc. Secondly, the proposal to create a buffer zone is imaginative and practical. While it is highly unlikely that the planning authorities will be successful in restricting urban growth in this area, it does provide a 'breathing space' during which consolidation of the conservation areas in the zone beyond may take place. The latter are critical elements in the strategy to control growth, and would very quickly be eroded if no buffer zone existed. In this way, the whole plan would be undermined. One can foresee, therefore, an encroachment upon the buffer zone which, while being a symbol of failure, might well ensure the implementation of strict controls in the area beyond.

Conclusion

In the past five years Mexico has embarked upon a concerted effort to tackle its problem of urban development. However, planning has had only very superficial impact upon the resolution of urban problems. All too often, regulations have been waived or ignored when confronted by the political or economic imperatives of the day. Elsewhere, planning has been used as a tool to secure loans from international agencies, to justify or increase budgetary allocation from cabinet or simply to validate decisions already taken. Public participation has been minimal; both politicians and planners have acted in either a paternalistic or patronising fashion. Recent overtures emphasising the importance of neighbourhood committees and consultative councils in the Federal District represent little more than mechanisms for exerting greater control for the Federal District authorities and for the local *Delegados.* Neither has the paramilitary-style voluntary weekend labour force organised by the Governor of the State of Mexico effected participation in decision-making; rather it represents a means of mobilising cheap labour to reduce the costs of community improvements.

Planning is weakened by the fact that so many facets of the Mexican political system act against it. The *sexenio* cycle[4] has meant a lack of continuity from one administration to another. The competition between sectors of public administration or different political entities means little horizontal cooperation and collaboration, which is absolutely essential if the problems of Mexico City's urban area are to be broached. The need for political stability and control makes unlikely any action that will disrupt the very sophisticated structure that exists via the PRI apparatus. Finally, economic vested interests will invariably be influential in overthrowing, stalling or undermining action that threatens them.

Although Mexico has a very real opportunity to use its future oil revenues to tackle many of the problems outlined in this chapter, and while the future of some sort of physical-planning ministry is assured, it is hard to see how the already acute problems of Mexico City may be resolved unless some of the so far 'untouchable' elements in the distribution of power are confronted head on. Elsewhere, urban centres that are growing from scratch will certainly benefit from a more structured and regulated development influenced by planners and planning departments. However, for the current citizens of Mexico City and their children, the prospects are grim.[5]

Notes

1. *Ejido* lands are those agricultural communities established after the Mexican Revolution in which lands are owned communally with individual rights of usufruct only. *Ejido* lands are, therefore, inalienable except for very small residential parcels (up to 2500 m^2) allocated to *ejidatarios* in an *ejidal* residential area.

2. In 1978 there were approximately 24.5 pesos to the US dollar and 45 pesos to the £ sterling.

3. Copies of the plan may be obtained by writing directly to the C. Sub-Secretario, Sub-Secretaria de Asentamientos Humanos, Constituyentes, Mexico DF.

4. The nonrenewable six-year term of office.

5. This chapter is in part a preliminary report of a research project financed by the Overseas Development Administration, 'Public Intervention, Housing and Land Use in Latin American Cities', co-directed by the author and Dr A.G. Gilbert. Full acknowledgement and thanks are also due to Ms Ann Raymond and Dr J. Murray, research collaborators on the project.

References

Arizpe, L., *Migración, etnicismo y Cambio Económico* (El Colegio de Mexico DF, 1975)

Balin, J., 'Migrant-Native Socioeconomic Differences in Latin American Cities: A Structural Analysis', *Latin American Research Review* (Winter 1969), pp. 3-29

Bataillon, C., 'La Geografia Urbana de la Ciudad de México', *América Latina*, vol. 7 (1964), pp. 71-88

Bataillon, C. and D'Arc, H.R., *La Cuidad de México* (Sepsetentas, 1973)

Bion Moore, W., *Industry and Water for the Valley of Mexico*, Banco de Mexico SA Agency Report (1968)

Brown, J.C., *Patterns of Intra-urban Settlement in Mexico City: An Examination of the Turner Theory*, Latin American Studies Program Dissertation Series No. 40 (Cornell University, August 1972)

Castells, M., 'La Urbanización Dependiente en América Latina' in M. Castells (ed.), *Imperialismo y Urbanización en América Latina* (Gustavo Gili, Barcelona, 1973), pp. 6-26.

CNSM (Comision Nacional de Salarios Minimos) Grupo de Estudio para el Problema del Desempleo Report (March 1974)

CONAPO (Consejo Nacional de Poblacion), *México Demografico* (Brevario, Mexico DF, 1978)

—— *Politica Demografico Regional* (1979)

Connolly, P., 'Uncontrolled Settlements and "self-build": What Kind of Solution?' in Peter Ward (ed.), *Self-help Housing: A Critique* (Alexandrine Press, Oxford, 1980)

COPEVI (Centro Operacional de Vivienda y Poblamiento), *La Producción de vivienda en la Zona Metropolitana de la Ciudad de México* (Mexico DF, 1977a)

—— *Investigacion sobre Vivienda*, vol. III *Las Politicas Habitacionales del Estado Mexicano* (COPEVI, AC, Mexico DF, 1977b)

Cornelius, W.A., 'Contemporary Mexico: A Structural Analysis of Urban Caciquismo' in Robert Kern (ed.), *The Caciques: Oligarchical Politics and the System of Caciquismo* (University of New Mexico Press, Alburquerque, 1973)

Cornelius, W., *Politics and the Migrant Poor in Mexico City* (Stanford University Press, 1975)

Cornelius, W.A., 'The Impact of Cityward Migration on Urban Land Markets: Problems and Policy Alternatives in Mexico City' in John Walton and L.H. Masotti (eds.), *The City in Comparative Perspective* (Halsted Press, New York, 1976)

DDF (Departamento del Distrito Federal), *Estudio de Económia Urbana del Plan Director*, vol. III (unpublished, 1976)

—— *Plan de Desarrollo Urbano: Plan General del Plan Director*. Versión abreviada (DDF, 1980)

Eckstein, S.E., *The Poverty of Revolution: The State and the Urban Poor in Mexico* (Princeton University Press, New Jersey, 1977)

Evans, H., *Towards a Policy for Housing Low-income Families in Mexico*. Unpublished thesis for dip. in Arch (Cambridge University, England, 1974)

Ferras, R., *Ciudad Netzahualcóyotl: Un Barrio en Via de Absorción por la Ciudad de México* (CES, Colegia de México, 1978)

Flores, E., 'El Crecimiento Urbano: Causas y Efectos Económicos' in *Tratada de Económia y Agricola*. Fondo de Cultura (1958); also in *Investigación Economica*, vol. XIX

Fox, D.J., 'Patterns of Morbidity and Mortality in Mexico City', *Geographical Review*, vol. 62, no. 2 (1972), pp. 151-86

Frieden, B., 'The Search for a Housing Policy in Mexico City', *Town Planning Review*, vol. 36 (1965/6), pp. 75-90

Fried, R., 'Mexico City' in W.A. Robson and D.E. Regan (eds.), *Great Cities of the World* (Sage, Beverley Hills, 1972)

Garza, G. and Schteingart, M., 'Mexico City: The Emerging Metropolis' in W. Cornelius and R.V. Kemper (eds.), *Latin American Urban Research*, vol. 6 (1978a), pp. 51-85

Garza, G. and Schteingart, M., *La Acción Habitacional del Estado Mexicano* (El Colegio de México, 1978b)

Gonzalez, C., *Democracy in Mexico* (Oxford University Press, London, 1970)

Grimes, O.F., *Housing for Low-income Families: Economics and Policy in the Developing World*, World Bank Research Publication (John Hopkins Press, Baltimore, 1976)

Grindle, M.S., *Bureaucrats, Politicians and Peasants in Mexico: A Case Study in Public Policy* (University of California Press, Berkeley, California, 1977)

Guerrero, Ma.T., Monroy, M. and Rios, H., *La Tierra, Especulación y Fraude en el Fraccionamiento Nuevo Paseo de San Agustin* (unpublished, 1974)

Hansen, R., *The Politics of Mexican Development* (John Hopkins University Press, Baltimore, 1971)

Huntingdon, S.P., *Political Order in Changing Societies* (Yale University Press, New Haven, 1968)

Jauregui, E., *Mesoclima de la Ciudad de Mexico* (Instituto de Geografia, UNAM, 1971)

Lavell, A., 'Regional Industrialization in Mexico: Some Policy Considerations', *Regional Studies*, vol. 6 (1972), pp. 343-62

LBI (Lloyds Bank International), *Bank of London and South America Review*, vol. 14, no. 11 (May 1980)

Lomnitz, L., *Como Sobreviven los Marginados* (Siglo Veintiumo, Mexico DF, 1975); English translation: *Networks and Marginality* (Academic, New York, 1977)

Mangin, W., 'Latin American Squatter Settlements: A Problem and a Solution', *Latin American Research Review*, vol. II, no. 3 (1967), pp. 65-98

Martin de la Rosa, *Netzahualcóyotl: Un Fenomeno*, Testimonios del fondo (Mexico DF, 1974)

Munoz, H., De Oliveira, O. and Stern, C., 'Migración y Marginalidad Ocupacional en la Ciudad de México in M. Castells (ed.), *Imperialismo y Urbanización en America Latina* (Gustavo Gili, Barcelona, 1973)

Munoz, H. et al., *Migración y Desigualdad Social en la Ciudad de México* (El Colegio de Mexico, DF, 1977)

Navarrete, I., 'La Distribución del Ingreso en México' in *El Perfil de Mexico en 1980*, vol. I (Mexico DF, 1972)

Oldman, O. et al., *Financing Urban Development in Mexico City* (Harvard University Press, Cambridge, Mass., 1967)

Padilla Aragon, E., *México, Desarrollo con Pobreza*, 3rd edn., Siglo XXI (Mexico DF, 1974)

Reyna, J., *Control Politico, Estabilidad y Desarrollo en México*, CES, no. 3 (El Colegio de México, 1974)

Rodriguez Araujo, O., *La Reforma Politica y los Partidos en Mexico*, Siglo XXI (Mexico DF, 1979)

SAHOP (Secretaria de Asentamientos Humanos y Obras Publicas), *Plan Nacional de Desarrollo Urbano*, Version abreviada (Mexico DF, 1978)

—— *Desarrollo Urbano: Zona de Conurbacion del Centro del Pais, Esquema de Ordenacion* (DGCP, 1979)

Scott, R.E., *Mexican Government in Transition* (University of Illinois Press, 1964)

Smith, P., *Labyrinths of Power: Political Recruitment in Twentieth-century Mexico* (Princeton University Press, New Jersey, 1979)

Suarez-Contreras, E., 'Migración Interna y Oportunidades de Empleo en la Ciudad de México in *El Perfil de México en 1980*, vol. 3, Siglo XXI (1972), pp. 361-421

Sudra, T. and Turner, J.F.C., *Housing Conditions and Priorities of the Lower Income Sectors of Population. Case Studies of Families in Metropolitan Mexico City*, unpublished paper (Mexico City, June-December 1973)

Tello, C., *La Politica Económica en México, 1970-1976* (Siglo Veintiuno, 1978)

Turner, J.F.C. *et al.*, *Government Policy and Lower-income Housing Systems in Mexico City*, Agency report to AURIS (Mexico City and Cambridge, 1971-2)

Unikel, L., *La Dinamica del Crecimiento de la Ciudad de México* (Fundación para estudios de la población, Mexico DF, 1972)

Unikel, L. and Lavell, A., 'El Problema Urbano en México', Manuscript 1979)

United Nations, *Statistical Yearbook, 1976* (New York, 1977)

Ward, P.M., *In Search of a Home: Social and Economic Characteristics of Squatter Settlements and the Role of Self-Help Housing in Mexico City*, PhD Dissertation (University of Liverpool, 1976a)

—— 'Intra-city Migration to Squatter Settlements in Mexico City', *Geoforum*, vol. 7, no. 5/6 (1976b), pp. 360-81

—— 'The Squatter Settlement as Slum or Housing Solution: Evidence from Mexico City', *Land Economics*, vol. 52, no. 3 (August 1976c), pp. 330-46

—— 'Self-help Housing in Mexico City: Social and Economic Determinants of Success', *Town Planning Review*, vol. 49, no. 1 (1978), pp. 38-50

Wionczek, M.A., *Inversión y Tecnologia Extranjera en América Latina* (Editorial Joaquin Mortiz, Mexico DF, 1971)

2 BOGOTA

Alan Gilbert

Introduction

The social sciences are undergoing a paradigm shift towards a political-economy approach to the analysis of society (Frank, 1967; Harvey, 1973; Castells, 1977; Palma, 1978). While no simple answers are likely to emerge from this new paradigm, at least new and interesting issues have been posed. In this chapter I wish to examine and illustrate issues which have emerged from the debates of the 1970s and which I believe focus attention on the key elements of how a city in Latin America functions.

First, a set of questions posed by Pahl (1975) is still highly relevant in the analysis of any city in the world: 'Who gets the scarce resources and facilities? Who decides how to distribute or allocate these resources? Who decides who decides?' These questions can no longer be limited to an examination of the behaviour of urban managers, that mysterious band of functionaries whose role has been extensively debated (Harloe, 1977; Williams, 1978). Rather, the question must be directed at each of the main resource areas in a city: why do the poor receive the worst land, the worst services and the worst housing; what role does the public sector play in the allocation of resources, what are the constraints on its actions and what are the relations with the private sector; what determines the allocation of resources and, perhaps most importantly, the quantity of resources to be distributed? Pahlian 'gatekeepers' are an interesting phenomenon and an important source of blockage to access on the part of certain low-income groups. But the most vital question is why those gates are established in the first place and who determines the width of the gates. For, gradually it is being realised that the procedures followed by urban bureaucracies are determined by the availability of resources. It is interesting to know how bureaucrats allocate council houses, but much more important to establish how the number of houses to be allocated is determined. The speed of the housing queue and the allocation procedures are, in essence, a function of the number of units to be allocated.

Second, the new paradigm has reminded us that governments do not act in a political or social vacuum. The social sciences have tended to

assume that governments in western democracies act in the best interests of the majority (Simmie, 1974); the ideology of an integrative
society is paramount. Debates over errors in policy have tended to
focus on the misinterpretations of planners, explicable in terms of bad
forecasts, assumptions or political intervention. The idea that governments may be the agents of particular groups within society has never
been entirely forgotten, but it has tended to disappear under the mass
of technocratic literature which has sought to explain how governments
could act more rationally and efficiently. Clearly, the new paradigm,
wherever it eventually leads, will not let us ignore the political dimensions of government decision-making; it forces an evaluation of why the
state acts in the way that it does. If we take a Miliband (1969) approach,
it requires that we look at the state as an instrument of a particular class
or alliance of class groups. It forces us to look at whom the government
represents and whom it fails to help and support. If we take a more
Poulantzian (1973) approach, the question becomes more subtle but no
less interesting. If the state is not an instrument of one particular
faction or class, if it operates autonomously of specific class interests in
order to maintain the system which favours the dominant classes, why
does it take particular actions at particular times? This approach raises
in turn questions about the conflicts that arise between the goals of
legitimacy and accumulation. At certain periods, governments act to
raise the rate of capital accumulation and economic growth; at others,
they are required, or forced, to introduce more equitable measures in
order to legitimise the social order. Without an understanding of the
changing pressures on governments we cannot understand why policies
change. In the past we have tended to assume that policies have changed
because of improved knowledge, resources or technology. Changes have
occurred because a rational decision has been made in the light of new
circumstances. Clearly, technology and changing resource availability
do affect decision-making but so too do the reactions of different social
groups. Many policies have changed, not because of new knowledge,
but because certain groups have registered disapproval of the old course
of action. What was of incidental importance yesterday may become,
through political pressure today, the critical issue of tomorrow. Governmental reactions must be seen not simply as technocratic responses to
politically neutral issues, but as the outcome of political and class
conflict.

Of course, elements of these issues have always been present in urban
geography and in development studies. But the paradigm shift has given
them greater emphasis and raised them from the second or third rank of

importance to top place. The shape of the present chapter has been influenced by that shift in priorities. Rather than pose the issue of what the government of Bogota should do to remedy the obvious problems of the city, this chapter poses the question of why the particular responses that have been taken have gained precedence. It is focusing on the issue of power and the subsequent allocation of resources. It is asking how decisions are made, why those decisions are made in the way they are, and who benefits and suffers as a consequence. In short, it is an analysis of the role of the state in an urban context.

The National Context

Until recently, Colombia was an essentially rural nation. In 1918, three out of four Colombians lived in the countryside and land was still the basis of economic and political power. While Bogota was the largest city and an important commercial and industrial centre in 1918, it did not control the economic life of the nation, being neither a port nor at the centre of the country's most prosperous agricultural region. Almost alone among Latin American capitals, therefore, Bogota was not a 'primate' city. Its lack of economic and political control over the regional economies limited its urban position to that of *primus inter pares.*

Gradually, as the nation has changed, the capital has gained more influence. During the past fifty years Colombia has been transformed from a rural to an urban economy. Since 1934 most governments have encouraged urban-linked development policies. Industrialisation has been favoured and manufacturing activity has increased its share of the gross national product from around eleven per cent in 1939 (IBRD, 1949) to 20 per cent in 1973. Industrialisation has been accompanied by investments aimed at improving transport, electricity and water provision and commercialising agriculture. As a consequence, the urban population has increased constantly, rising from 31 per cent of the national total in 1938 to 61 per cent in 1973 (DANE, 1978b).

Urbanisation has been precipitate throughout the country, as rural dwellers have moved to the cities to escape from agricultural poverty and, at times, rural violence. Between 1951 and 1964 every city with more than 30,000 people grew by at least four per cent annually; the average rate was 5.9 per cent. Commercial, construction and industrial activities expanded in most of the larger cities. Indeed, by the standards of most Latin American countries, the distribution of economic activity in Colombia is still remarkably decentralised (Gilbert, 1974). While Bogota, Medellin and Cali have increased their shares of industrial activity, foreign and local enterprise have established major plants throughout the country (Gilbert, 1975).

It is only really since the 1950s that Bogota has slowly increased its dominance over the country. Despite the omission of several shanty towns from the 1973 census, its intercensal growth rate was higher than that of all its main rivals (Table 2.1). Other economic indicators reflect

Table 2.1: Populations of the Major Colombian Cities, 1951-73

City	1951	1964	1973	Annual change (%) 1951-64	1964-73
Bogota	664,506	1,673,370	2,870,594	7.4	6.2
Medellin	397,738	948,025	1,410,154	6.9	4.5
Cali	245,568	633,485	926,264	7.6	4.3
Barranquilla	296,357	530,651	728,533	4.6	3.6
Bucaramanga	107,887	224,876	377,149	5.8	5.9
Cartagena	111,291	217,910	356,424	5.3	5.6
Pereira	89,675	179,133	245,214	5.5	3.6
Cúcuta	70,375	147,176	216,509	5.8	4.4
Manizales	92,030	195,542	204,024	6.0	0.5
Ibagué	54,347	125,233	180,734	6.6	4.2
Armenia	72,805	155,364	158,388	6.0	0.2
Palmira	54,293	106,502	140,481	5.3	3.1
Santa Marta	37,005	89,161	126,719	7.0	4.0
Pasto	48,853	82,546	119,339	4.1	4.2
Buenaventura	35,087	70,079	115,770	5.5	5.7
Neiva	33,040	75,886	105,595	6.6	3.7

Source: DANE, *Censo Nacional de Población* (1951, 1964, 1973).

this slow but consistent increase in Bogota's urban position (Table 2.2). The proximate cause of this trend has been the increasing dominance of national government in the political and economic life of the country and the government's location in Bogota. Since the National Front government came to power in 1958, the executive has taken an increasing share of activity in all aspects of national life. Government has become involved in labour relations, transport, sport, rural credit, the construction industry, industrial development and export promotion

Table 2.2: Measures of Bogota's Urban Dominance

	1954	1964	1978
Building construction (m^2) (% of largest seven cities)	36.0^a	51.0	54.4
Electricity consumption (% of largest ten cities)	30.2	29.7	35.5
Water subscribers (% of largest eleven cities)	28.8	32.8	38.2
Cheques cashed (% of nation)	32.9	37.6	38.5
Manufacturing employment (% of nation)	–	27.7^c	29.0^d
Population (% of national total)	5.8^b	9.6	12.8^e
Population (% of national urban total)	14.9^b	18.4	20.9^e

a. 1953. b. 1951. c. 1965. d. 1975. e. 1973.

Sources: *Revista del Banco de la República; Censo Nacional de Población* (1951, 1964, 1973); *Boletin Mensual de Estadistica.*

in a sustained effort to 'modernise' the country. While the government's share of the gross national product is still low by Latin American standards (6.7 per cent of GNP in 1973 compared to 4.5 per cent in 1951), its influence is all-embracing. More than ever before, Bogota is the centre of Colombian life; no longer can the regions ignore the decisions made in the capital, and regional elites have increasingly become national élites. Regional businesses have established headquarters in Bogota; regional politicians whose wealth was concentrated in their home areas have sought investment opportunities in Bogota. If for no other reason, what happens within the city is of national importance.

Bogota's Growth and Problems

Since 1951 the population of Bogota has grown from just over 650,000 to something over four millions. Much of this growth has been directly attributable to migration; in 1974 only 27.6 per cent of the population aged between 15 and 59 years had been born in Bogota. Most of the migrants came from the mainly rural areas within one hundred miles of the city, 36 per cent of the population in 1964 having been born in Cundinamarca (the surrounding department) and 26 and 10 per cent, respectively, from the nearby departments of Boyacá and Tolima. Among the migrants, females were by far the most numerous; in 1964 the city contained 485,000 female migrants compared to 387,000 males.

This pattern is most adequately explained by the characteristics of the labour market; women rather than men are employed in domestic service. Migrants do not face insuperable problems in obtaining employment in the city. Indeed, among men there were few differences in the occupational status of recent migrants in 1964 and those who had been born in the city or had lived there for more than five years (Lubell and McCallum, 1978). Among women there was a heavy concentration of recent migrants employed in domestic service (61.4 per cent, compared to 28.6 per cent among longer-term residents). These figures and more recent data from Mohan and Hartline (1979) suggest that Bogota is still a place of opportunities for the migrant and that 'migrants recent or of long standing, are not very different from natives and, if anything, are better off'. They also reflect the fact that all migrants are Spanish speakers and, while many are initially distinguishable from residents in terms of speech, dress and behaviour, they are easily assimilated. Indeed the sheer volume of in-migration makes assimilation easy for the newcomer; everyone has a brother, sister or friend in the city.

Opinions differ over whether migration will continue in such large numbers in the future. As a percentage of the future population growth of the city, it is probable that migration will become less important as the essentially young population of Bogota pushes up the rate of natural increase of the city. In 1973, for example, 51.2 per cent of the city population was under 20 and 83.1 per cent under 40. But fertility rates are falling quite rapidly in the city, and it is possible that the late 1980s will see a rise in the contribution of migration to city growth. What remains certain is the continuation of current rates of population growth.

Rapid population growth is clearly a complication for the city authorities, but would be little more were it not for the problems posed by inadequate employment opportunities and low incomes. By Colombian standards, however, Bogota hardly has an unemployment problem; figures from 1963 show that unemployment has varied from a low of 6.1 per cent to a high of 16.1 per cent (in June 1967). There is no tendency for the unemployment rate to deteriorate; the low of 6.1 per cent was the figure recorded for June 1979. By comparison with the situations in the three other major Colombian cities, the Bogota position looks very favourable (Table 2.3). The employment problem in Bogota is less the shortage of jobs than the low productivity of so many economic activities. Large numbers of workers are employed for long hours in unremunerative activities such as construction, handicraft production, street vending and domestic service. There were 82,000

Table 2.3: Unemployment in Colombia's Largest Cities

	June 1976	June 1977	June 1979
Bogota	8.4	7.8	6.1
Medellin	13.1	15.5	13.9
Cali	11.0	10.0	10.4
Barranquilla	11.2	8.8	6.2

Source: *Revista del Banco de la República* (September 1969), p. 1300.

domestic servants in 1973 among a total labour force of 831,000
(DANE, 1978b). Among the poor, 20 per cent of male workers work
over 60 hours per week and only eight per cent less than 40 hours
(Mohan and Hartline, 1979).

Perhaps it is not surprising that large numbers of workers earn little.
The minimum wage has certainly never been generous and many
workers in the factories are paid at that rate. Outside the formal sector,
particularly among street vendors and construction workers, many
receive much less. Indeed, according to the 1973 census, 62 per cent of
all income earners were earning 50 pesos or less per day. In 1978 dollar
values this meant that 49 per cent of the Bogota population in 1973
were earning less than 70 dollars per month.

The consequence of low incomes is that a considerable proportion
of the city population is suffering from inadequate living conditions. In
terms of housing, the average number of persons per room was 1.6
(DANE, 1977). Altogether, 63.2 per cent of houses had an occupancy
of more than one person per room, and among the rental population
(around half of the population) some two-thirds occupied less than
110 m² (DANE, 1978a). In terms of education, 22 per cent of seven
to nine year olds in 1973 received no primary school education, and
among 15 to 19 year olds 41 per cent had received no secondary education (DANE, 1978b). In terms of health, detailed figures are unavailable,
but the 1977 Bogota health plan noted that malnutrition was common
among children under five, that one third of the population make no
use of the health services, that the incidence of infectious diseases is
very high and that there were only 2.5 hospital beds for every 1000
inhabitants (Bogota, 1977).

By Third World standards, and even by the standards of rural Colombia, these statistics are quite respectable. What is worrying is that there
are few consistent signs that welfare levels among the poor are

improving, even though the city's economy has been expanding rapidly. Between 1960 and 1975, Bogota's average per capita income increased by 30 per cent in real terms, sufficient to have improved the living standards of the poor quite markedly (Svenson, 1977). Unfortunately, there is *prima facie* evidence to support the case that most of the benefits of this increase have gone to the more affluent and little to the poor (Table 2.4).

Table 2.4: Social Indicators for Bogota

Housing	1951[a]	1964[b]	1973[c]
Houses without water (%)[d]	22.8	13.1 (28.7)	8.8 (25.7)
Absolute number of houses without water[d]	19.232	27.803 (60.616)	32.268 (96.953)
Number of persons per room	1.63	1.90	1.63
Houses with more than one person per room (%)	55.5	70.5	63.2
Houses with renters (%)	53.3	47.0	49.9
Education[e]	1951	1964	1970
Proportion of 7-11 age group attending school (%)	44.9	63.2	64.5
Number of 7-11 year olds not attending	51.613	79.557	157.929
Health[f]	1960	1967	1974
(1) Hospital beds in city	5951	6618	8366
(2) Free public and charity beds	4168	3575	4824
City population ÷ (1)	219	314	361
City population ÷ (2)	313	540	626

Sources: a. Housing census (1951). b. Housing census (1964). c. DANE (1977). d. Bracketed figures are the differences between the total houses recorded in census minus the number of residential water accounts recorded by the *Empresa de Acueducto y Alcantarillado*. e. Secretariat of Education (unpublished data). f. City Health Plan and *Anuario Estadistico de Bogota*.

It is clear that the top three deciles in the population distribution have benefited from the economic expansion of the past three decades. It is also clear that the absolute and relative numbers of people living at an acceptable standard have increased — a fact reflected in the increased membership of social-security schemes, the rising numbers of personal bank accounts, the expansion in professional and white-collar occupations, the rise in the number of middle-income homes and the proliferation of private cars. Many poor families also benefited from the city's economic growth. The continued expansion of illegal settlement areas suggested that many poor families were managing to purchase lots on which to build homes, an increasing proportion of which were provided with basic infrastructure. The expansion of the school system allowed a higher proportion of children to receive primary and even secondary school education.

Unfortunately, there is evidence of a less favourable side to the picture. Firstly, although the distribution of income improved to some extent during the 1950s and 1960s (Urrutia and Berry, 1975), during the 1970s it almost certainly worsened. As the inflation rate leapt, so real industrial wages fell, as a result of the inability of manufacturing workers to achieve matching wage rises; between September 1970 and March 1976 the real wages of blue-collar manufacturing workers fell by 15 per cent (Fedesarrollo, 1976). In most societies, manufacturing workers are numbered among the more affluent manual workers, and their failure to maintain their standard of living in Bogota poses the question of what has happened to those people employed in the so-called 'informal' sector. For the poor employed in commerce, construction and services, information is scarce, but it would be surprising if these groups had done much better than maintain their real standards of living during the 1970s. The trend is unfortunate, to say the least, in a city where in 1970 the top five per cent of income earners received the same 30 per cent share of income as did the bottom 70 per cent.

Secondly, although there was a dramatic increase in the availability of services such as water, telephones and electricity, the relevant agencies were unable to cope with the pace of urban growth. Thus, although the relative numbers of houses with services increased markedly, the absolute numbers of houses without services such as drainage and water increased gradually. By 1973, some 700,000 people in the city may have been living in houses without water. Provision of certain other services may well have deteriorated. The number of hospital beds in the city, for example, increased annually by just under 2.4 per cent compared to population growth at least twice as high. Worse still, the rate at which free hospital beds became available slowed, and the ratio between the total city population and the number of free beds worsened (Table 2.4).

Thirdly, the pace and form of urban expansion has lengthened the journey to work, has increased real land prices and has accentuated levels of pollution and traffic congestion. While all groups have suffered to some degree from these urban diseconomies, the poor have suffered more, in the sense that they have had less access to compensatory benefits. Thus, they have suffered from worse traffic congestion and pollution, without the compensation of possessing their own car. They have suffered from rising land prices, without relief from income tax or easy access to credit facilities. There are also signs that, despite higher rates of home ownership among the higher-income groups, the proportion of houses with renters has remained more or less constant during the past thirty years (Table 2.4). Increasing prosperity, therefore, has not brought the advantages of home ownership, even in an illegal settlement, to around one-half of the population.

In sum, while the overall picture of the conditions of the poor has not obviously worsened, they have clearly not improved as rapidly as the expansion in the urban economy would have warranted. And, given the appalling conditions in which so many of the urban population live, merely maintaining those standards is a major indictment of the city's economic organisation.

Land and the State

Throughout Latin America it is possible to distinguish between regular and irregular housing developments. The first is generally confined to higher-income groups, is serviced, has planning permission, occupies the more desirable city locations, is designed by professional architects and built by construction companies. The second provides accommodation mainly for the poor in the form of spontaneous housing, outside the planning framework, is initially unserviced and is located on less desirable and less valuable tracts of land. Within this second group, two categories can be distinguished according to their formation: the land invasion, that is, the settlement of illegally occupied land; and the illegal subdivision, that is, the settlement of land purchased by the occupier without adequate servicing or planning permission. In some cities, such as Lima, Peru, or Valencia, Venezuela, most low-income settlements originate as land invasions. In other cities, such as São Paulo and Mexico City, the poor mostly buy land in pirate urbanisations. Bogota falls into the second category.

In Bogota, the state is involved in land allocation in the following ways:

(1) it decides, though zoning laws and the designation of the urban

perimeter, which land can legally be serviced and which cannot;

(2) it determines the forms of land use and the servicing and density levels in different parts of the city;

(3) it intervenes in the case of disputes between individuals over the use and ownership of land;

(4) it protects the owners of land against the incursions of non-owners.

In this section, I shall be concerned with the role of the state in the allocation of land to the poor. Specifically, I shall ask why land invasions generally are not permitted in the city, why such an extensive illegal mechanism as pirate urbanisation has developed, and how the state seeks to intervene and to legitimise this form of land allocation. Essentially, I am attempting to answer Pahl's question about resource allocation in the context of the availability of land for the poor.

Land Invasions

Land invasions are uncommon in Bogota. A major survey carried out in Colombia by the National Housing Institute in 1972 stated that only 0.7 per cent of Bogota's housing was located in invasion areas (ICT, 1976). This was something of an underestimate, because excluded from the invasion total were settlements which had been formed through invasion but later legalised. Nevertheless, it is true that invasions are rare. A review of newspaper records, various documents of the planning department and the ICT inventory shows that only 21 settlements of the city have ever been referred to as invasions; a small number in comparison with Bogota's 800 or so *barrios*. Included in this total are some settlements which were hardly invasions; in *Barrio* CLAS, for example, most of the population had purchased lots and only a few families had actually invaded land.

Bogota is neither typical nor atypical of Colombian cities as a whole, for the incidence of invasions appears to be a local phenomenon. In some cities, invasions are almost totally absent. Thus the ICT inventory records the following percentages of homes founded in invasion settlements in different cities: Pasto, 0.2 per cent; Manizales, 0.4 per cent and Armenia, 1.5 per cent; Cúcuta, 58 per cent; La Dorada, 20 per cent; Valledupar, 19 per cent; Ibagué, 11 per cent and Barranquilla, 9 per cent.

The difference in the frequency of invasions between cities has no legal basis; the same law applies in all urban areas. It prescribes that the police take action within 48 hours of a written complaint against a group of invaders. If the invaders cannot demonstrate a rental contract, or if they hide themselves, they will be removed immediately. The only real limit on this power is that removal must take place within 30 days of the act of invasion or within 30 days of the date when the complainant first knew of the invasion. If removal does not take place within 30 days, however defined, the invader can only be removed when the authorities are granted a possession order from a civil judge. Civil action can be supplemented, however, by the much stronger criminal law. Article 424 of the penal code declares invasion to be a crime and punishable by imprisonment of from two to 20 months. The law applies whether the land invaded belongs to a private individual or to the state, and has been increasingly invoked since a new security statute was introduced by the Turbay government in 1978. In Bogota, at least, it is now especially difficult to invade land.

If the difference between cities is not explained by the letter of the law then it must be explained by how the law is applied. In cities such as Cúcuta the police are not called in to remove invaders; in Bogota they are always called in. In turn, this difference affects the propensity of poor people to invade land in different cities: the more probable ejection, the less likely people are to take the risks involved in invasion.

In the case of Bogota, the absence of invasions is usually explained in terms of the following factors. First, it is claimed that the weather discourages invasion. This is a poor explanation, because invasions have taken place, and do take place, despite the inclement conditions. Similarly, harsh winters in other areas such as southern Chile have not prevented land invasion (Cleaves, 1974). It is true that in the Colombian cities where invasions are common conditions are much warmer than Bogota, but this is an inadequate explanation. If people are prepared, as they most certainly are, to build shacks on purchased land in Bogota despite the weather, then they would invade land if they believed that they would be allowed to remain there. Second, Bogota is located on the end of a fertile and prosperous agricultural area. This means that most of the land on the edge of the city is cultivated and is valuable. In addition, most of the land has a legal owner, usually a private individual or company. The government does own land but on the whole it belongs not to local government but to particular government or semigovernment agencies who act like private owners. Thus the water company owns most of the mountainside to the east of Bogota and the *Beneficencia de Cundinamarca* (Charity of Cundinamarca) owns a large wedge of land two miles to the west of the city centre. What Bogota lacks is an area of land reserved under colonial Spanish law for public and specifically indigenous population use. These *resguardos indigenas* have been prime areas for invasion in certain cities such as Cali and Ibagué. Their absence in Bogota means that almost every plot of land has an owner with an *escritura* (legal title) who is prepared to call in the police. Third, when the police have been called in to act in Bogota they have usually done so promptly and efficiently. This has been true even when invaders have been eventually allowed to stay. When the police have been ordered to move in, the invasion has usually been successfully repulsed. Fourth, it is said that there is no tradition to invade in Bogota. In some cities there are recognised invasion leaders. During the 1950s in Cali, Rincón and Barborena were renowned for the number of invasions they led. In Bogota, there is only one group which has been actively involved in invasions; a communist group known as the *Central de Provivienda* (Central for Housing). Recently, however, even they have been reluctant to organise or support invasions, and have turned on occasion to the purchase of land to house their members.

There are two additional and, to my mind, more significant factors which explain the infrequency of invasions in Bogota. First, there is an alternative form of land acquisition for the poor in Bogota, the illegal subdivision or, as it is known locally, the 'pirate' urbanisation. For reasons which I shall discuss below, this mechanism seems to work fairly well in Bogota, in the sense that the poor do not seem to be generally dissatisfied with the process and the cost of land, while rising fast, is still within the range of many poor families' budgets. But this alternative presumably would be gladly forsaken for free land if it were possible to invade. The presence of the 'pirate' urbanisation market does not explain why there is less pressure on the poor to invade land. It serves in fact as a safety valve permitting substantial numbers of people access to land and thereby reducing the need to invade. Second, the political system in Bogota has not used land as a source of patronage. In most cities where invasions have become the normal form of obtaining land for the poor, politicians have been active in terms of organising, or arbitrating, the process. Thus, in Lima, the government and politicians have been involved in the invasion process at least since the 1950s. In Chile, the wave of invasions which characterised the last years of the Frei administration were encouraged both by opposition and later by governmental groups (Cleaves, 1974). In Venezuela, the city of Valencia has been the scene of frequent invasions, some at least of which were directly encouraged by both the party in power and the opposition. Recently, in Barranquilla, the fourth largest Colombian city, members of the council have been accused by the National Council

of State of encouraging the invasion of three hectares of land belonging
to private owners. The Council of State has ordered the removal of the
50,000 families and the payment of compensation to the owner, according to *El Tiempo* (19 June 1979). In Bogota, by contrast, invasions
have never become the major tool of cooption and control of the major
parties. They have been encouraged only by opposition groups who
have had relatively little electoral support. In short, the political system
has been as well served by the use of employment and servicing patronage as by invasions. And in this they have been helped by the 'pirate'
urbanisation process and recent accommodations made by the planning
authorities to ease that process.

Invasions, therefore, have been an occasional rather than a recurrent
phenomenon and have tended to succeed only in exceptional circumstances — notably when there has been doubt about the ownership of
land or where the owners have acted inefficiently and tardily in establishing their claim to the land. Thus Policarpa Salavarrieta was founded
in 1961 on land intended for the construction of a new hospital. Inefficiency on the part of several state organisations with responsibility for
the land prevented the speedy removal of the initial invaders. A major
police attack on the settlement in 1966 led to the deaths of a man and
two children and to the gradual de-escalation of the conflict. Today the
barrio is well established, even if it still possesses contraband services.
In another Bogota invasion, in Nuevo Chile, the owners also acted
slowly and although the invaders were removed the authorities eventually ordered that the police move the imprisoned invaders back to
the settlement. This settlement is now serviced by the official agencies.
In sum, therefore, invasions occur infrequently and only when there is
indecision on the part of the owners and the authorities. In contrast to
many other cities, Bogotano politicians do not actively encourage the
invasion process.

Pirate Urbanisation

Pirate urbanisations in Bogota have been extensively discussed in the
literature (Vernez, 1973; Doebele, 1975; Losada and Gomez, 1976),
though certain elements of the phenomenon merit further attention.
Pirate urbanisations are normally created on land fringing the city which
is divided into small lots and sold at low prices with at best limited
services. Their illegality stems from the fact that the subdivision does
not fulfill the local planning norms in terms of the services provided,
the areas of open land designated, the width of the roads and so on. In
addition, while the subdividers normally give contracts (*promesas de*

compraventa) to the purchasers, there are usually legal complications
and deficiencies in the documentation.

In Bogota the pirate urbanisation is the principal means by which the
poor acquire land. Arias calculated that 59 per cent of Bogota's population lived in such areas (DAPD, 1973) even if many of these were
renters, while Vernez (1973) calculated that 45 per cent of families
were living in pirate urbanisations. The area of land covered by pirate
urbanisations was estimated as 38.4 per cent in 1973 (DAPD, 1973)
and between 1972 and 1974 as much as 52 per cent of urban expansion
was through this illegal process (DAPD, 1978). Clearly, it is a well-
established process which is tolerated by the local authorities.

Nevertheless, it is interesting to ask why the pirate urbanisation
exists. After all, it does offend the planning regulations; it poses major
problems for the service agencies; it creates a group of pirate urbanisers
who are on the fringe of the law and who are generally suspected of
making large profits and of exploiting the poor; and it is a process
which cannot be controlled either by politicians or by the planning
authorities. On the other hand, its major virtue is that it allows the poor
access to land and thereby reduces the risk of invasions. Indeed, I will
argue that the pirate urbanisation movement seems to create few serious
problems for the authorities, and hence is permitted as a very necessary
safety valve. It is a safety valve, moreover, which is useful to a number
of powerful groups within Bogota, providing profits, patronage and
protection. In short, it is a mechanism which is highly functional to the
Bogota political and economic system. Let us examine the specific
advantages to different groups.

First, the poor gain access to land and, in the absence of any alternative, they are satisfied. As Doebele (1975) has argued, it provides the
only way in which they can obtain a stake in the property market. The
system is organised so that they can gain credit; indeed, no other institution within Bogota is prepared to lend money to the poor and, once
obtained, land is inflation-proof. It allows the poor to build and consolidate their own housing. It provides the opportunity to improve the
building and rent rooms, thereby increasing their income. Finally, it is
partially legal and most poor people believe, rightly as it happens, that
they will not be removed. Of course, there are certain disadvantages.
Services do take a long time to arrive, especially drainage. Sometimes
the pirate urbaniser provides nothing in the way of services, defaults on
promises or charges high prices. Sometimes the settlements are involved
in long battles with the authorities and with the pirate urbaniser over
servicing. In some cases, it may be supposed that the poor are paying

too high a price for land. Doebele argues that pirate urbanisers charge high enough prices to provide all services. On the basis of returns for 135 'pirate' urbanisations to the *Superintendencia Bancaria*, however, Carroll (1980) concludes that the rate of return to the average pirate subdivider is not excessive. 'The top 25 per cent of pirate subdivisions in sample earned a mean nominal rate of return of 166 per cent annually, compared with a mean of 55 per cent for all 'pirate' sub-divisions studied.' Some urbanisers are forced to pay out considerable sums in bribes to the authorities, and others lose out because their urbanisations are expropriated by the government. Undoubtedly, the mechanism is a second best, and could be improved if the political and technical planning system in Bogota were more honest, neutral and competent. But, surprisingly perhaps, there is confidence in the system. Few among the poor complain bitterly about the system or the urbani-ser. Losada and Gomez, in a study of five pirate urbanisations, found that there was no general distrust or opprobrium towards the pirate urbaniser. Doebele (1975) found that only eight per cent of his sample thought that the pirate urbaniser had deceived them. Our own visits to pirate *barrios* in Bogota revealed no general criticism of the mechanism. Discussions with *barrio* leaders in 16 pirate settlements found definitely hostile attitudes in five cases, neutral views in four and definitely posi-tive views of the urbaniser in five others; in two other cases the attitudes were unclear or conflicting. Since, on the whole, we were talking to *barrio* leaders who often had good reason to criticise the urbaniser, this represents a remarkably favourable view of the process. Overall, the poor in Bogota do not seem to believe that the mechanism treats them any worse than any other aspect of the politico-economic system. Perhaps that is not high praise, but it is sufficient reason for them to accept the system and to gain access to the advantages which it un-doubtedly provides for that portion of the poor who are able to purchase land in this way. Carroll (1980) argues that 'for the most part the pirate market successfully and competitively supplies a relatively low-quality good for which there is a high demand at a modest price and for which there is no satisfactory alternative.'

Second, the pirate urbaniser is clearly a believer in the efficacy of the system. These urbanisers are by necessity out-and-out entrepreneurs who are prepared to take risks and skate on very thin ice. Some see themselves as serving the poor; others are involved only because they owned land on the fringe of the city; others are out to make large profits; others see the process as an entry point to politics. Perhaps surprisingly, there seem to be few links between the pirate urbanisers and the major construction and urbanisation companies in the city. The pirate urbanisers come, on the whole, from lower-middle-income groups who view the mechanism as a risky but legitimate route for upward social mobility. Some exploit the poor; some gain the poor's respect; but most view this mechanism as a first step to something else. In our interviews with pirate urbanisers we found aspirant politicians, land developers and building contractors.

Third, landowners throughout the city clearly benefit directly from the system. Owners of land close to low-income areas in many cities are threatened by invasion. In Bogota, they are not free of unwanted pressures; it is not unknown for pirate urbanisers to threaten the owners of land fringing the poorer parts of the city with an invasion as an incentive to sell out. But, on the whole, the owner has the opportunity either to subdivide his own land or to sell to a pirate urbaniser. In either event, the sanctity of private property is upheld. If it can be upheld in the poorer fringes of the city, then it is quite safe in the higher-income areas. Thus, the pirate-urbanisation movement, by offering the poor some stake in the property system, upholds the property concept throughout the city and maintains the inequality of land holding in Bogota. In other cities, invasions serve a similar purpose when restricted to low-value or public land, but the pirate-urbanisation mechanism serves landowners still better. Thus landowners throughout the city are well served by this strictly illegal system.

Fourth, local politicians are not averse to the system, because it provides them with a source of patronage. Most pirate urbanisations require help in negotiating with the public utilities for services. The presence of a councillor or congressman is a help to a community; our visits to *barrios* in Bogota revealed numerous cases where a councillor had arranged a bus service, reduced the cost of water provision or obtained a grant to pave a road. It is my contention that the politician is less effective in obtaining services than he would claim — such of course is one of the arts of politics — but, insofar as *barrio* populations believe that politicians can help them, the presence of an unserviced population demanding assistance creates obvious political and electoral opportunities. The only major difficulty facing the politician is if services are generally unavailable and no mediation on his part can hasten the process of servicing. In this respect, Bogota suffers less than many other cities, because the water, electricity and telephone companies are quite effective. Most services are available, even if a wait is required. Thus, in short, the populations of pirate urbanisations offer a potential source of support for the politician and their lack of legality and services are an obvious means of mobilising that support.

Fifth, the presence of pirate urbanisations offers relatively cheap housing to the poor of Bogota, which allows higher-income groups to pay lower wages. From this perspective the pirate urbanisation is less adequate than an invasion. Nevertheless, it still represents a means of accommodating the poor at low cost. Despite complaints from the middle classes that these urbanisations are the sources of crime and other social evils, those groups gain more from the presence of poor *barrios* than they lose. The lack of services and high-quality physical accommodation for the poor is an implicit source of subsidy for employers of industrial, commercial and domestic labour.

In general, therefore, my argument is that the pirate-urbanisation mechanism performs a highly necessary role in the city. It serves politicians, land owners and business interests, and to an extent satisfies the poor. At the same time, it is clearly a system which creates numerous difficulties and problems, and requires careful control on the part of the state.

The major problem, of course, is that the poor are often paying as much for unserviced lots in pirate urbanisations as they might pay under a different politico-economic system for serviced lots. If there were adequate taxes on land speculation, an efficient government sites-and-services programme and a larger budget to provide necessary infrastructure and community services, the poor would fare much better than they do now. In this respect the pirate-urbanisation mechanism is inadequate. The mechanism also creates problems for the service agencies. Since pirate urbanisation occupies land without planning permission, there is no effective control on the process of urbanisation. This means that pirate urbanisations often occupy land which is difficult and expensive to service. Settlement along the mountainside or below the level of the River Bogota raises the costs of drainage and water supply. Thus, the public utilities are often forced to provide facilities where rational land-use allocation would have precluded such servicing. In one sense this does not pose a problem for the service agencies. Since they operate on a commercial basis they charge higher prices to consumers than would be the case if the services were more rationally organised. Through cross-subsidisation and higher charges the peripheral *barrios* are serviced; indeed the service agencies are on the whole quite keen to service the *barrios* to prevent illegal use of water and electricity (Fuentes and Losada, 1978). But, from the point of view of the rational use of land and the cheap provision of services, the pirate-urbanisation mechanism is an absurdity. Finally, the system creates many opportunities for graft and corruption. Frequent references are made in Bogota about the bribes required to obtain planning permission for urban development. It is not unknown for councillors to offer their services to pirate urbanisers at a price. Clearly, corruption would exist without pirate urbanisations, but is exacerbated by a process which is so obviously ripe with potential sources of illicit wealth.

But, if the process works neither equitably nor efficiently, it does work well in the context of the way the city of Bogota functions. At the same time it cannot be assumed that it will always work well; it requires careful control by the state if it is to maintain the stability of the system. For this reason, the state has established a series of mechanisms to control pirate urbanisation, which have become both more insistent and more realistic through time. These changes have not occurred in a political vacuum but have been an outcome of pressure from the poor. The most important source of pressure came between 1966 and 1970 when ex-dictator Gustavo Rojas Pinilla and his party ANAPO offered a major threat to the hegemony of the two major political parties. Gaining his support mainly from the low-income population, and attracting much support in Bogota's pirate urbanisations, he won the presidential vote in 1970 but lost the election. This political threat was neutralised after 1970 in part by a major campaign to improve the conditions of the poor in the *barrios* of Bogota. In 1971, a major initiative was launched by the country's president to provide water for the peripheral *barrios* of Bogota. In 1972, a policy was introduced by the government of Bogota, of restricting the growth of new pirate urbanisations and servicing existing areas. New decrees were approved which reduced the level of services required of an urbaniser; it was hoped that more urbanisers would establish legal rather than pirate urbanisations and that subsequent servicing would be easier and therefore less costly. The same decrees made legalisation of illegal *barrios* possible through three stages: first, the *barrio* had to be upgraded through the provision of basic services; second, the *barrio* would be *legalised*, thereby permitting the issue of legal titles to the occupiers; finally, the full range of infrastructure and community services would be provided, which would finally *regularise* the settlements. This correction policy was complemented by the prevention of new illegal settlements through stiffer penalties and firmer application of the law. Essentially, the policy was to help the poor in existing settlements while holding back the growth of new pirate urbanisations.

The programme has not been unsuccessful. Many *barrios* have been legalised, and services have been provided for large numbers of people.

massive increase in the capacity of the water and elec-
he policy has ensured that the proportion of unserviced
has not increased. It is also claimed that the rate of
...e urbanisations has been slowed. In the five years to
...y, 36 urbanisations were established under the minimum-
norms decrees. From December 1974 to February 1977, 24 per cent of
the land in Bogota was developed under the minimum-norm decrees,
compared to 30 per cent through pirate urbanisations (DAPD, 1979).
If the prevention element in the programme has been less successful
than had been hoped, the cause has been the cost of the land and the
shortage of land suitable for minimum-norms urbanisations (Carroll,
1980). Whether because of inappropriate zoning regulations, bureaucratic delay, the concentration of land in the hands of the large
companies or the shortage of land available for low-income settlement
in Bogota, there has been a constraint on the supply of land for this
settlement form. Such a policy, realistic though it clearly is, cannot
work without more fundamental reforms to the land market.

The other initiative of the government to control the pirate-urbanisation process operates through the *Superintendencia Bancaria* (SIB).
Responsibility was given to the SIB in 1968 to intervene in real-estate
companies which failed to satisfy the rules of good business behaviour.
The SIB is thus concerned with urban developments at all income levels,
but has been most occupied with low-income urbanisations. Its most
important powers are to freeze the assets of irresponsible companies
and to jail the urbanisers for up to six years. In fact, the law is inadequately applied and, except for a short period in the later 1970s, has
not been a satisfactory control over pirate urbanisers. It has been
claimed that the office is both inefficient and corrupt; certainly the
agency has taken some very strange decisions (Losada and Gomez,
1976). On the other hand, the SIB faces a genuine problem. As Paredes
and Martinez (1977) put it, they have the power to stop the pirate-
urbanisation process completely, but if this were done it would cause
more problems than it solved. Too strict an interpretation of the law
would severely restrict the poor's access to land. As a consequence, the
SIB in its more responsible periods has acted merely to control the
worst excesses of the pirate-urbanisation process. Where a *barrio* population has complained to the SIB about the urbaniser and where a major
issue has been involved, the SIB have intervened. Some urbanisers have
been put in prison and fines applied. The difficulty for the Superinten-
dency, however, is what to do with the pirate urbanisations once they
have been intervened. The normal procedure has been to appoint ICT,

the national housing institute, as the agent to supply services for the
barrio and to legalise its existence. Unfortunately, ICT have been unable
to perform this role adequately. Indeed, it has been claimed that they
are less able to service the *barrios* than the pirate urbaniser under pressure from the community and the SIB. In 1979, relations between the
SIB and ICT deteriorated to such a point that the SIB began to appoint
its own agents to intervened *barrios*, in the hope that the pace of
servicing and legalisation would be accelerated.

Whatever the deficiencies of both the District of Bogota's planning
agency and of the *Superintendencia Bancaria*, there is today much
closer control of the pirate-urbanisation process than previously. This
reflects the growing awareness among politicians that the pirate-urbanisation mechanism has innumerable flaws and that its worst excesses
must be controlled if the mechanism is to work at all. Most planners
and some politicians want all low-income developments to occur
through the minimum-norms procedure. But government in Bogota
does not function on rationality principles, nor aim to provide the best
possible solutions for the less privileged. It is rather a response to the
pressures exercised by several powerful interest groups. And, in general,
with all its faults, pirate urbanisations serve the powerful groups in the
city sufficiently well to impede any substantial attempt at reform. The
poor undoubtedly suffer from the process but they accept the situation
as the best available in an unfair world.

At the same time there are forces for change. First, the support
proffered to politicians by the poor of Bogota is diminishing. Apathy at
election times has been very high for a number of years, and respect for
politicians as a group is notable for its absence. In addition, there are
real economic pressures undermining the process. Land prices are increasing faster than wages or the prices of other commodities. It would
appear to be more difficult to purchase a lot in a pirate urbanisation
today than ten years ago. Carroll (1980) calculates that purchase is now
possible for families earning around the median city income level but
not to those in the lowest third of the income distribution. Since the
system's main rationale is that it provides the poor with land, any major
limitation of access is likely to lessen the poor's belief in the system.
The point is being reached where the state has to act to modify the
balance of power between those who own land and those who demand
access to it. At present the balance of advantage lies with the landowners, and the Bogota land market represents a major area for capital
accumulation and speculative profits. But if the system of private
profit is to continue in Bogota it must be accepted by all groups, or at

least tolerated. Pirate urbanisation has been a major method of legitimisation and cooption of the poor. If it is undermined because of the failure to hold down land price rises due to the absence of effective land and profits taxes, then the legitimacy of the system may well be threatened. I believe that fear of this legitimacy being threatened was a major force influencing the introduction of the *normas minimas* legislation in 1972 and of the various servicing programmes which were characteristic of the 1970s. It may be time for a more radical change in the way that the land market operates. Unless it is, major landowners will be gaining at the expense not only of the poor but also of many other powerful groups in the industrial, commercial and even the construction sectors. At that point change must occur to maintain political and economic stability.

The Local State in Bogota

The state is forced to respond to the problems of the city. Indeed the influence of government is everywhere affecting the provision of services, controlling the conditions of employment, building houses, roads and hospitals and providing jobs. But, while there is government, there is no single government. Rather, each one of the gamut of public agencies that operate in Bogota tends to operate for itself and fails to coordinate its actions with other government institutions. Notorious cases abound where anarchy results. The national housing agency built a housing estate without obtaining planning permission from the city planning department. The city authorities replied by refusing to service the estate, and it remained unoccupied for several years. The electricity and water agencies supply *barrios* which are outside the official urban perimeter. The local planning department declare that they should not be serviced; the agencies service the *barrios* (Fuentes and Losada, 1978). The district of Bogota establish a mechanism for controlling the growth of illegal settlements, but the mechanism does not apply in the neighbouring department of Cundinamarca, where future urban expansion will take place.

At this level there appears to be no real government but a succession of agencies doing governmental tasks in a way not dissimilar to the operation of a series of private companies. Government works in Bogota, but it works according to its own implacable logic; some public agencies are efficient and others inefficient. Some agencies are efficient because there is a consensus that those services are vital for the wellbeing of the city. A political decision has been made that these agencies will be provided with the funds and the autonomy to perform a task that is deemed to be necessary to the interests of particular, perhaps all, groups in the city. Thus, the telephone, water and electricity companies operate efficiently; not every house is serviced, but the companies are regarded as essentially technical agencies which are capable of providing services and gradually do so. There are occasional shortages but the services generally work very well. Politics, in the sense of special favours being granted to particular settlements or individuals, are not absent from these agencies, but are certainly contained. Essentially, these agencies operate according to a routine, established on technical grounds, and services are costed and priced accordingly. Independent of one another they may be, but they get their respective jobs done.

But there is a second type of agency in Bogota which is not efficient. A past mayor described the public bus company as demonstrating 'all the ills to which a mistaken and improvised management can lead' (Alcaldia Mayor, 1976). In 1979 the company had ten drivers for every bus and an accumulated debt of about £13 million. The shortage of buses was due to the large number of units which needed repairs, and to the fact that some 199 new imported buses had been embargoed for five years by the Colombian customs in Cali and Buenaventura because the duties had not been paid. Similarly, the garbage company, while performing a reasonable service in some parts of the city, is consistently criticised for failing to remove rubbish in the poorer areas. In addition, it is criticised for taking on more employees than it can afford to pay or even pension off – 'the curse of the demagogic race between the political parties', as *El Espectador* puts it (12 November 1978).

Such agencies have often been dismissed as typically Latin American governmental institutions; nothing else could be expected of them. This is too glib an explanation. It is more accurate to think of such agencies as serving two separate functions. The formal function – to provide a bus service or to collect rubbish – they perform more adequately. In fact, I would argue that politics and indeed political stability in Bogota could not function without this second kind of agency. Councillors gain votes by getting jobs in the bureaucracy for political allies among the poor.

Thus, the government in Bogota – indeed at every level of government in Colombia – is a mixture of what we might designate as political and technical agencies. Both are political, in the sense that their formal or informal function serves to maintain the existing political and economic system. But the first kind of agency performs this political role through the efficiency with which it provides a specific service; the second performs its political role through favours and the exercise of partisanship. There are some cities in Colombia where nearly all agencies are of the second kind; Bogota and Medellin are perhaps exceptional in having so many efficient kinds of agency. Bogota has achieved this position because it is the national capital and the country's largest city. Since the kind of coalition government that has existed since 1958 has followed a modernisation strategy which included the industrialisation of the country, it is perhaps not surprising that special efforts have been made in the national capital. Since the city is the largest industrial and commercial centre in the country, there has been no shortage of pressure from the private sector for the efficient provision of services.

Thus, the technical agencies are allowed to operate largely without partisan political pressures; they are allowed to raise their tariffs, can refuse to service particular settlements and choose their directors and staffs primarily on technical grounds. They are also supported in their applications for the foreign loans required to expand services. Water, drainage and electricity expansion has come essentially with the support of the World Bank, and telephone expansion through loans from Eriksson. The nontechnical agencies are also provided with resources, but at a limited level. There are constant financial deficits in these agencies, constant crises, constant changes of directors and personnel, but enough funding is usually provided to pay the staffs. However, these are relatively small budgets. In 1974, the combined budgets of the public transport and the garbage company were 600 million pesos (about £15 million) compared to the 1700 million pesos of the electricity agency or the 1300 million pesos of water. Thus a strict, or at least a degree of, control is maintained even over the nontechnical, politicised agencies. They are inefficient within a limited area, one that is deemed to be less than critical for the city, or for particular influential groups in the city. Within this area, politics reigns.

Control in Bogota, as elsewhere, is maintained through the budget. This control applies not only to the scope for political manoeuvring and patronage but to the servicing of the poor. Even the efficient agencies find that their choice of policies is severely limited by their budgets. Essentially, they act like private corporations charging for what they provide. They are required to repay their loans together with a certain level of interest. They do not make profits, but the prices they charge are determined by their efficiency and by the presence or absence of a subsidy. The outcome of the requirement to break even, reasonable or otherwise, is that the agencies operate to supply those groups in the city who can best afford the services they supply. Electricity, water and telephones are provided on demand for those that can pay the full cost of the service. The rich in Bogota actually pay premium tariffs, because these agencies have a pricing structure which favours poorer groups. Thus higher-income residential areas are supplied with services by the combined action of the agencies and the urbanisers. The servicing is efficient and rapid; the agency benefits by operating in this way. Their response to the poor, however, is different. Servicing the poor is more complex, the *barrios* are often laid out in a way which increases costs, or are located on hilly land or on terrain that is liable to flooding. They are serviced at a price, but may have to wait because, given the tariff structure, they are less remunerative and more trouble to the agency. The outcome is that the rich are serviced immediately, while the poor, because they cannot pay so readily and because they are often outside the urban perimeter or lack planning permission, have to wait. The agencies are not to be criticised for this response; it is a consequence of the way they are organised and are expected to operate.

Any criticism that pertains to this process must be directed to higher levels of government. It is not the gatekeepers who are culpable, but those who placed the gates. The poor could be supplied more rapidly if the agencies were allowed to provide a subsidy. Perhaps more pertinently, they could afford to buy the service if the distribution of income in the city were fairer. But the poor are excluded on both counts; the services are not subsidised, and real incomes seem to be declining, at least for industrial workers, which makes it more and more difficult for them to purchase services. Thus, the efficiency of the technical service agencies, which is admirable, works not against the poor but as a reflection of the economy of the city. Because the agencies operate essentially on the basis of 'whoever shall pay, shall receive', the distribution and level of income in the city are the critical elements. It is not the actions of the service agencies which are inequitable, but the structure of demand for their services.

I would characterise the technical agencies in Bogota as acting both for accumulative and legitimisation goals. They maintain economic growth in the city by providing light, water and telephones. But they do not actively discriminate against the poor; the servicing routines are broadly understood by the poor and accepted by them. Occasional crises and protests occur, but there is no legitimacy crisis in this sector in Bogota. The nontechnical agencies, on the other hand, are operating mainly for legitimisation purposes. Their function is to give jobs and favours to poorer groups. More specifically, they are used to coopt settlement leaders and political groups who might otherwise oppose the political system. Incidentally, they also provide a service. Some rubbish is collected; education at primary school level is supplied; and some health facilities are available. Such services are not essential to the powerful in Bogota, because the private sector supplies those groups. Education and health is provided expensively, somewhat variably, but for the better off very effectively. They are covered by social security or private insurance against the most expensive illnesses, and can pay for the best medical care available. The poor, on the other hand, are totally dependent on the public services. But these services do not function according to technical criteria; all of the services on which the poor are primarily dependent perform partisan political roles. Thus the education secretariat is highly politicised; road sweepers and doctors are appointed largely on political grounds. Not only do the agencies supplying services for the poor operate inefficiently but the funds available to them are limited. Budgets are deliberately held back, both because the services are regarded as nontechnical and because those services are regarded as unimportant by the major decision-makers. More accurately, the choice between better services for the poor and higher taxes on land and incomes is normally resolved in favour of higher-income groups.

The real problem areas in Bogota therefore relate to those services which are provided by the state and which the poor cannot provide for themselves. Insofar as electricity and water costs are too high, the poor do not receive services; insofar as hospital beds are not made available, they do not gain access to hospital. On the whole, the technical agency providing the first kind of service works well, because it also serves industry, commerce and high-income groups. On the whole, the second kind of agency, characterised by underbudgeted and politically riven bureaucracies, does not work well, because their services are irrelevant to the needs of the powerful. This latter kind of service is only improved in cases where a crisis arises. Improvements occur when there is a threat to the legitimacy of the regime. A major electoral threat to the National Front coalition in 1970 induced a major effort to service the poor; health centres proliferated; subsidised water was pumped into the hillside *barrios*; more schools were provided.

But such threats to the system have been rare in Bogota. On the whole, urban protests rather than social movements are the rule. As a consequence, the political system responds to the poor in *ad hoc* fashion rather than through a well-planned offensive to remove the problems. If one settlement protests about its school, its health centre or its drains, then a politician or an agency takes up the cry and makes some real or token responses. But such responses are limited, and tend to benefit one group of the poor at the expense of another. They get electricity for one *barrio* a few months earlier than it might otherwise arrive. Another *barrio* with less political *palanca* (influence) waits a few months longer. On the whole, these responses have little overall effect. Politicians make a lot of noise in Bogota, but the presents the system lets them hand out are very limited. Councillors have a few jobs to offer, some funds to allocate; they can speed up servicing in some cases or may get a bus service; but the key decisions which really affect the way that the poor live are decided at the highest political levels. It is the national president and his cabinet, subject to major influences from the principal Colombian pressure groups and politicians, who decide the critical issues. The distribution of income, as affected by decisions on minimum salaries, taxation levels and pricing policies, the sums of money available to the city of Bogota to spend on health and education, the subsidies which can or cannot be provided to service poor areas, are all determined at the national level and not in Bogota. Urban managers exist in Bogota, but they do not have the power to make the critical management decisions; real decisions are essentially in the hands of national managers.[1]

Notes

1. This paper is a first fruit of a major research project underway at University College, London, entitled 'Public Intervention, Housing and Land Use in Latin American Cities'. The project, directed by the author and Dr Peter Ward, is financed by the Overseas Development Administration and involves a comparative analysis of the cities of Bogota, Mexico City and Valencia, Venezuela. Fieldwork took place between September 1978 and October 1979. Thanks and recognition are due to James Murray, Ann Raymond and Carlos Zorro Sanchez for their contributions to the project's success and vitality.

Bibliography

Alcaldia Mayor, *Informe del Alcalde Mayor de Bogota al Honorable Consejo 1976* (Bogota, 1976)
Cardoso, F.M., 'Dependency and Development in Latin America', *New Left Review*, vol. 84 (1972), pp. 83-95
— 'Current Theses on Latin American Development and Dependency: A Critique' *Boletin de Estudios Latinoamericanos y del Caribe*, vol. 22 (1977), pp. 53-64
Carroll, A., *Pirate Subdivisions and the Market for Residential Lots in Bogota*, City Study Project Paper 7 (World Bank, Washington DC, 1980)

Castells, M., *The Urban Question: A Marxist Approach* (Edward Arnold, London, 1977)

Cleaves, P.S., *Bureaucratic Politics and Administration in Chile* (California University Press, Berkeley, 1974)

DANE, *La Vivienda en Colombia 1973* (Bogota, 1977)

— *Boletin Mensual de Estadistica*, no. 328 (1978a)

— *La Población en Colombia 1973* (Bogota, 1978b)

DAPD *(Departamento Administrativo de Planeación Districal), Mercadeo de Tierras en Barrios Clandestinos en Bogota* (1973, mimeo)

— *Normas Minimas de Urbanización y de Servicios. Consideraciones a Sus Aplicación* (1978, mimeo)

Doebele, W., *The Private Market and Low Income Urbanization in Developing Countries: The 'Pirate' Subdivisions of Bogota,* Discussion Paper D75-11 (Harvard University, Department of City and Regional Planning, 1975)

Dos Santos, T. 'The Structure of Dependence', *American Economic Review*, vol. 60 (1970), pp. 231-6

Fedesarrollo, *Coyuntura Economica*, vol. 6 (1976)

Frank, A.G., *Capitalism and Underdevelopment in Latin America* (Monthly Review Press, New York, 1967)

Fuentes, A.L. and Losada, R., 'Implicaciones Socio-económicas de la Ilegalidad en la Tenencia de la Tierra Urbana de Colombia', *Coyuntura Economica*, vol. 8, no. 1 (May 1978), pp. 1-28

Gilbert, A.G., *Latin American Development* (Penguin, Harmondsworth, 1974)

— 'Urban and Regional Development Programmes in Colombia since 1951' in W.A. Cornelius and F.M. Trueblood (eds.), *Latin American Urban Research*, vol. 5, *Urbanization and Inequality* (Sage, Beverley Hills, 1975), pp. 241-76

— 'Bogota: Politics, Planning and the Crisis of Lost Opportunities' in W.A. Cornelius and R.V. Kemper (eds.), *Latin American Urban Research*, vol. 6, *Metropolitan Latin America* (Sage, Beverly Hills, 1978), pp. 87-126

Harloe, M., *Captive Cities* (Wiley, New York, 1977)

Harvey, D., *Social Justice and the City* (Johns Hopkins, Baltimore, 1973)

IBRD (International Bank for Reconstruction and Development), *Basis of a Development Program for Colombia* (Johns Hopkins, Baltimore, 1949)

ICT, *Inventario de Zonas Subnormales de Vivienda y Proyectos de Desarrollo Progresivo* (Bogota, 1976)

Losada, R. and Gomez, H., *La Tierra en el Mercado Pirata de Bogota* (Fedesarrollo, Bogota, 1976)

Lubell, H. and McCallum, D., *Bogota, Urban Development and Employment* (International Labour Office, Geneva, 1978)

McGreevey, W.P., *An Economic History of Colombia, 1845-1930* (Cambridge University Press, London, 1971)

Miliband, R., *The State in Capitalist Society* (Weidenfeld and Nicholson, London, 1969)

Mohan, R. and Hartline, N., *The Poor of Bogota: Who They Are, What They Do, and Where They Live* (World Bank, Washington DC, 1979, mimeo)

Pahl, R., *Whose City?* (Penguin, Harmondsworth, 1975)

Palma, G., 'Dependency: A Formal Theory of Underdevelopment or a Methodology for the Analysis of Concrete Situations of Underdevelopment', *World Development*, vol. 6 (1978), pp. 881-924

Paredes, A. and Martinez, R., *Alternativa para la Solucias del Problema de la Vivienda para Grupos de Bajos Ingresos: El Sector Privado Tradicional y las Normas Minimas,* Paper presented to INTERHABITAT, Sixth Inter-American Conference on Housing (Medellin, November 1977)

Poulantzas, N., *Political Power and Social Classes* (New Left Books, London, 1973)

Servicio Seccional de Salud, *Plan du Salud 1977* (Bogota, 1977)

Simmie, J., *Citizens in Conflict* (Heinemann, London, 1974)

Svenson, G., *El Desarrollo Económico Departamental 1960-75* (Inandes, Bogotá, 1977)

Urrutia, M. and Berry, A., *La Distribución del Ingreso en Colombia* (La Carreta, Medellin, 1975)

Vernez, G., *Bogota's Pirate Settlements: An Opportunity for Metropolitan Development*, Unpublished doctoral thesis (Berkeley, 1973)

Williams, P., 'Urban Managerialism: A Concept of Relevance', *Area*, vol. 10 (1978), pp. 236-40

3 TUNIS

Richard I. Lawless and Allan M. Findlay

Tunisia has known a remarkable urban continuity. Its urban system, characterised by a high degree of primacy, was already well established long before the French protectorate, and the primacy of Tunis, the capital, was substantially reinforced by the advent of European colonialism. The restructuring of the Tunisian economy during the colonial era established Tunis more strongly than ever before as the economic, social and political core of the nation. The relationships between this urban 'core' and the regional 'periphery' have become increasingly strongly manifested in the flow of raw materials, people and investments towards Tunis from the less fortunate areas of the country. Miossec (1978) has shown, for example, how the banking system established by the French has tended through time to become polarised within Tunis, draining capital and savings from all over Tunisia towards the core city. The flow of human resources towards the capital has been equally dramatic, as many as one in three of the population of Tunis in 1966 being in-migrants. By 1975, Greater Tunis, with a population of 900,247, was four times larger than the second city of Sfax, and accounted for 16 per cent of the total and one in three of the urban population of Tunisia (Table 3.1).[1]

Table 3.1: Evolution of the Population of Tunis and Tunisia, 1921-75

| Census year | Tunis | | | Tunisia | Ratio Tunis: Tunisia (%) |
	Tunisian (Muslim) population	European population	Total		
1921	98,204	73,472	176,676	2,093,939	8.1
1926	106,860	79,136	185,996	2,159,078	8.6
1936	142,460	115,653	258,113	2,608,313	9.9
1946	303,829	144,991	448,820	3,230,952	13.9
1956	397,234	163,882	561,116	3,783,159	14.8
1966	654,610	24,993	679,603	4,533,351	15.0
1975	—	—	900,247	5,572,128	16.2

Source: The census.

94

The City since Independence

Although space does not allow detailed discussion of the pre-twentieth-century city here, it is essential to remember that the colonial period had a profound impact on both the pre-colonial 'Islamic' foundation and on the structure and development of the modern city. Declaration of the French Protectorate in 1881 was followed by the laying-out of a planned grid-iron settlement (*villeneuve*), replacement of the central medina walls by a ringstrasse, and development of an artificial port and major industrial zone. As the colonial period progressed, European garden-suburbs spread rapidly, to become the dominant form of urban development, and in the early 1940s an important new element in the city structure appeared around the edges of the central city, in the form of spontaneous settlements (*gourbivilles*) to house the massive influx of Moslem migrants. For further details of this period in the city's history, see for example, Callens (1955); Sebag (1958, 1974); Taieb (1960); Cleveland (1978); Revault (1978); and Findlay (1980b).

Independence inaugurated profound changes in the social organisation of the city. In the space of a few years, the vast majority of the Europeans (an estimated 150,000 French, Italians and Maltese) departed for France or Italy, and most of the Tunisian Jews emigrated to either France or Israel. Whereas the European community represented almost a third of the city's total population in 1956, by 1966 it had declined dramatically to below four per cent (Table 3.1). Even more dramatic were the internal movements of the Tunisian Arab bourgeoisie, who quickly abandoned the medina for a more comfortable lifestyle in an apartment in the former colonial town or a villa in the suburbs left vacant by the departing Europeans. From there it became a dazzling tale of upward mobility, including such accoutrements as secondary residences — 'progress' in both space and time away from the medina. So long as the French dominated the Tunisians politically, the latter stayed in the medina and adhered to its old value system; once independence was achieved, it was the new government's overwhelming desire to sweep away everything which recalled the colonial period and which seemed to have justified it, the backwardness of the country and above all the cities. Because of this national commitment to a modernising state and a secular society, the medina became a 'haven of archaisms' to a class that rejected it as a place to live, as a place to conduct business and, most importantly perhaps, as a place to learn and worship. A move to the modern city and the acceptance of the value systems and the conduct which it imposed was therefore easily accomplished.

Paradoxically, the Tunisification of the European city was accompanied by the Europeanisation of the Tunisians who occupied it. The medina, abandoned by its bourgeoisie, was invaded by refugees from certain *gourbivilles* destroyed when the government launched a *dégourbification* programme and by a stream of new migrants from the rest of the country, the vast majority from rural areas. The newcomers quickly occupied the fine old houses and palaces which were subdivided and rented out room by room by their absentee owners (Lawless, 1980a).

As a result of these population movements, Tunis is no longer a city ordered by ethnicity or caste but increasingly is ordered according to more contemporary principles of class. The cleavages to emerge since independence are different in kind from those which were the dominant form in the past, and the new spatial patterning is one of marked segregation of the different socio-economic groups, divisions which appear to be increasing rather than decreasing. The sharp class cleavages that characterise independent Tunisia have highly visible projections in the physical form of the city. Government policies during the last two decades, and especially since 1970, aimed at solving the city's acute housing problems, have accentuated rather than alleviated these divisions, which today are vividly reflected in the extreme disparity in housing types within the city (Figures 3.1 and 3.2).

Figure 3.1: Tunis: Location and Place Names

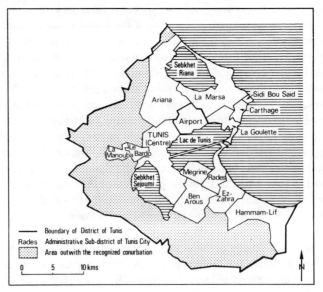

Figure 3.2: The Housing Areas of Tunis, 1976

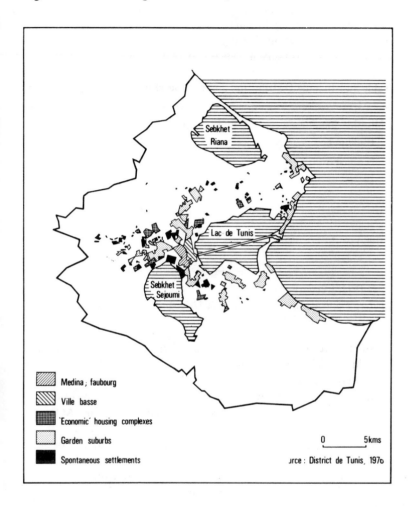

Sebkhet Riana

Lac de Tunis

Sebkhet Sejoumi

Medina; faubourg

Ville basse

'Economic' housing complexes

Garden suburbs

Spontaneous settlements

0   5kms

ırce : District de Tunis, 197ь

Every effort has been made by the state to encourage private construction, and bank loans are available to cover up to 80 per cent of the cost of building a new dwelling. In the early 1970s some 88 per cent of all investment in real estate was by the private sector and a mere twelve per cent by the public sector, municipalities and parastate organisations. The government also encourages a system of rent-purchase (*location-vente*), with monthly instalments repayable over a period of 15-20 years at modest rates of interest. Both of these schemes effectively exclude the vast majority of the urban population, almost two-thirds of which has an average monthly income of less than 50 Tunisian dinars (Table 3.2) and benefits the privileged groups, the upper and middle classes and some skilled workers in regular employment. Weak rent-control

Table 3.2: Income Distribution among Households in Greater Tunis

Monthly income (dinars[a])	Proportion of all households in Greater Tunis (%)
Less than 10	11.1
10-29	21.6
30-49	27.2
50-79	18.5
80-99	6.6
100-119	4.8
Over 120	7.3

a. In 1972, 1 Tunisian dinar = £0.84.

Source: *Enquete Migration et Emploi 1972-73* (Institut National de la Statistique, Tunis, 1975)

measures have encouraged property speculation, and the fact that the most luxurious dwellings form a category entirely free of all regulations has merely channelled private investment towards this type of construction, which is completely beyond the means of the mass of the population, the low-income groups and the petit bourgeoisie. At the same time the *Société Nationale Immobilière Tunisienne* (SNIT), the major state organisation involved in housing construction, has not only failed to respond to the needs of the low-income groups but has actively discriminated against them by, for example, increasing the deposit demanded under the rent-purchase scheme to at least a third of the total cost of the dwelling (Fakhfakh, 1977).

The spatial manifestation of these elitist policies can be seen in the pattern of urban growth since 1956 (Micaud, 1974, 1977; Abdelkafi, 1978). Beautiful villas or *pavillons* set in spacious grounds have invaded the more attractive hillslopes to the north of the city from Belvédère Supérieur, Mutuelleville, El Menzah to Ariana and along the northern coastlands between Carthage and La Marsa; and since 1974 the first apartment blocks have appeared in these northern suburbs. This wave of construction continues, and has greatly extended a pattern of suburban development established during the last decade of colonial rule. In 1971 the university campus marked the limit of the built-up area; today villas and apartments extend 4 km to the north of it and have spread over the eastern, western and southern flanks of the Jebel Nahli. These fine neighbourhoods are the home of the privileged classes, and present the actualisation in space of the ideals of the political élite. Their spatial extent is entirely out of proportion with their population; and a small but privileged minority absorbs, and will continue to absorb, far more than its share of services and infrastructure.

To the west of the city around Le Bardo and Manouba, a series of 'popular cities' (economic or 'low-cost' housing complexes) have been built either directly by the municipalities or in some cases by SNIT and are occupied by the petit bourgeoisie and the more affluent workers under the rent-purchase scheme. Estates such as *cité* Ibn Khaldoun, *cité* Ez Zouhour and *cité* El Khadra were initially destined to rehouse the population living in spontaneous settlements, but they have been rapidly taken over by the middle-income groups, which have increased in number as a result of the dramatic expansion of the tertiary sector within the upper circuit of the urban economy during the last two decades. These so-called *logements économique et social*, which can cost between 5000 and 8000 dinars, requiring a monthly repayment of 32 to 65 dinars, have failed to solve the housing problems of the majority of the urban population, who are simply too poor to afford them. Excluded by their poverty from state assistance, the city's low-income groups have been forced to seek shelter either in the medina and its faubourgs or in the *gourbivilles*, where densities of between 500 and 1,000 per hectare are common, rising to 1,200 in places. The older central *gourbivilles* are scarcely recognisable today as the same residential areas described by studies carried out a decade or more ago. The inhabitants have consolidated their position by illegal improvements of their dwellings, until the majority of the houses are constructed with 'modern' materials. In some cases the city has reluctantly extended electricity, public sources of water, elementary sewage, some paving and a compulsory numbering of houses and streets. Spontaneous settlements such as Melassine, Saida Manoubia, Djebel Lahmar, Borjel, Jebel Jelloud and Kabaria are now quarters like others, and attempts to dislodge a population that has entrenched itself against every obstacle has proved virtually impossible. Djebel Lahmar, for example, occupies some of the choicest real estate near the centre of Tunis. But although the older *gourbivilles* have become legitimised, physical and legal constraints have severely limited their expansion, so that densities within them have risen sharply as a result of an influx of newcomers unable to find shelter elsewhere in the city. Such pressures have also resulted in the creation and rapid expansion of several new *gourbivilles* far from the centre. One, known as Kram-Aeroport after its site on a projected road tying the international airport to the northern littoral, can be explained by its proximity to the new port at La Goulette (Figure 3.2). Another has grown rapidly adjacent to El-Riana, about 8 km north of El Menzah, the first colonial suburban extension to be built after World War II. Each is the site of a large weekly market catering for a marginal and still semirural population. Other new *gourbivilles* have mushroomed along the south-eastern edges of the Sebkhet es Sedjoumi, at Douar Hicher and north of Ariana on the road from Raouad.

Table 3.3: Patterns of Residential Land Use

	Area (hectares)	Population (1975)	Population density (per hectare)
Medina and faubourgs	270	135,000	500
Ville basse (old colonial city)	270	85,000	315
Garden-suburbs	3000	315,000	105
Spontaneous settlements	320	296,000	925
Economic or 'low-cost' housing complexes	700	126,000	180
Total	4560	960,000	211

Source: Poncet (1978).

Poncet has demonstrated conclusively how the largest number of people are confined to the smallest amount of urban space. His calculations, set out in Table 3.3, reveal that 45 per cent of the city's population, the vast majority earning less than 50 dinars a month, are squeezed into the medina and its two faubourgs and the spontaneous settlements which together occupy little more than one-tenth of the city's total residential area; 13 per cent of the population, mainly drawn from the middle-income groups (50-80 dinars per month) live in the so-called 'popular cities' built as a result of state initiatives, and occupy 15 per cent of the total area; while just under a third of the population, predominantly the upper and middle classes, live in the garden-suburbs, appropriating two-thirds of the city's total residential area. The medina and two faubourgs shelter almost as many people as the old colonial city, now known as the *ville basse*, the preserve of the middle-income groups, on exactly the same area.

The rapid spatial growth of Tunis during the first two decades after independence – the city nearly doubled in area between 1956 and 1966 – occurred without urban planning (Micaud, 1974, 1977). A master plan produced in 1962 by the *Bureau d'Etudes Quaroni Carlo*, and later updated, was essentially a classic plan of zoning for land-use and transportation patterns. It cast the state in the ineffective role of *gendarme* rather than the active agent in innovative intervention. Lack of planning, rapacious land and property speculation and the dominance of private investment, local and foreign, have produced a seriously distorted urban structure, characterised by a number of socially segregated, monofunctional quarters converging on a polysocial, multifunctional centre. Those neighbourhoods which have developed along the northern and western communication axes are overwhelmingly residential. The southern suburbs on the other hand are predominantly industrial, and some three-quarters of the total area devoted to industrial land use in the city is concentrated in this zone, located along the railway line running south from the old port of Tunis (which has lost most of its activities to the new port of La Goulette) through Jebel Jelloud and Sidi Fathallah, industrial centres established during the colonial period, to Ben Arous and Megrine, where the city's major new industrial estates have been created during the last ten years. Pollution is a major problem in this southern zone and housing provision is poor in both quality and quantity, so that, whereas the northern and western suburbs have attracted the upper- and middle-income groups, the residents of these southern suburbs are drawn mainly from lower-income groups. This basically sectoral character of the city's structure suggests comparisons with Hoyt's (1939) sectoral theory of urban land use, which emphasises the *directional* element controlling land-use contrasts rather than *distance.*

In contrast to the socially segregated, monofunctional suburbs, the central zone of the city contains the complete spectrum of socioeconomic groupings, and performs a wide range of functions; indeed its polysocial character is directly related to its multifunctional economic structure. In addition to important residential areas, there are numerous industries and crafts, but above all a major concentration of service activities. Some 70 per cent of all tertiary establishments in Greater Tunis and 80 per cent of all jobs in the city's tertiary sector are located here, with a major concentration in what has been described as the

hypercentre, a rectangular area of 35 hectares with its major axis along
the Avenue Habib Bourguiba and delimited by the Rues Farhat Hached,
Nahas Pacha, El Jazira and the Place d'Afrique. The hypercentre contains
over 2,000 tertiary establishments, including government departments,
the major banks, insurance companies, the head offices of major private
and state industries and corporations, transport services, a wide range of
wholesale and retail trades, the international hotels, modern restaurants,
cinemas and theatres. Together they employ over 40,000 people or
one-third of all workers in the city's tertiary sector.

Since independence, the tertiary sector has expanded rapidly —
notably after 1970, with the liberalisation of the Tunisian economy and
the influx of private foreign capital. The concentration of this growth
in Tunis has resulted in the tertiarisation of the urban economy. Official
statistics for 1975 reveal that approximately 56 per cent of the city's
active population were employed in services (District de Tunis, 1975).
Miossec (1978) found that employment in the banking sector, for
example, has been increasing by 10 per cent annually in recent years
and office space by 10-20 per cent.

This *explosion tertiaire tunisoise*, linked to the internationalisation
of the Tunisian economy, has produced a profound transformation in
the spatial structure of the central zone. Until independence, most
tertiary establishments were located in the Kasba, in the medina along
the major axes of the *suqs* and in the *ville basse* around the railway
station and in the zone between the Porte de France and the Colisée.
Between 1956 and 1970, new establishments appeared along the
Avenues Habib Bourguiba, Farhat Hached, Paris and Carthage and
soon dominated the facades of the principal axes of the hypercentre.
Since 1970, however, a dramatic increase in the number of new offices
and shops has resulted in a spectacular spatial expansion of the tertiary
sector into the zone situated between the Avenue Carthage-Paris and
the port, but notably into the northern quarters of the *ville basse* and
beyond — into Lafayette, Belvédère and Cité Jardin. This expansion
has been accompanied by a much greater spatial separation of the major
branches of tertiary activity, for example, the separation of banking
and commerce following the construction of the new central bank. In
addition to many new tertiary establishments, a number of existing
activities, particularly government offices and the head offices of industrial companies, have migrated from the Kasba and hypercentre to
modern premises, better adapted to their needs, in the northern quarters.
The process whereby tertiary activities are attracted by the upper-
class residential neighbourhoods (zones of assimilation) but repelled by

the industrial areas, the port, the station and physically degraded areas such as Petite Sicile (zones of discard) has been identified as a common feature of cities in market economies, and serves to reinforce the new pattern of social segregation which has appeared since independence.

The increasing demand for office space in the central zone has resulted in the loss of important residential accommodation. One-third of all offices in the centre occupy former dwellings. This 'conquest' of the central zone by the tertiary sector is seen vividly in the northern quarters of the *ville basse* near Place Pasteur, where many of the villas have been transformed into banks, the head offices of industrial firms or consultancies, and vacant lots are rapidly occupied by new office buildings. The same process is at work in the hypercentre, where an estimated $11,414 \text{ m}^2$ of land around the railway station has been converted from residential to office use, and there are strong pressures to transform the few remaining apartments along the Avenue Habib Bourguiba into offices. Indirectly, this process has led to a sharp rise in the price of land and rents. Land values throughout the *ville basse* have risen with few exceptions to over 100 dinars/m^2 (Figure 3.3), with the peak of land-value intensity rising to 300 dinars/m^2 at the intersection

Figure 3.3: Land Prices in 1976 (Dinars/m^2)

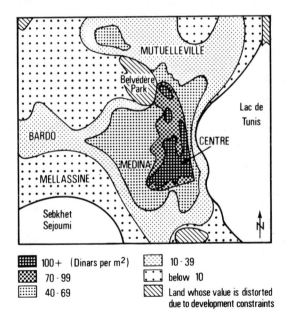

of the Avenues Habib Bourguiba and Carthage-Paris, while office rents
rose annually by more than 12.5 per cent between 1970 and 1977;
office rents in the hypercentre now exceed 3 dinars/m². Unable to
resist the pressure of the tertiary sector and the rise in the price of land
and property, residential areas have been pushed out of the zones of
strong centrality towards the periphery. In 1956 the majority of the
population lived less than 3,000 m from the city's central point; in 1975
half the population lived 4.5 km from the centre, and a quarter more
than 7 km away. The long distances which now separate place of residence and place of work, in a city where 80 per cent of the inhabitants
do not own their own car, have placed intolerable strains on systems of
public transport. As all principal routes converge on the urban core, this
zone now suffers from serious traffic congestion and parking difficulties
at peak hours — problems which are aggravated by the volume of north-
south traffic between the residential quarters and the industrial zones
which must pass through the city centre.

The rapid horizontal expansion of the central business district into
the inner residential areas of the colonial city has also been accompanied
by an even more dramatic vertical development. Today, numerous
multistorey office blocks and hotels line the major avenues, dwarfing
the buildings constructed during the colonial period; examples include
the *Office du Commerce Extérieur, Banque Centrale de Tunisie* and the
Hotel du Lac along the Avenue Mohamed V; *Hotel Africa* and *Tunisia
International* on the Avenue Habib Bourguiba; the head offices of the
Société Tunisienne d'Electricité et de Gaz on the Avenue Jean-Jaures;
and the headquarters of the *Agence de Promotion des Investissements*
in Rue du Royaume d'Arabie near Avenue Mohamed V. A major new
axis between Place d'Afrique and Ariana has been constructed at right
angles to the Avenue Habib Bourguiba, the dominant axis of the traditional hypercentre, and the parallel avenues, Paris, Liberté-Palestine and
Mohamed V, have been extended northwards towards Ariana.

Miossec (1978) has recently identified a number of distinct nuclei
along this new north-south axis, the hypercentre, Lafayette, Place
Pasteur and the intersection of Avenue Charles Nicolle and 'route X' at
Ariana, and has suggested that the city is developing a multinuclei
structure. This trend appears to be confirmed by the *plan regional
d'aménagement* (PRA) published by the District of Tunis (1977), which
lays down major guidelines for the spatial development of Greater Tunis
to the year 1986, with a second stage to 2000 (Dlala, 1979). In place of
a *hypercentre mononucléaire* the PRA seeks to create a *centre poly-
nucléaire*. Tertiary activities of international and national importance,

such as the major banks and specialist services, will remain in the central zone, but other activities are to be concentrated in a number of new *centres peripheriques* (Figure 3.4). The first and most important *centre regional*, including offices, shops and social and cultural amenities, is to be located at Ariana, close to the *Cité Olympique* and the future International Fair, with smaller centres, *centres locals*, at El Ouardia, El Mourouj and Manouba to serve the northern and western suburbs. These new *poles d'animation* are to be linked by an integrated transport

Figure 3.4: The Planned Development of Land Use in the Tunis Conurbation

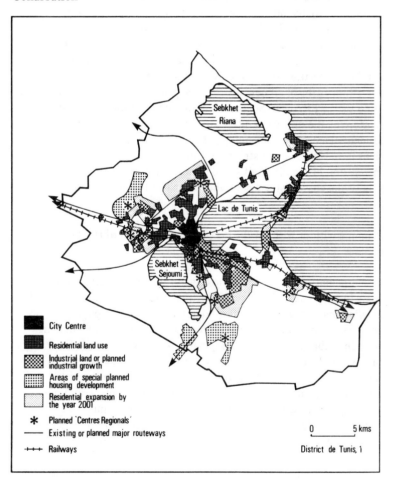

network consisting of fast urban motorways and a surface metro system. The plan does not envisage the creation of a major new centre in either the western or southern districts until after 1986, when the development of zones reserved for future urban expansion to the south-west and northwest of the present urban area (Naassen, Fouchana, Kassar Said and M'Nihla) is scheduled to begin.

The aim of the plan is to counterbalance the dominance of the hypercentre, avoid the complete tertiarisation of the *ville basse* by maintaining its multifunctional character and reduce traffic congestion in the central zone. Paradoxically, by attempting to weaken the domi-nance of the traditional hypercentre, the creation of a major *centre regional* at Ariana must strengthen the new north-south axis, trans-forming it into the dominant axis of future development and relegating the southern and western axes to a secondary role. At least three-quarters of all office buildings now under construction are situated within this north-south axis, notably along the Avenue Mohamed V, while four-fifths of all new office space planned for Greater Tunis until 1986 by the PRA is to be located in the *centre regional* at Ariana, reinforcing the migration of tertiary activities towards the high-class residential areas. Such planning policies can only produce new distor-tions in the city's urban structure, enforce an even greater spatial segregation of the different social groups and complete the marginalisa-tion of the city's historic core, the medina and its two faubourgs.

Planning with or without the People — the Problem of the Tunis Medina

In sharp contrast to the dramatic transformation of much of the *ville basse* in recent years, little new construction has occurred in the medina, *la ville ancienne*, and with a few notable exceptions its physical struc-ture has survived virtually intact. Yet, paradoxically, the medina has been the subject of lively scrutiny and numerous recommendations by a number of different planning bodies, each of which has sought to modify or even entirely recast the present vocations of the historic core. Whereas the rest of the city has evolved with only a minimum of planning, the medina has captured the attention of planners of every nationality, who have used it as a sort of magical mirror in which they have seen reflected their vision of what the country has been or ought to become (Micaud, 1978).

In the immediate post-independence period the medina, abandoned by anyone of consequence, was perceived both aesthetically and ideologically with distate by the Tunisian élite. It was seen as an obstacle to progress that had to be overcome if the country was to have a capital worthy of the modernising image projected by Tunisia's new leaders. Caught between the administrative centre around the Kasba and the bustling commercial life of the Avenue Habib Bourguiba and Avenue de Carthage, its destruction seemed not only imminent but logical. In 1961 President Bourguiba organised an international colloquium to try and resolve the problem. Many of the projects recommended the opening up of the medina to traffic, while the Israeli planner Yona Friedman, leading proponent of space city theory, put forward a plan to avoid demolition or radical surgery by adding a second storey (Kultermann, 1969), a proposal which would have relegated the medina to the basement level of a two-storey city. None of the proposals received were actually implemented, but the colloquium did succeed in forestalling the onset of demolition. Gradually, the Tunisian élite became resigned to the irrelevancy of the medina inhabited and used by poverty-stricken newcomers to the city. For the planners, the historical core became a sort of natural obstacle, rather like the Sebkhet es Sedjoumi or the Lac de Tunis, to be avoided, and they began to plan for a new national administrative centre near the present campus of the University of Tunis. Antagonism therefore turned into indifference, and it was more than a decade after independence before renewed interest in the fate of the medina became apparent.

The factor which prompted the Tunisian élite to take a new look at the medina was international tourism. As the Tunisian tourist industry got underway during the late 1960s a new policy emerged: the preservation of the medina in the interests of economic development. In order to acquire international aid, the project for renovating the medina was linked to that of Carthage, the focal point of an extensive archaeological site with Punic, Roman and Byzantine remains scattered throughout the suburbs on the northern littoral of Tunis. In what became known as the *Projet Tunis-Carthage* (PTC), sponsored by UNESCO, a range of consultants prepared a nine-point programme, seven of which concerned facilities for tourists. It was designed to create a Carthage-medina package for 'cultural tourism' that would contribute to the economic development of Tunisia by making Tunis a metropolis with first-class amenities.

For three years, the foreign experts of the PTC worked in liaison with the *Association Sauvegarde de la Medina* (ASM) and its *Atelier d'Urbanisme*, which had been founded in 1967 to prepare a master plan for the medina. The results, however, were negligible. From the outset there was much greater enthusiasm for Carthage than for the city's Islamic monuments, and proposals for turning the medina into a museum city like Carcassone in southern France seemed at variance with the actual situation as revealed in studies carried out by ASM.

Their sociological analyses revealed the extent to which the medina had been transformed from a citadel of urbanity to city-centre ghetto. The ASM census undertaken in 1968 revealed that two-thirds of households in the central medina were occupied by migrants possessing few resources, compared with less than one-third at the time of independence. A quarter of all residential properties in the central medina were found to be subdivided and rented out room by room. The number of rented rooms in traditional *oukalas* and in private dwellings converted into rooming houses had quadrupled between 1956 and 1968. Throughout the medina and faubourgs population densities averaged 500 per hectare (or 2.7 to a room), compared with 211 per hectare for the Greater Tunis area, rising to 1313 per hectare in parts of the central medina (Table 3.3). There was severe overcrowding, with some 46 per cent of all households living in one room. Some housing cells were even rented to one group for the day and another for the night.

This transformation of the historic centre into a low-income popular zone had brought about the rapid physical deterioration in the medina's traditional fabric. A number of factors were found to have contributed to the lack of investment in the repair and proper maintenance of residential properties. The ASM discovered that not only were few properties owned by their occupants, but multi-ownership of single dwellings by absentee landlords was common, and many houses abandoned by the Europeans and Jews were either occupied illegally or administered by private agents for a fee. The fine old houses of the medina are not particularly well-built, although they are very carefully finished, and so, once the facade deteriorates, water seeps into the earthen or poorly lain stone walls and decay quickly follows. Palaces and mansions formerly occupied by the upper and middle bourgeoisie and more modest dwellings had equally succumbed to neglect and decay. Housing conditions were therefore extremely bad – 50 per cent of dwellings were in a poor state of repair, and some lay in ruins. Infrastructures were inadequate and outdated – 60 per cent of houses did not possess piped drinking water and 53 per cent were compelled to use communal lavatories. A sewage system originally designed for 40,000 was expected to serve almost four times as many people (Lowy, 1970, 1975; Lawless, 1980a).

Against this background, proposals to instal large-scale tourist facilities of the European type seemed totally unrealistic. By 1973, when the PTC project was terminated, only one project had received official recognition. A second, for the renovation of the Hafsia area – part of the former Jewish quarter which had undergone extensive demolition (Danon, 1955) – gained approval within a year. This project, which involved rebuilding one section of a covered bazaar (Souk el Hout) and the construction of 100 'low-cost' housing units, merely took the form of yet another speculative real-estate venture. The monthly rent of each new apartment was 80-92 dinars, effectively excluding the low-income residents of the medina, half of whom possess an average monthly income of less than 20 dinars.

The failure of the PTC led to a new phase in urban planning and the creation of a new high-level planning board, the District of Tunis, to deal with the key problems of the capital – housing, transport, industry and municipal finances. At the same time, the ASM was reorganised, placed under the control of the Tunis municipality and under the direction of a predominantly Tunisian staff, and given instructions to return to its original tasks. Ambitious plans to renovate the medina involving large-scale demolition and reconstruction were abandoned, and replaced by specific proposals for rehabilitation, meaning the gradual improvement of the existing urban fabric. Equally important, attention shifted from a preoccupation with the major monuments and the architectural heritage towards the rehabilitation of existing housing stock in the residential quarters. Preservation of the present urban fabric and the assurance of its correct functioning in the interests of the residents became the principal concern of the ASM. This was made clear in one of the first ASM reports, which states (Projet Tunis/Carthage, 1974):

> The present housing shortage and the poverty of the medina residents prevents any large scale rehousing in new buildings or a reduction in densities. The traditional housing stock must therefore continue to fulfil a social role for a long time to come. Because it is impossible to renew the housing stock or to reduce densities the major effort must favour the preservation of the existing fabric by repairing and maintaining it, and by improving living conditions.

Drawing on data collected from earlier ASM studies, a series of new recommendations were published early in 1974. They proposed a differentiated zoning of the medina (Lawless, 1980b), in which the upper central medina containing the major historic monuments became the responsibility of the Ministry of Culture's *Institut National d'Art et d'Archéologie* (INAA) and the rest that of ASM. It was recognised that the problems associated with the restoration of historic monuments were quite different from those posed by the rehabilitation of the average commercial and residential architecture. For that reason, responsibility for restoration and for finding new uses for historic monuments was left to the INAA; ASM in turn devoted its attention to the residential areas.

The proposals of ASM concerning the plight of residential areas included sound arguments against demolition and renovation. They pointed out that not only was it more costly than rehabilitation schemes, but renovation resulted in a further deterioration of the urban fabric, especially on the fringes of those sectors subject to extensive demolition; it displaced the low-income residents, who were forced to seek shelter elsewhere, often in the already overcrowded *gourbivilles*, and by introducing higher-income groups it encouraged segregation and thereby aggravated social tensions. Rehabilitation of existing housing stock on the other hand, they argued, was much less expensive; it mini-mised displacement of residents, gave tenants the possibility of eventual ownership of their lodgings and thereby encouraged participation and integration in the community – factors which could, in turn, lead to a reduction in social tension, a decline in crime and the maintenance of political stability.

Even more important, the ASM proceeded to show what medina residents could do for themselves within the *existing* legal and financial framework. As an example of this kind of intervention, a detailed proposal for a new pilot project was put forward (Projet Tunis/Carthage, 1974). Paradoxically it concerned what had originally been designated as stage two of the Hafsia project for urban renewal. This sector, known as Ilot IIIE-50, is situated immediately to the north of the area redeve-loped as stage one of the Hafsia project between the Rue des Djerbiens and the Rue el Mechnaka. Within this sector there were 35 dwellings in a poor state of repair and lacking basic amenities, occupied by 103 households, a total of 560 people. Two-thirds of the households had monthly incomes of less than 30 dinars, and the average monthly rent was 5.500 dinars. The intervention proposed by ASM recommended that demolition should be kept to a bare minimum, that the residents should be provided with decent living conditions and tenants be given the opportunity of eventual ownership of their lodgings. The improve-ments recommended included the repair and remodelling of premises to fulfil certain basic specifications. All walls were to be made safe to bear their loads and surfaces protected against humidity. Buildings were to be restructured to permit the installation of electricity and electrical equipment and to provide a minimum of one window in every room. In addition, proper sanitary facilities and piped drinking water were to be provided, together with access to a sewage system for every three families or for every floor. Each household was to have at least two usable rooms, including basic facilities and, wherever possible, access to a patio or terrace. Rents were to be adjusted to a rate compatible with the quality of the lodging. The second type of intervention concerned the vacant lots which were to be filled with constructions of traditional design — i.e., courtyard houses — serving the same social needs as the surrounding buildings. Priority would be given to those residents displaced as a result of the improvement schemes, and the new occupants were to be given the opportunity of eventual ownership of their lodgings by means of a rent-purchase scheme. Significantly, the minimum monthly payment for a single room, kitchen, lavatory and patio, with the opportunity of adding a second room, was fixed at six dinars, while the maximum monthly payment for a two- or three-room dwelling was not to exceed 15 dinars. If the sector had been entirely rebuilt following the strategy adopted for Hafsia 1, the figures presented by ASM reveal that the monthly payments would have been at least 72 dinars, possibly rising to 170 dinars. Indeed the report on ASM's proposals for this sector concludes by comparing the financial investment needed to implement these two very different planning policies, and shows conclusively that the cost of rehabilitation is only one-third that of renovation.

The problems facing projects of this type are obvious. How are the poor residents of the medina to secure the necessary funds, however small, to pay for these improvements? Most of them cannot afford bank loans, because of the high rates of interest, and the municipality does not give improvement grants. To this problem, the ASM appears to have found a solution in the form of the *Fond National pour l'Amélioration de l'Habitat* (FNAH), a little-known fund available since 1956, which should be capable of financing rehabilitation projects solely by applying funds that accrue to it from taxes on medina properties. The fund is also empowered to make direct grants to very poor families, as well as loans with or without interest to other low-income groups.

Although the dissolution of *habous*[2] properties after 1956 made the municipality of Tunis the proprietor of approximately 20 per cent of medina properties, the pattern of private property ownership still

presents problems which are difficult to resolve. A very low rate of
owner occupation in the medina, the large number of absentee landlords
and the widespread occurrence of multi-ownership of single properties
discourages both the maintenance and improvement of housing stock by
tenants and landlords alike, and has contributed significantly to the
marked deterioration of the physical fabric of the old city. A radical
reform of the present structure of property ownership would appear to
be a prerequisite for the successful implementation of improvement
schemes if they are to benefit the actual residents of the medina. Such
a programme is not included in the ASM proposals, although a number
of possible solutions are offered to the problem of multi-ownership.

But possibly the most serious obstacle to the ASM programme is the
residents' collective psychology of poverty. The inhabitants of the
medina may well be extremely resistant to all efforts to help them help
themselves. Their participation in improvement schemes requires confidence in the authorities, which is by no means a characteristic of the
more marginal of the city's residents. It remains to be seen whether a
characteristic improvidence and reliance on luck rather than planning
can be easily overcome (Boardieu, 1973).

Nevertheless, in spite of these criticisms, the new ASM proposals
mark a significant shift in attitudes among at least some of the planners
concerned with the problems of Greater Tunis, and they are confirmed
in the *plan regional d'aménagement* (PRA) published by the District of
Tunis in 1977, which is opposed to extensive demolition in the medina
and in favour of improvements to the existing housing stock; the PRA
also encourages the municipality of Tunis to take more vigorous action
against landlords who refuse to cooperate in the rehabilitation of their
properties (District de Tunis 1977). The ASM's planning policies are no
longer characterised by romantic idealism, disregard of socio-economic
realities and an obsession with international norms. Imported Western
planning traditions have been firmly rejected, because it has been
recognised that they cannot provide a solution to the housing problems
of the majority of the city's inhabitants; the medina and the large
squatter settlements escape the comprehension of such planners. These
areas defy urban renewal, which has come to mean extensive demolition, relocation of many thousands of people and then reconstruction
of new dwellings, because modern construction cannot be scaled down
to the financial capabilities of the majority of the urban population in
Third World countries. Tunisia's modern construction industry provides
a classic example. It has nearly priced itself out of the housing market
in recent years, and new housing projects have revealed again and again

the fallacies of government-sponsored 'low-cost' housing schemes and their inability to answer real and urgent needs. For example, the fifth development plan estimates that 280,000 new houses will be needed during the period 1977-81 but that actual construction is unlikely to exceed 125,000. The cheapest housing unit built by SNIT costs around 4500 dinars and requires a monthly repayment of 30 dinars. As an alternative, ASM proposes 'advocacy planning', which involves the participation and interests of the residents of areas being considered for rehabilitation. Wherever possible, the ASM will provide preliminary studies and technical aid in order to encourage the residents to reconstruct their own environment with the help of traditional artisans. Such a programme, they argue, will preserve the form and function of this quarter, improve the living conditions of the residents, preserve civil peace and cost far less than any other response to the housing problems of the city.

Similar arguments have been used by other planners to discourage the authorities from demolishing the *gourbivilles* or merely ignoring them, and to encourage a more positive response, including legalising the status of some of the older and larger spontaneous settlements. Some progress appears to have been made and the government, with financial aid from the World Bank, has recently inaugurated a rehabilitation programme for the major *gourbivilles* which aims to improve living conditions by providing basic services — sewage, piped drinking water and electricity — without displacing the residents (Group Huit, 1978a, b).

These developments suggest that for the first time there is a measure of official acceptance of 'advocacy planning', planning with or by rather than for the people, autoconstruction and evolutive housing. If tacit acceptance can be translated into positive action, there is at least a glimmer of hope that a deceleration of Tunis' worsening housing crisis can be achieved by giving the majority of the urban population, who are too poor to benefit from the new public housing programmes, security and decent living conditions in their current places of residence.[3]

Problems of the Tunis Labour Market

The inequalities resulting from the malfunctioning of the Tunis housing system are accentuated by the spatial and structural rigidities of the urban labour market. Regrettably it is the same segment of the city's population which is underprivileged in both the housing and labour markets.

Analysis of the pattern of economic activities in Tunis reveals that specific branches of employment are concentrated within certain zones of the city, and that the location of economic activities as a whole is distinctly different from the residential distribution of population. Not surprisingly most of the city's 20,000 agricultural workers are to be found around the fringes of the city, but industrial, commercial and service activities are much more localised. To the south of the city, Megrine, Ben Arous and Bir Kassaa all have over 40 per cent of their workforce involved in industry, while to the west of the city very little employment in secondary activities is to be found. The port area near the city centre and the Petite Sicile quarter of the *ville basse* also possess a wide range of important manufacturing activities, including several noxious industries which pollute the densely populated neighbourhoods nearby. The highest level of concentration occurs in the pattern of tertiary activities, the majority of which are located in the *ville basse* and medina, with the major concentration in the hypercentre (Houidi, 1977). The immense concentration of manufacturing, commercial and service employment in the polyfunctional city centre has led to the congestion of this area and to its absolute dominance as the economic, social and political hub of Tunis and Tunisia. Equally important, its economic prosperity has deprived other parts of the city and also other less favoured areas within the nation of 'modern' secondary and tertiary sector activities. Concentration of employment opportunities within a very small area of Tunisian space reflects the persistence of the highly centralised decision-making procedures inherited from the colonial administration but greatly strengthened since independence by the national government.

Few parts of the city offer more jobs than there are residents of working age. Only the *ville basse* and medina with 45 per cent of the city's jobs and the industrial quarters to the south with 23 per cent of all jobs have significant surpluses of jobs over resident working population (District de Tunis, 1976b). A small excess of jobs over residents is also to be found in the vicinity of the airport. In contrast, major deficits occur in the majority of the city's suburbs. Large areas of western Tunis are almost entirely devoid of any local job opportunities and are far from the main zones of employment. In the Bardo-Manouba district, for example, there was a deficit of 32,000 jobs in 1976. A consequence of spatial imbalance of this magnitude is the massive daily redistribution of workers between their homes and places of work. The city's transport system experiences acute stress, particularly in coping with peak-demand traffic between the western residential areas and the hypercentre.

Commuter rail links with settlements on the southern periphery of
the conurbation, such as Rades and Hammam Lif, and also with garden
suburbs to the north-east of the city, such as Le Kram, Carthage and La
Marsa, offer reasonably rapid access to the city centre. Bus links with
Bardo and Manouba are much less adequate particularly for peak rush-
hour requirements. But the most poorly served areas are not those most
distant from the city's major employment nodes. Spontaneous settlements such as Saida Manoubia, which lies between the medina and
Sebkhet es Sedjoumi, are poorly located relative to the city's transport
network, and the journey to work for their residents can often take
much longer than those coming from the more distant garden-suburbs.
The majority of the residents of Saida Manoubia are employed in secondary and tertiary activities (Table 3.4) and many therefore commute
daily to other parts of the city (District de Tunis, 1976c).

Table 3.4: Employment by Sector of 'Residents' in Saida Manoubia

Sector	Percentage of the active population
Industry (both formal and 'informal')	15.3
Artisanal activities	4.7
Construction	9.1
Commerce	16.2
Administration	9.1
Transport	19.5
Day labourers	7.4
Other	5.3
Persons working abroad	4.4
Retired persons	4.2
'Unemployed'	3.5

Source: Groupe Huit (1978a).

While spatial imbalances in the distribution of employment have
been shown to create a variety of social and economic stresses within
the city, much more serious problems arise from the overall shortfall of
jobs in the conurbation. Employment provision has been identified by
the District of Tunis (1975) as the most critical problem facing the
city's planners, exceeding in severity the problems of housing, sanitation
and public transport. Reducing the overall shortfall in labour supply is

almost a prerequisite to the solution of the other problems facing the city, as this is the source of many of the hardships experienced by the urban poor.

Labour Demand

Examination of the sectoral distribution of employment in Tunis reveals that disappointingly little restructuring of the urban economy has occurred in the post-colonial era (Table 3.5). The level of *demand* for labour in both Tunis and in the rest of the country has consistently

Table 3.5: Sectoral Distribution of Employment in Tunis

Sector	1966	1974
Agriculture	19,000	20,000
Mines and energy	3500	5000
Manufacturing	39,000	62,000
Building and public works	10,000	16,000
Total secondary activities	52,500	83,500
Transport	11,000	18,000
Commerce	22,000	32,000
Administration	45,000	60,500
Tourism	2000	3500
Other services	14,000	16,500
Total tertiary activities	94,000	130,500

Source: District de Tunis (1975).

lagged behind the growing *supply* of labour, even though there has been a modest expansion of jobs in recent years (Findlay, 1980a). The most striking characteristic of the employment structure of the Tunis labour market at the time of the first census after independence (1966) was the dominance of the tertiary sector. Of all actively employed persons, 56.8 per cent worked in this part of the urban economy. Most of these were employed in administration or commerce, reflecting the continuing role of Tunis as administrative and commercial capital of the country. By contrast, secondary activities were poorly developed and employed less than one-third of the active population in 1966. The absolute

number of employees in the secondary sector appears to have grown by
only 30 per cent between 1952 and 1966, lagging far behind the rate of
urban population growth (Table 3.1). The weakness of the manufacturing sector following the departure of the few French entrepreneurs who
had invested their skills and capital in Tunis was particularly marked. In
1966 there were substantially fewer employees in industry than in the
swollen ranks of the Tunisian administration. During the first post-
independence decade the government favoured industrial decentralisation and the creation of a number of important new industries, mainly
for import substitution, outside the Tunis conurbation. After the return
to economic liberalism in the 1970s, however, the volume of employment in secondary activities in Tunis increased considerably and the
character of industrial growth changed dramatically. An optimistic
estimate of the size of the manufacturing labour force in Tunis by the
end of 1974 suggests it involved 62,500 persons, most of whom had
found work in foreign-owned, export-oriented industries. These new
industries had been attracted to Tunisia following the introduction in
1972 and 1974 of new laws on industrial investment, which transformed
the country into a virtual free zone for foreign industrialists. For example, under this 'open-door' policy 32 new textile firms set up factories
in the central area of Tunis, and many more located in suburban areas
such as the four large new clothing factories established on the northeast coast in the La Goulette-La Marsa area.

The 'open-door' industrial policy has undoubtedly contributed to
the growth of employment in the Tunis labour market. By the end of
1977, the *Agence de Promotion des Investissements* (API), the government agency responsible for promoting industrial investment by foreign
companies, claimed that the Tunis conurbation had received 19,955 new
jobs since the beginning of 1973 as a result of the policy (API, 1978).
The significance of the new industrial strategy in influencing trends in
the labour market has been considerable; in the years 1973 to 1975 86
per cent of job expansion in manufacturing in the Tunis conurbation
was in export-oriented industries established under the new investment
laws. Indeed, Tunis has received the lion's share of investment arising
from the new industrial policies, attracting no less than 43 per cent of
all new enterprises (Table 3.6).

Investment in export-oriented industries has been imbalanced in both
its spatial and sectoral distribution. Most new jobs have been concentrated in one sector, textiles, thereby increasing the potential instability of
the Tunisian labour market (Table 3.7). In Tunis the textiles sector has
grown in importance and whereas it employed only 13.1 per cent of the

Table 3.6: Industrial Development at 31 December 1977 as a Result of New Foreign-owned Industrial Projects Initiated in the Period 1973-6

	Number of projects	Investment achieved (1000 dinars)[a]	Employment achieved
In Tunis	1088	103,900	19,955
Tunisia	2505	313,058	51,421
Tunis as percentage of total	43.4	33.2	38.8

a. In 1977 1 Tunisian dinar was worth £0.78.
Source: API (1978).

Table 3.7: Industrial Development by Sector, 1973-6

	Tunis	Tunisia	Proportion in Tunis (%)
Food industries	2025	6004	33.7
Construction	2604	8081	32.2
Mechanical and electrical engineering	3812	6185	61.6
Chemical and rubber industries	767	1782	43.6
Textiles	8021	23,579	34.0
Other	2726	5790	47.1
Total	19,955	51,421	29.5

Source: API (1978).

manufacturing labour force at the beginning of 1970, by the end of 1976 this figure has risen to 17.4 per cent. The only other manufacturing activity to experience a significant expansion within Tunis as a result of the new investment policy has been mechanical and electrical engineering, the capital city receiving 62 per cent of all new jobs in this sector. The dangers inherent in overdependence on growth in only one branch of manufacturing have been made tragically clear, following the collapse of West European demand for Tunisian textiles and the imposition of crippling tariff barriers by the EEC on imported clothing in 1978.

While manufacturing employment in Tunis experienced only moderate expansion in the 1970s, the growth of the tertiary sector of the urban economy has continued unabated. Statistical sources differ in their estimates of the precise size of the sector, but they are in agreement about its relative importance. The District of Tunis has suggested that, at the end of 1974, 55.9 per cent of the active population of the city was involved in administration, commerce and service activities, while the 1975 census registered 56.7 per cent of the Tunis labour force in the tertiary sector. The continued dominance of tertiary activities in Tunis is not surprising in view of the persistence of centralised national decision-making procedures. These have resulted in Tunis preempting approximately half of the country's administrative employment. Ironically, the return to economic liberalism has encouraged at one extreme the proliferation of small commercial enterprises in the tertiary sector, and at the other the emergence of branches of many of the world's largest international corporations, retailing complexes and banks. One of the most serious consequences of the penetration of international capital has been the partial forfeiture of the country's independence from foreign decision-makers.

Labour Supply

The size and rapid rate of growth of the population of Tunis have already been discussed. In 1966, 43.1 per cent of the population were less than 15 years of age. Consequently, the population entering the active age groups has increased, causing the active population to expand even faster than the population of Tunis as a whole. Those in the age cohorts 15-60 years of age accounted for 52.3 per cent of the population in 1966 and 60 per cent in 1975. During the same period the female activity rate rose from 17 per cent to approximately 23 per cent, further contributing to the potential labour supply. The increase in the female activity rate has occurred because of the growth of female employment opportunities and the aspirations of a growing proportion of female school leavers to become wage earners.

At the present time labour supply greatly exceeds labour demand. In 1975, 76,000 persons were officially recorded as unemployed. This estimate is optimistic; it does not account for the many members of the 'active' population who had irregular, part-time or extremely insecure employment. For example, in the city centre itself 39 per cent of the labour force is involved in so-called 'informal' activities in the lower-circuit or small-scale sector of the urban economy, reflecting a situation of gross underemployment. Despite this grim picture, the Tunis labour market has in recent decades continued to attract jobseekers from other parts of the country, exacerbating the already alarming problem of over-supply of labour in the city. The overall balance of labour supply and demand is, however, only one aspect of the difficulties resulting from labour surplus in Tunis.

Since independence, changes have occurred not only in the character of labour supply but also in the aspirations of jobseekers. This is not surprising in view of the relatively high levels of educational and profes-sional training attained by a large part of the population. Tunis, both as the capital city and national educational centre, had the highest rates of literacy in the country in 1975. Amongst the active labour force, 61 per cent had received at least some primary schooling, while 27 per cent had attended secondary school. The 1975 census indicated that 10 per cent of the active population could be termed highly skilled, and this may be compared with a national average of only 5.4 per cent. A fundamental mismatch exists between the levels of educational attainment of the workforce and the levels of skill required on the labour market (Findlay, 1978). In the case of Tunis there is a particularly acute imbalance between the low rate of expansion of male employment in manufactur-ing activities and the much more rapid rise in the supply of young semiskilled and skilled workers seeking jobs in these sectors of the urban economy. Semiskilled and skilled workers from all parts of Tunisia, per-ceiving Tunis as the focal point in the national economy, come and seek jobs in the manufacturing industries of the Tunis agglomeration.

A twofold influx of jobseekers has thus invaded the Tunis labour market. When taken in conjunction with only limited expansion of manufacturing industries, it is not surprising that the Tunis labour market has been unable to absorb this increase in skilled and semiskilled labour. It is ironic but understandable that, according to the 1975 cen-sus, Tunis boasted the largest concentration of 'modern' employment opportunities in the country and at the same time had the largest pool of officially registered unemployed persons. This duality poses a major dilemma for Tunisian manpower planners who must seek by job creation to absorb the urban unemployed without further increasing the existing spatial and economic imbalances between Tunis and the rest of the country, hence accelerating in-migration of jobseekers to the capital.

Jobseekers in the Tunis Labour Market

A survey of jobseekers in Tunis carried out in 1977 by Findlay (1980b) offers some interesting insights into the current employment situation in Tunis. Amongst a sample of 235 jobseekers in Tunis, 60 per cent were in-migrants to the city. It was found that the migrants in the sample had come from all over Tunisia to seek employment, but particularly from the mountainous northwestern districts. The majority of migrant jobseekers came from other urban centres within the less favoured regions, rather than from rural communities. The survey also revealed that 38 per cent of migrant jobseekers had some level of professional qualification, hence reinforcing the fact that the Tunis labour market faces problems not only of job provision but of employment creation in those sectors of the urban economy appropriate to the skill levels and aspirations of the workforce. Skill levels were even higher amongst jobseekers native to the city. Many were young men with little professional experience yet nevertheless with high aspirations of finding employment in Tunis.

The Tunis labour market, in addition to Tunisois jobseekers and in-migrants, also receives workers returning from foreign employment, mainly in France or Libya. These migrants prefer to seek work in the urban labour market in Tunis, rather than return to their villages or towns of origin. In the survey six per cent of jobseekers native to Tunis and 17 per cent of those from other parts of Tunisia were found to have previously worked abroad. These jobseekers, accustomed to relatively high wages, aspired to much higher incomes than other jobseekers. Unfortunately, the industrial experience which they had acquired while working abroad appeared to be of little relevance in their search for employment in Tunis.

While the problem of matching skill levels with job creation is an important task, Tunis manpower planners must also grapple with the problem of the many jobseekers with little or no professional training, approximately 60 per cent of the sample survey. Although not of the magnitude common to many Third World cities, this problem remains serious. The District of Tunis in 1975 admitted that one-third of all employment was in the so-called 'informal' sector. About half of all in-migrants to the city are forced to find work in small-scale activities such as street vending when they first arrive in the city (Hay, 1974).

Although employment in the lower circuit of the urban economy is characterised by very low incomes and unstable employment prospects, investigation has shown that this sector is far from a disorganised chaos

of marginal manufacturing, vending and service activities. A study of
the second-hand-clothes (*la friperie*) traders of one of the spontaneous
settlements, Melassine, and the Hafsia quarter of the medina (Group
d'Etudes Tunis, 1976) indicated that, although many of the traders had
no shop, they competed for trade in a highly organised and structured
system controlled by a few entrepreneurs and wholesalers who alone
had access to sources of imported bales of clothes. The very limited
number of traders with official licences for selling second-hand clothing,
combined with this highly organised system, has given rise to an active
black market. Street traders are highly dependent on the superstructure
of wholesalers, and operate with very low profit margins and considerable insecurity of employment. It is very difficult for them to improve
their status, as their low income level means that they cannot raise sufficient capital to establish their own formal retail outlets. The traders
interviewed from Melassine had been selling second-hand clothes, on
average, for 16 years, while those from the Hafsia quarter had been in
the trade for an average of 21 years.

The example of the second-hand-clothes trade is no exception, and
is repeated in other branches of the small-scale sector of the urban
economy. It demonstrates the familiar and depressing tale that for the
poorly educated, poorly qualified worker the city of Tunis provides a
highly structured and relatively immobile labour market, which offers
little opportunity for upward occupational mobility.

Conclusion

Although housing and employment have been identified as the most
critical problems facing planners responsible for the city of Tunis, a
wide spectrum of other physical, economic and social constraints also
demand urgent action. If the dual role of Tunis as haven of international
capitalism and home to one in five of the Tunisian population is to be
resolved satisfactorily, planners can no longer afford to neglect analysis
of the socio-economic processes underpinning the acute pressures on
the city's structure. Planning policies for the city, if constructed in isolation from broader strategies of regional development and the more
equitable distribution of human and physical resources, cannot hope to
be more than cosmetic in character and are doomed to failure. Reorganisation of planning goals towards greater spatial and sectoral integration
within the national economy would lay a more satisfactory foundation
for Tunisian development. The spatial manifestation of this would be

more balanced urban and regional development and an increased
potential for social and occupational mobility within the housing
and labour markets of Tunis.

Notes

1. The population of Tunis expressed as a percentage of the total Tunisian
population has increased continuously between 1921 and 1975. It did not
decline in the decade 1956-66 as suggested by some demographers (e.g., Picouet,
1975).
2. Religious foundations whose role was to manage donated properties; part
of the profits was used to maintain the foundation, the rest was distributed to
the inheritors.
3. Early in 1980, rehabilitation schemes were underway in a number of
spontaneous settlements, Djebel Lahmar, Melassine and Saida Manoubia, but
little progress has been made towards implementing the rehabilitation project
known as Ilot III E-50 in the medina. The ASM has not succeeded in securing an
executive role to ensure the implementation of its proposals, and its relations
with the District of Tunis, responsible for the formulation of planning policies
throughout Greater Tunis, are nonexistent. The District, for their part, appear
to have established a working relationship with the municipality of Tunis (to
whom the ASM nominally belongs) which totally bypasses the ASM.

Bibliography

Abdelkafi, J., 'Tunis: Les Conditions de l'Urbanisation', *Maghreb Machrek*, vol.
80 (1978), pp. 63-73
Abu-Lughod, J.L., 'The Legitimacy of Comparisons in Comparative Urban Studies
– A Theoretical Position and an Application to North African Cities', *Urban
Affairs Quarterly*, vol. 11, no. 1 (1975a), pp. 13-35
— 'A Comparative Analysis – Cairo, Tunis and Rabat-Salé', *Ekistics*, vol. 233
(1975b), pp. 236-45
— 'Moroccan Cities: Apartheid and the Serendipity of Conservation' in J. Abu-
Lughod (ed.), *African Themes: Essays in Honour of Gwendolen Carter*
(Northwestern University, Evanston, 1975c), pp. 77-111
— 'Developments in North African Urbanism: The Process of Decolonization' in
Urbanization and Counter-urbanization, Urban Affairs Annual Review 11
(Sage, Beverley Hills, California, 1976), pp. 191-211
API (*Agence de Promotion des Investissements*), *Investissement Industriel en
Tunisie* (API, Tunis, 1976), p. 70
— *Réalisations des Projets Agrée Au Cours du Quatrième Plan, 1973-76, Enquete:
Année 1977* (API, Tunis, 1978)
Aydalot, P., 'La Structuration de l'Espace Economique Tunisien', *Revue Tunis-
ienne de Sciences Sociales*, vol. 5 (1966), p. 71
Bourdieu, P., 'The Algerian Subproletariat' in I. William Zartman (ed.), *Man,
State and Society in the Contemporary Maghrib* (Praeger, New York, 1973),
pp. 83-92
Brown, L.C., *The Tunisia of Ahmad Bey, 1837-1855* (Princeton University Press,
1974)

Callens, M., 'L'Hébergement Traditionnel à Tunis', *Les Cahiers de Tunisie*, vol. 3, no. 10 (1955), pp. 165-79

Clarke, J.I., 'Tunisia: Population Patterns, Pressures and Policies' in J.I. Clarke and W.B. Fisher (eds.), *Populations of the Middle East and North Africa: A Geographical Approach* (University of London Press, London, 1972), p. 365

Cleveland, W.L. 'The Municipal Council of Tunis, 1858-1870: A Study in Urban Institutional Change', *International Journal of Middle Eastern Studies*, vol. 9, no. 1 (1978), pp. 33-61

Danon, V., 'Les Niveaux de Vie dans la Hara de Tunis', *Les Cahiers de Tunisie*, vol. 3, no. 10 (1955), pp. 180-210

Dardel, J.B. and Klibi, S.C., 'Un Faubourg Clandestin de Tunis: Le Dj. Lahmar', *Les Cahiers de Tunisie*, vol. 3, no. 10 (1955), pp. 211-24

DAT (*Direction Amenagement du Territoire*) Group Huit, *Villes et Developpement* (DAT, Tome 1, Tunis, 1973)

Despois, J., 'La Répartition des Industries de Transformation dans l'Afrique du Nord' in *Industrialisation de l'Afrique du Nord*, Bibliothèque Génerale de l'EPHE, Sixième Section (Colin, Paris, 1952)

District de Tunis, *Schéma Directeur d'Aménagement et d'Urbanisme: Rapport d'Orientation* (Tunis, 1975), p. 17

— *Le Centre de Tunis Analyse et Propositions* (Tunis, 1976a), pp. 10-21

— *Elements pour une Politique de Localisation des Emplois* (Ministère de l'Intérieur, Tunis, 1976b)

— *Elements pour une Politique des Transport* (Ministère de l'Intérieur, Tunis, 1976)

— *Plan Regional d'Aménagement*, vol. 3, *Schemas de Zones* (Ministère de l'Intérieur, Tunis, 1977), pp. 8-11

Dlala, H., 'Compte Rendu du Plan d'Aménagement Regional du District de Tunis', *Revue Tunisienne de Geographie*, vol. 2 (1979), pp. 177-80

Fakhfakh, F., *Une Banlieue de Tunis Depuis l'Independance: l'Ariana*, Fascicule 1, Urbanisation, Reseaux Urbains, Regionalisation au Maghreb (CNRS, Centre Interuniversitaire d'Etudes des Milieux Naturels et de l'Aménagement des Pays Mediterranéens, Poitiers, and Conseil Scientifique de l'Université de Tours, 1977), pp. 167-202

Findlay, A.M., 'Tunisia: Country Case Study', *Working Paper for the International Migration Project* (University of Durham, England, 1978), pp. 41, 53

— 'Planning for Migration: The Case of Tunisia', Unpublished paper presented to the Institute of British Geographers' Conference on Population and Development (Cambridge, 19-20 September 1979)

— 'Spatial Dimensions of Tunisian Manpower Planning' in H. Bowen-Jones and J.I. Clarke (eds.), *Change and Development in the Middle East* (Methuen, London, 1980a)

— *Patterns and Processes of Tunisian Migration*, Unpublished PhD thesis (University of Durham, England, 1980b)

Ganiage, J., *La Population Européene de Tunis au Milieu du Dix-neuvième siècle* (PUF, Paris, 1960)

Groupe d'Etudes Tunis, *La Structure et l'Organisation de la Friperie à Tunis* (DAT, Université Libre d'Amsterdam, Amsterdam, 1976)

Groupe Huit, *Activites Tertiaires du Centre de Tunis* (Ministère de l'Intérieur/ District de Tunis, 1977), pp. 42-8

— *Réhabilitation du Quartier de Saida Manoubia* (Ministère de l'Intérieur/Municipalité de Tunis, Tunis, 1978a), p. 13

— *Project de Réhabilitation du Quartier de Jebel Lahmar* (Ministère de l'Intérieur/Municipalité de Tunis, Tunis, 1978b)

Hay, M., *An Economic Analysis of Rural-urban Migration in Tunisia*, Unpublished PhD thesis (University of Minnesota, 1974)

Houidi, T., *L'Hypercentre de Tunis*, Mémoire de maitrise (Université de Poitiers, 1977)

Houidi, T. and Miossec, J-M., *La Population Tunisienne en 1975* (DAT/Ministère de l'Equipement, Tunis, 1975)

Hoyt, H., *The Structure and Growth of Residential Neighbourhoods in American Cities* (US Government Printing Office, Washington, 1939)

Kultermann, U., *New Directions in African Architecture* (George Brazilier, New York, 1969)

Lawless, R.I., 'Industrialisation in the Maghreb – Progress, Problems and Prospects' *Maghreb Review*, vol. 1, no. 2 (1976), pp. 6-9, 18

— 'Social and Economic Change in North African Medinas: The Case of Tunis' in H. Bowen-Jones and J.I. Clarke (eds.), *Change and Development in the Middle East* (Methuen, London, 1980a)

— 'The Future of Historic Centres: Conservation or Redevelopment?' in G.H. Blake and R.I. Lawless (eds.), *The Changing Middle Eastern City* (Croom Helm, London, 1980b), pp. 185-93

Lowy, P., 'L'Artisanat dans les Médinas de Tunis et de Sfax', *Annales de Géographie*, vol. 470 (1970), pp. 473-93

— 'Les Villes Fermées d'Afrique du Nord: Méthodes de Recherche', *L'Espace Géographie*, vol. 1 (1975), pp. 31-43

Micaud, E.C., 'Belated Urban Planning in Tunis: Problems and Prospects', *Human Organization*, vol. 33, no. 2 (1974), pp. 123-37

— 'Urban Planning in Tunis' in R.A. Stone and J. Simmons (eds.), *Change in Tunisia* (State University of New York Press, New York, 1977), pp. 137-58

— 'Urbanization, Urbanism and the Medina', *International Journal of Middle Eastern Studies*, vol. 9, no. 4 (1978), pp. 431-47

Miossec, J-M., L'Affirmation de la Fonction Economique de Tunis', *Revue Francaise d'Etudes Politiques Méditerranéenes*, vol. 30-1 (1978), pp. 91-120

Miossec, J-M. and Signoles, P., 'Priorité de l'Echelle Nationale dans l'Urbanisation et l'Organisation Spatiale de la Tunisie', *Travaux de la Table Ronde, Urbanisation au Maghreb* (AIEM, Poitiers, 1978), pp. 243-70

Pellegrin, A., *Histoire Illustrée de Tunis et de La Banlieue* (Saliba Editions, Tunis, 1955)

Picouet, M., 'Evolution Récente du Peuplement de l'Agglomeration de Tunis', *Cahiers ORSTOM Seree Sc. Humaines*, vol. 12, no. 4 (1975), p. 346

Poncet, J., 'Continuites Urbaines et Discontinuites Sociales à Tunis', *Revue Francaise des Etudes Politiques Mediterraneenes*, vol. 30-1 (1978), pp. 198-204

Projet Tunis/Carthage, *Sauvegarde et Mise en Valeur de la Medina de Tunis, Dossier 6 Operations de Rehabilitation de l'Ilot III E-50* (UNESCO, Institut National d'Archeologie et d'Arts, Association Sauvegarde de la Medina, 1974), p. 20

Revault, J., *L'Habitation Tunisoise: Pierre, Marbre et Fer dans la Construction et le Decor*, (CNRS, Paris, 1978), pp. 15-24

Sebag, P., 'Le Bidonville de Borgel', *Les Cahiers de Tunisie*, vol. 6, no. 23-4 (1958), pp. 267-309

— 'Le Faubourg de Sidi Fathallah', *Les Cahiers de Tunisie*, vol. 8 no. 29-30 (1960), pp. 75-136

— 'La Decolonisation et la Transformation des Quartiers Traditionnels de Tunis' in *Les Influences Occidentales dans les Villes Maghrebines a l'Epoque Contemporaine*, Etudes Mediterraneenes 2 (Editions de l'Universite de Provence, 1974), pp. 247-55

Signoles, P., 'Villes, Industries et Organisation de l'Espace en Tunisie' in *Travaux du Centre Géographique, d'Etudes et de Recherches Rurales*, vol. 5 (Université de Poitiers, 1975)
— 'Les Inégalités Régionales entre Tunis et la Tunisie', *Revue Francaise d'Etudes Politiques Méditerranéenes*, 30-31 (1978a), p. 50
— 'L'Armature Urbaine Tunisienne', *Revue Tunisienne de Géographie*, vol. 1 (1978b), pp. 65-96
Taieb, J., 'Une Banlieue de Tunis: L'Ariana', *Les Cahiers de Tunisie*, vol. 8, no. 32 (1960), pp. 33-76
Valensi, L., *Fellahs Tunisiens: l'Economie Rurale et la Vie des Campagnes aux Dixhuitième et Dixneuvième Siècles* (Mouton, Paris, 1979a), pp. 15-17
— *On the Eve of Colonialism: North Africa before the French Conquest* (Africana, London, 1977b), p. 41

4 LAGOS

Bola Ayeni

Lagos, the largest metropolitan area in Nigeria, is located along the southwestern coast at the only outlet to the sea of a lagoon that extends from West of Cotonou in the Republic of Benin to the Niger Delta in Nigeria. The fact that this was the only natural break along some 2,500 kilometers of the West African coastline made Lagos a very important port in the trading activities of the eighteenth and nineteenth centuries. However, the growth of Lagos is due to the growth of the colonial economy of Nigeria (Table 4.1). As the seat of government since 1914,

Table 4.1: Land Area and Population Growth in Lagos, 1866-1976

Year of census	Area (km^2)	Total population	Intercensus increase	Annual growth rate
1866	3.97	25,083	–	–
1871	3.97	25,518	1.7	0.6
1881	3.97	37,452	46.8	3.9
1891	3.97	32,508	-33.2	-1.4
1901	–	41,847	28.7	2.5
1911	46.08	73,766	76.3	5.8
1921	51.64	99,690	35.1	3.1
1931	65.51	126,108	26.5	2.4
1941				
1950	69.68	230,256	82.6	3.3
1952	69.68	267,407	16.1	7.8
1963	69.68	665,246	188.9	11.9
1952[a]	–	341,569	232.6	11.5
1963[a]	–	1,136,154	–	–
1974[a]	178.36	2,437,335	–	–
1976[a]	271.20	3,519,000	–	–

a. These figures are for the metropolitan area of Lagos.

Sources: Population Census of Nigeria (1952, 1963); Population figures given for 1974 and 1976 were estimates (Ayeni, 1978; Lagos State Government, 1977).

the largest sea-port and the most important railway and air terminus, the city had maximum significance in the predominantly export-oriented economy of the country. In 1950, the city was given the status of a municipality, and its area was subsequently extended to incorporate parts of the mainland (Figure 4.1). Today, the metropolis includes six local-government areas in the fastest-growing part of the country.

Figure 4.1: Metropolitan Lagos

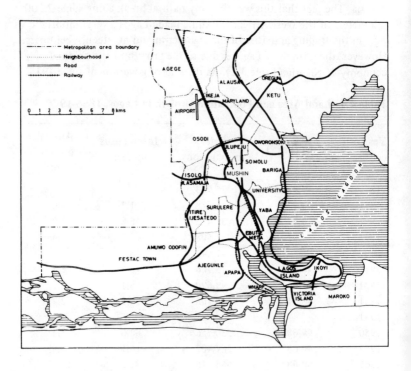

The Location of Economic Activities and Patterns of Land Use

In 1970 and 1971, Lagos contained more than one-third of the total number of wholesale establishments in the country and about one-quarter of the total number of retail outlets in the formal sector, which accounted for over 60 and 50 per cent, respectively, of total employment.

Trading in the informal sector in Lagos is organised through a number of market places that are known all over the country. Thus, the traditional market centres of Obun Eko, Ebute-Ero (Haven of Visitors), Egerton Square, Faji, Olowu Street, Great Bridge and Obalende play important roles in the distributive trade, while the Central Lagos Slum Clearance schemes of the 1950s gave room for the development of a modern Central Business District along the Marina, Broad Street and Nnamdi Azikwe Streets (Figure 4.2). Today, this Cental Business District shows most of the characteristics of similar districts in other major cities. It is an area of intense land use, indicated by the large number of multistorey buildings and skyscrapers, and there is clear evidence of both functional and areal differentiation (Mabogunje, 1964).

Moreover, as the break-of-bulk point in the import-substitution industrial-development process that began in about 1955, Lagos became the major industrial centre in the country. By 1965, it accounted for 37.8 per cent of industrial activities, and this proportion increased to 50 per cent in 1969. In 1975, metropolitan Lagos accounted for over 65 per cent of the value added by manufacturing, with these activities located mainly on industrial estates at Apapa, Ebute-Metta, Ikeja, Ilupeju and Isolo.

In addition to the industrial and commercial functions of the city, Lagos remains the *de facto* headquarters of the Federal government. Consequently, it houses and provides work places for civil servants and members of the diplomatic corps. Furthermore, the capital of Lagos State is at Ikeja, part of the Lagos metropolis. In all, the Federal government provided employment for over 118,170 people, while the state government gave employment to 19,063 in 1975 (Table 4.2). Undoubtedly, Ikoyi and Lagos Island are the most important locations for civil-service employment in the metropolis. This concentration of activities

Table 4.2: Federal- and State-government Employment in Major Employment Zones in Lagos, 1975

Zone	State	Federal	Total
Ikoyi	1404	23,919	25,323
Lagos Island	7147	87,582	94,729
Victoria Island	515	1609	2124
Ikeja	7468	795	8263
Others	2529	4265	6794
Total	19,063	118,170	137,233

Source: Federal and State Government, Annual Estimates (1975).

on the two islands is a major cause of heavy traffic flows between the islands and the mainland of the metropolitan area.

The metropolitan area of Lagos differs from many Nigerian cities in that urban land uses are so mixed that it is difficult to spatially differentiate them. Residential land occupies only about 50 per cent of the total built-up area of the metropolis, while industrial usage occupies 11.31 per cent (Table 4.3). Other major uses of land are educational

Table 4.3: Urban Land Use in Lagos, 1975

Types of use	Area (hectares)	Proportion of total (%)
Residential[a]	12,063	48.02
Educational	1440	5.73
Health	179	0.71
Commercial	985	3.92
Industrial	2843	11.31
Administrative	760	3.02
Transportational	2230	8.88
Sports and recreation	467	1.86
Special installations (army, etc.)	4095	16.30
Cemetries	64	0.25
	25,126	100.00

a. The figures given for residential use by Doxiades differ from the estimates of the Metropolitan Planning Unit (see Table 4.4).

Source: Based on Doxiades Associates International (1977).

institutions, which occupy 5.73 per cent; commercial activities, which occupy 3.92 per cent; transport, which occupies 8.88 per cent; and administration, which occupies 3.02 per cent (Figure 4.2).

Spatial variations in the density of residential land use occur over the metropolitan area. The largest residential tracts are found in Agege, Mushin, Ijeshatedo, Ikoyi East and Maroko, where residential land occupies more than 80 per cent of total built-up area (Table 4.4). In contrast to these heavily built-up residential zones are places like the Airport-Sogunle, Ketu-Oregun, Mushin NW, the Central Business District (CBD), Ikoyi West and Lagos Island, where more buildings are used for other purposes than residential. An important characteristic of residential land use in Lagos is the areal separation of people by socio-economic characteristics. For instance, certain neighbourhoods like

Figure 4.2: Land Use in Lagos, 1979

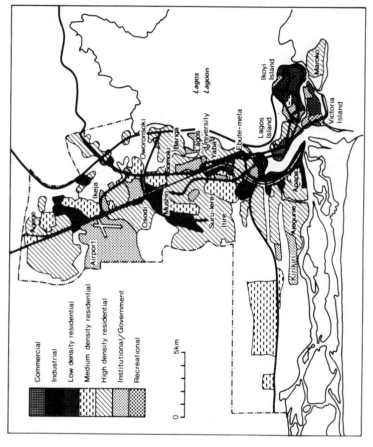

Table 4.4: Some Characteristics of Residential Land Use in Lagos, 1976

Zones	Total area (hectares)	Built-up area	Gross residential area	Fraction residential (%)	Estimated inhabitants (thousands)	Number of houses
Agege	2428	1139	910	79.9	393.6	13,404
Airport-Sogunle	2783	2414	403	16.7	131.8	4006
Ikeja	2010	1353	820	60.6	144.2	6040
Oregun-Ketu	2358	590	293	49.7	138.0	2513
Mushin NW	940	624	197	31.6	30.6	1115
Ijeshatedo, Itire	876	704	615	87.4	250.3	5943
Mushin W, Surulere N	565	506	388	75.7	298.8	4627
Mushin Central	323	302	193	63.9	289.7	4301
Mushin E, Bariga	1837	881	697	79.1	480.5	9431
Surulere S, Ebute-Metta	1274	1012	537	53.1	143.6	5762
Yaba S, Ebute-Metta E	980	834	427	51.2	242.6	5864
Amuwo Town, Festac Town	4553	1716	553	32.2	12.2	721
Iganmu, Ajegunle, Apapa	2586	1771	1044	59.0	519.0	9318
Lagos Island N	361	281	128	45.6	243.1	5487
CBD and institutions	163	158	6	3.8	9.5	–
Ikoyi West	409	317	114	36.0	33.8	1247
Ikoyi East	720	591	524	88.7	51.3	2332
Victoria Island	505	358	194	54.2	14.4	939
Maroko	514	234	222	94.9	85.4	3117
	27,120	16,177	8288	51.0	3519.0	86,197

Source: Lagos State Ministry of Works and Planning (1977).

Victoria Island, Ikoyi East, Government Reservation at Ikeja, Ilupeju and Palmgrove residential estates are inhabited by the higher-income group. These areas (Figure 4.2) are low-density residential areas and are generally characterised by the presence of tracts of open land. Medium to high residential areas exist in Yaba, Surulere, Ebute-Metta and in numerous privately owned residential estates such as Maryland, Anthony Village and Okupe. Elsewhere are low and sometimes very poor and substandard residential areas, within which there is a high mix of residential and other activities.

Urban Problems in Lagos

Nowhere are problems of Nigerian urbanisation and urban development more starkly depicted than in Lagos. Here urban problems range from unemployment to traffic congestion and environmental deterioration. Green and Milone (1972) summarise the situation as follows:

> Chaotic traffic conditions have become endemic; demands on the water supply system have begun to outstrip its maximum capacity; power cuts have become chronic as industrial and domestic requirements have escalated; factories have been compelled to have their own wells and to set up stand-by electricity plants; public transport has been inundated; port facilities have been stretched to their limits; the conditions have degenerated over extensive areas within and beyond the city's limits in spite of slum clearance schemes; and city government has threatened to break down amidst charges of corruption, mismanagement and financial incompetence. Moreover, although employment opportunities have multiplied in industry, commerce and public administration, there is no doubt that thousands of in-migrants have been unable to find work, and the potential for civil disturbances has increased.

The above 'litany of ills' constitutes an efficient summary of the dimensions of urban problems in Lagos today.

Inadequate and Inefficient Provision of Basic Services

The provision of certain basic services and conveniences such as housing, health facilities, educational institutions, recreational facilities, water and electricity remains the greatest failure of the metropolis of Lagos. Even when these facilities are provided, they are often inadequate or are not efficiently maintained. The failure of the metropolis in this endeavour cannot be disassociated from the phenomenal rate of population growth by in-migration, the corresponding spatial expansion of the built-up area and the fact that the metropolis possesses very limited resources to meet these increasing demands on its infrastructure.

The inadequacy of housing structures in metropolitan Lagos constitutes one of the greatest problems. This problem is reflected not only in the rocketing rents a prospective house or room occupier has to pay but also in the fact that, even in high-class residential areas, there is great overcrowding. For instance, while the average number of people per room in Lagos in 1976 was 4.1, the high-class residential area of Ikoyi and the lower to medium residential areas of Yaba and Ebute-Metta also had 4.1 (Table 4.5). Higher densities are found on Lagos Island (5.4), Mushin Central (4.5) and Agege (5.0). The extent of overcrowding is also reflected in the very high ratios of inhabitants per house. The average for Lagos metropolis is 40.8, although higher figures are recorded in Mushin Central (67.4), Mushin West (64.6), Ajegunle (55.7), Oregun and Ketu (54.9). The lower figures of 15.3 for Victoria Island, 21.9 for Ikoyi East and 27.1 for Ikoyi West indicate the lower densities in these high-class residential zones.

The high densities of people per room and per house lead to over-utilisation of space and household facilities like water, electricity and toilets. This constitutes one major reason why these facilities never function efficiently in many homes. Furthermore, because almost all available space has been utilised for the construction of the rooming houses in which most of the inhabitants reside, the development of other social and neighbourhood amenities such as parks and recreational grounds near residential areas has been hindered.

In spite of the poor quality and the immense overcrowding all over Lagos, house rents keep on rising. Rent edicts meant not only to standardise house rents but also to keep them low have not succeeded because the supply of residential quarters is grossly inadequate. For instance, as far back as 1964, Koenigsberger *et al.* (1964) estimated the annual requirements of housing at 2,000 units. This was undoubtedly above what the city was capable of providing at that time. Unfortunately this annual requirement has risen in recent years. Table 4.6 shows that, between 1975 and 1985, 9000 housing units would be required annually. The heavy financial implications of this for government and private entrepreneurs as well as the low capacity of the economy are inhibiting factors to the provision of adequate housing in Lagos.

The supply of household amenities like water and electricity is constrained by the rapid areal growth of Lagos. This has meant that the

Table 4.5: Housing Characteristics in Lagos, 1976

Zones of the Metropolis	Total number of houses	Inhabitants per house	Inhabitants per household	Inhabitants per room
Agege	13,404	29.4	3.1	5.0
Airport-Sogunle	4006	32.9	8.2	3.7
Ikeja	6040	23.9	5.7	3.8
Oregun, Ketu	2513	54.9	4.7	3.2
Mushin NW	1115	27.4	4.5	2.5
Ijeshatedo, Itire	5943	43.1	5.9	4.0
Mushin W, Surulere N	4627	64.6	5.1	3.5
Mushin Central	4301	67.4	6.1	4.5
Mushin E, Bariga	9431	50.9	5.1	3.1
Surulere S, Ebute-Metta	5762	24.9	–	–
Yaba S, Ebute-Metta E	5864	41.4	5.1	4.1
Amuwo, Festac Town	721	16.9	3.7	1.6
Iganmu, Ajegunle-Apapa	9318	55.7	5.8	4.2
Lagos Island N	5487	44.3	8.8	5.4
CBD and institutions	–	–	–	–
Ikoyi West	1247	27.1	7.6	4.1
Ikoyi East	2332	21.9	–	–
Victoria Island	939	15.3	–	–
Maroko	3117	27.4	5.4	3.7
Total	86,197	40.8	5.8	4.1

Source: Lagos State Ministry of Works and Planning (1977).

authorities simply cannot cope with the demands on these facilities. A study of the slums that exist both on the peripheries and in the central parts of Lagos (Ayeni, 1977) discovered that while overuse and deterioration were the main problems in the central slums of Lagos Island and Mushin, basic amenities were either simply inadequate or nonexistent in the peripheral slums of Ojota, Maroko and Ajegunle (Table 4.7). For example, at the time of the survey, both piped water and electricity were not supplied to Maroko while piped water was absent in Ojota. On

Table 4.6: Housing Requirements in Metropolitan Lagos, 1975-85

Type of need	Dwellings	Housing units
Demographic requirements	482,340	80,390
Replacement for road development	20,000	3333
Replacement for substandard units	10,000	1667
Vacancy and commercial reserves	7234	1206
Total	519,574	86,596

Source: *Survey and Planning of the Lagos State Economy*, Lagos State Population and Housing Report No. 8 (Planning Studies Programme, University
of Ibadan).

Table 4.7: The Nature of Household Amenities in Slum Areas of Lagos, 1975

Type of amenities	Maroko (%)	Ajegunle (%)	Ojota (%)	Mushin (%)	Central Lagos (%)
Houses with piped water	0.0	76.0	0.0	42.0	50.0
Houses with wells	36.8	15.0	10.0	0.0	0.0
Houses with electricity	0.0	97.0	100.0	100.0	97.5
Types of toilet:					
pail	54.0	78.0	0.0	8.0	33.3
pit	33.3	18.0	100.0	62.0	27.3
water closet	2.1	0.0	0.0	20.0	39.3
Kitchen with adequate facilities	21.5	23.0	35.0	56.0	50.0

Source: Ayeni (1977).

the other hand, many houses in Mushin and central Lagos had both
facilities. Constant breakdown of these facilities is, however, a common
feature in Lagos. For electricity many houses and firms have had to rely
on standby generators, while for water supply many households depend
on water from wells, ponds and flowing streams.

In 1973, there were only 274 primary schools and 82 secondary
schools. These enrolled 226,700 and 33,608 people, respectively. With
a metropolitan population of approximately two and a half million,
this provides one primary school for every 9124 inhabitants and one
secondary school for every 30,487 inhabitants, respectively. At a

government standard rate of one primary school for every 4000 people and one secondary school for every 10,000 people, it is obvious that these educational facilities are inadequate. Even these ratios have been obtained not by building new schools, but by causing existing schools to run two sessions, a morning session between 7.30 a.m. and 12.30 p.m. and an afternoon session from 12.30 p.m. to 5.00 p.m. daily. Apart from the strain borne by students in afternoon sessions, such overcrowding as this constitutes serious overutilisation of existing facilities.

Gross inadequacies also exist in the provision of medical facilities. In 1973, there were only 164 health establishments in the metropolitan area. This was made up of 117 in Lagos Division and 47 in Ikeja. In all, these facilities offered 4275 hospital beds at the rate of one bed for every 585 people. Although by Nigerian standards this is a very low figure, the total number of health facilities can be said to be inadequate on account of the number of health personnel per member of the population, as well as of the types of health facilities. Although Lagos again has a disproportionate share of medical personnel, many of these work in specialised medical institutions like the Lagos University Teaching Hospital, which alone has more than 600 of the 4275 hospital beds. Furthermore, the inadequacy of medical personnel is also reflected in the fact that a visit to a hospital takes the best part of two days, the first to see the doctor and the second to collect the drugs. The fact that private clinics which do not necessarily meet government standards mushroom in Lagos attests to this shortage of medical-care facilities.

The Problem of Environmental Deterioration

Environmental deterioration is one of the most alarming and uncomfortable problems of metropolitan Lagos, because it can be seen almost everywhere, in the form of heaps of garbage and other waste material and also in the structure of houses in the central slums of Lagos Island and the peripheral *bidonvilles* of Ojota, Maroko, Ajegunle and elsewhere. These two expressions of environmental deterioration are opposite sides of the same coin.

Solid wastes in Lagos include food waste, combustible materials, glass, ceramics, dead animal matter, automobile parts and solid industrial wastes. The problem of solid-waste accumulation arises because of the imbalance between the production of waste and the capacity of existing clearance facilities. An important and uncomfortable consequence of the accumulation of solid waste is the characteristic filth and

bad air of such low-income areas as Mushin, central Lagos, Apapa
Ajegunle and many parts of Agege and Ikeja (Figure 4.2).

In the past, the collection, storage, transportation to dumping sites
and final liquidation of waste materials were the responsibility of local
government areas but recently these duties have been constituted into
the responsibility of a newly created Refuse Disposal Board. Failure to
perform this function successfully in the past led to the emergence of
various methods of refuse disposal. For instance, in large parts of the
metropolis, refuse is disposed through self-help, either by burning or
by dumping into swampy areas. In low-density residential areas, there
is a government-organised house-to-house collection, while in the high-
density areas people are expected to dump refuse at a central location.
Since the rate of refuse removal by the authorities is low, garbage
accumulation is inevitable, while the inadequacy of dumping sites
encourages the indiscriminate dumping of refuse on public open spaces,
undeveloped lands, streets and even into the drainage system.

The high rate of garbage accumulation may be deduced from the
observation that a housing unit generates as much as 12 m³ of domestic
refuse in a single month. In 1975 alone, it was estimated that about 4.5
million m³ of domestic refuse required disposal within the metropolitan area each month (Lagos State Government, 1977). Lack of money
on the part of local government to deal effectively with problems of
refuse disposal, as well as the lack of effective management of refuse
collection and transportation, are major problems.

Sewage-disposal schemes, on the other hand, have been a topic of
intense research in the search for a clean environment in Lagos. Initial
studies began as early as 1916, while subsequent studies were conducted
in 1926, 1928, 1956 and 1973. In spite of these, the methods of sewage
disposal have remained unchanged over the years. Essentially, sewage
disposal in Lagos, as in many cities of Nigeria, takes one of three forms:
a pail system whereby wastes are removed in pails by night-soil men and
then transported to a disposal site; the pit or *salanga* system, whereby
holes are bored near houses and covered on the surface by a flat slab
with a small hole to let in the waste; and the septic-tank system whereby
human wastes are disposed of through water closets. In Lagos, the pail
system is in use in about 50 per cent of all households, especially in
Agege, Oshodi, Ketu, Ojota, Bariga, Isolo Mushin and a wide area of
central Lagos (Lagos State Government, 1977). The system is not only
unhealthy and unsatisfactory, but may also be dehumanising. The pit
system, on the other hand, serves about 3.8 per cent of metropolitan
Lagos, and is found mostly in older residential areas in both urban and

suburban parts of the city; it is found widely in Mushin, Ketu, Agege, Oshodi, Ojota and Bariga. Finally, the septic system is found in the newer residential areas such as Surulere, Ikeja (GRA), Maryland, Yaba, Iganmu, Apapa, Ikoyi-Victoria Island and the rebuilt areas of Lagos Island. Houses that use this system constitute only some 38.5 per cent of all houses in the metropolitan area.

There is no doubt that the sewage-disposal system in Lagos demands serious attention. In the past, many grandiose schemes for sewage disposal have been proposed by firms and organisations like Doxiades and Associates, the Lagos State Property Development Corporation and GKW Planning Associations; finance has always been an inhibiting factor in the implementation of these programmes.

Other aspects of environmental deterioration include atmospheric waste from the emission of gases by industries or automobiles, and the discharge of industrial effluent into streams. Another is noise pollution, whether generated by aeroplanes, car horns or publicly placed loud-speakers and stereophonic sound systems. At present, these problems are not regarded as serious. One serious problem which is emerging is that there have been annual floods since the early 1970s. These floods are commonest during the rainy season and result from a number of causes, primarily the lack of foresight by engineers and construction workers who design and construct roads and buildings without making adequate provision for drainage facilities. In many parts of the metropolis, the situation is exacerbated because existing drainage networks have been unwittingly blocked by residents, who utilise them for the disposal of solid wastes. Consequently, the fear of floods has grown in recent years, especially in most of the CBD on the Marina and even in parts of Surulere, Yaba and Itire.

The Problem of Intracity Movement

The problem of intracity movement in the Lagos metropolitan area is clearly apparent all over the city. Tamar Golan (1975) described the situation as follows:

> Driving into Lagos centre . . . be it from the Mainland, Ikoyi or Victoria Island, is an experience not to be repeated, and only the ordeal of coming into the city from Ikeja Airport can be compared with it . . . Driving into Lagos, you have ample time to look around, as your car is stuck in innumerable traffic jams, your driver gets into

long arguments with others who are trying to get an inch ahead of him.

Golan's description of the traffic situation, very true in 1975, is less true today, because of the great efforts made to improve the situation. However, the problems still remain and planners are far from achieving a total and lasting solution.

Although Lagos metropolitan area possesses ample resources for the development of rail and water transportation, most of the traffic in Lagos is by road. Further congestion arises because the external road networks that link the metropolitan region with the rest of the nation pass through the city; these same roads are the major links between Lagos Island and the outlying parts of the metropolitan areas such as Ikeja, Agege, Yaba, Mushin and Apapa. Furthermore, many roads in Lagos are narrow, the exceptions being the newly constructed Agege-Western Avenue road, Lagos-Badagri express way, the Ikorodu Road dual carriageway and the Apapa-Ikeja express way. The narrowness of the roads make them inaccessible to mass-transit systems such as the buses of the Lagos State Transport Service. In recent years, the phenomenal growth of population and rising standards of living have meant the purchase of many vehicles (cars, buses, motor cycles and bicycles), with the attendant overcrowding and congestion of the roads.

Traffic is generated in Lagos, as elsewhere, by the desire to go to work or to school, to purchase services or to engage in recreational activities. Consequently, the spatial juxtaposition of residences *vis-à-vis* these functions could be crucial to traffic generation. In Lagos (Figure 4.2) there is a concentration of work sites on Lagos Island, Ikoyi and Victoria Island, while workers live mainly in Ebute-Metta/Yaba; Mushin/Idioro; Surulere; and Ikeja. In a survey of the distribution of employed people *vis-à-vis* the location of their employment, the above residential districts housed 23, 22, 14 and 12 per cent of the population, respectively. On the other hand, the major work centres of Lagos Island, Ebute-Metta, Apapa and Ilupeju/Ikeja house 28, 18, 13 and 11 per cent of job opportunities, respectively (Table 4.8). The final column of Table 4.8 represents the proportion of people who must necessarily commute to work, by different zones of the city.

The desire to commute easily to work meets with serious problems in Lagos, partly because of the awkward spatial relations of work and residential areas (Figure 4.2) and partly because of the way in which the residential areas housing different socio-economic groups have developed. A major outcome is that the pattern of interaction has a trend rather

Table 4.8: Percentage Distribution of Employed People in Lagos according to Place of Residence and Place of Work, 1975

Area	Workers residing in in area (%)	Those working in area (%)	Those working in some other area (%)
Victoria Island	1.9	2.7	54.8
Ikoyi	1.7	2.8	21.8
Obalende, Lagos Island	13.7	28.2	63.3
Ebute-Metta/Yaba	22.5	18.4	30.4
Apapa	4.5	13.3	55.1
Ajegunle/Ajeromi	5.3	2.4	19.0
Surulere/Ijora/Iganmu	11.7	6.3	21.6
Igbobi/Shomolu/Bariga/ Akoka	7.9	2.3	18.0
Mushin	21.9	7.5	27.4
Oshodi	3.1	1.3	16.2
Ilupeju/Palm Grove, Ikeja	2.2	10.5	33.3
Agege	4.6	2.5	42.4
Others	–	1.8	–

Source: O.J. Fapohunda (1975).

inefficiently from north to south (Figure 4.3). Attempts to ease the interaction are complicated in that a considerable number of commuters own motor vehicles (Table 4.9), and also because there are no

Table 4.9: Percentage of Workers in Residential Areas of Lagos who Earned more than N2000 and Owned Cars, 1975

Residential areas	Those earning N2000 or more	Those owning cars (%)
Apapa	51.0	54.1
Ilupeju/Ikeja	47.9	54.2
Oshodi	27.9	30.9
Victoria Island	23.8	33.3
Ikoyi	21.6	18.9
Surulere/Iganmu	19.4	17.7
Igbobi/Shomolu/Bariga	7.0	12.8
Ajegunle/Ajeromi	3.4	15.5
Ebute-Metta/Yaba	7.6	10.0
Obalende/Lagos Island	4.7	10.8
Mushin/Idi Oro	1.5	8.4
Agege	0.0	0.0

Figure 4.3: Patterns of Interaction on the Journey to Work in Lagos, 1974

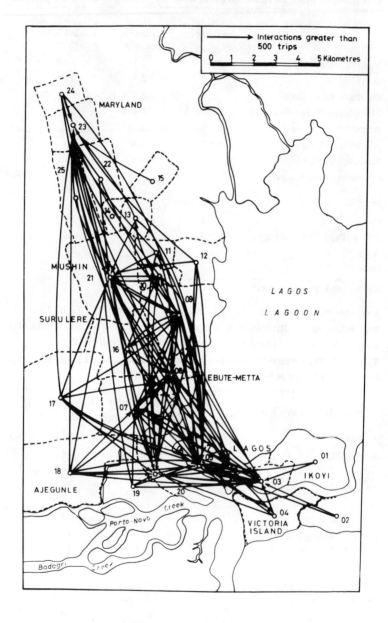

alternative routes to the centres of employment. Consequently, when the volume of traffic on the journey to work is combined with that on trips to service centres, recreational facilities and educational institutions, severe congestion of the road network develops.

In spite of the reconstruction of some roads and widening of others (Figure 4.4), the traffic congestion in recent years is alarming.

Figure 4.4: The Road Network in Lagos, 1979

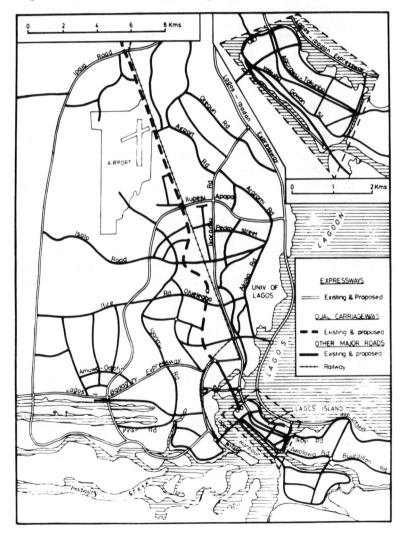

Consequently, within the last four years, the urban administrators have tried to alleviate matters by promulgating an edict which restricts the number of cars reaching municipal Lagos. This, the Lagos State Traffic edict, permits only those motor cars whose registration numbers begin with an odd number to enter the municipal area on specified days of the week, and only those with a registration number that begins with an even number to enter on the next day. Because there is no efficient mass-transit system, this edict has inflicted hardship on some car owners, while many families who can afford to do so have reacted by buying a second car, so as to have cars with both even and odd initial numbers in their registrations. This edict, therefore, cannot be said to have solved the problem of congestion on the roads.

Urban Unemployment

A major problem of urbanisation in Lagos is unemployment. Although there are no systematic data on the unemployed in Nigerian cities, there is enough evidence to discern the nature of urban unemployment. Falae (1971) reported that, while the unemployment level in the country was 1.7 per cent, it varied between 5 and 20 per cent for the urban centres. High levels of unemployment in urban centres in general and Lagos in particular are not unconnected with the rapid rates at which cities grow through rural-urban migration. Between 1952 and 1963, migrants accounted for an increase of 393,000 in the city's population, representing 75 per cent of total increase during the same period. Until very recently, the only jobs available in the cities were civil-service jobs but, in recent years, the pace of industrialisation has increased, and a substantial percentage of the labour force of Lagos has been able to move into the manufacturing sector. Nevertheless the rate of growth of job opportunities has not matched that of migration into Lagos.

In a more recent survey of the unemployed in Lagos (University of Lagos 1974), 525 of the 1480 people interviewed (that is, 45 per cent) were aged 20-4 years, while another 28 per cent were 15-19 and 18 per cent were 25-9 (Table 4.10). One can safely conclude that the unemployed people in Lagos are mainly able-bodied men and women. Furthermore, more than 88 per cent of these unemployed people come from states of the Federation other than Lagos State. In addition, a detailed analysis of the unemployed showed that, while only 3 per cent had no formal education, 90 per cent had a minimum of full primary school education, and 30 per cent had a minimum of secondary

Table 4.10: Sample of Unemployed Persons by Age and Sex, Lagos, 1974

Age group	Male		Female		Total	
	No.	%	No.	%	No.	%
Below 15	4	0.35	1	0.30	5	0.34
15-19	272	23.82	136	40.24	408	27.57
20-4	525	45.97	145	42.90	670	45.27
25-9	218	19.09	41	12.13	259	17.50
30-4	69	6.04	10	2.96	79	5.34
35-9	29	2.54	3	0.89	32	2.16
40-4	16	1.48	1	0.30	17	1.15
45-9	5	0.44	0	0.00	5	0.34
Above 50	4	0.35	1	0.30	5	0.34
Total	1142	100.00	338	100.00	1480	100.00

Source: *Characteristics of the Unemployed in Lagos*, Research Bulletin 2/003
(Human Resources Research Unit, University of Lagos, Lagos, 1974)

school education. Generally, people with a secondary school education constituted about one-third of the unemployed, while people with primary school education formed some 28 per cent.

It is not surprising that the bulk of the unemployed had at most a secondary school certificate. Falae (1967) made the same observation about unemployment in the country's urban centres. The reason often given for this is that the country's education system, lacking an emphasis on vocational training, has produced people who find that their job desires can only be met in the urban centres, especially in civil-service employment. Since these people, usually migrants into Lagos, shun agriculture and possess few skills, they do not readily find employment and are usually forced after long stays in unemployment to join the apprenticeship system to learn a trade (Calaway, 1964). This apprenticeship system is the source of the large labour force employed in the informal sector of the economy.

In Lagos, urban unemployment has a major component that is not readily seen. This component, better described as underemployment or hidden unemployment, comprises the large number of street traders and hawkers that are found all over Lagos. These hawkers, selling articles that range from foodstuffs to electronic materials, are often to be seen at traffic holdups, near offices and at recreational centres. A

closer look at their wares reveals the small size of their capital, as well
as their possible standards of living. Although very little is known about
the socio-economic characteristics of this group, it is possible that they
are young primary school leavers and people with little or no education.
It would seem that their primary concern is to eke out some living from
one form of odd job or another.

The Problem of Urban Management

It is often argued that urban problems in Nigeria have reached such
alarming proportions because of the lack of effective urban management
(Mabogunje, 1974). Furthermore, it is argued that urban governments
are ineffective because they are poor, while their insolvency derives
partly from the inability of the urban administration to tap all the
available revenue-yielding resources, such as property rating and property taxation, sales taxes and so on, and partly from the structure of
government. That the quality of urban administration is poor and
management and technical personnel are in short supply complicates
the issue. While these observations are generally true for Lagos, it must
be noted that the capital, nevertheless, has been treated more fairly
than any other Nigerian city.

The need for efficient urban management in Lagos was first evident
in connection with instituting proper public-health and sanitation
measures in the city. As far back as 1899, a General Sanitation Board
consisting of nine members was created as advisory body to government
for the municipality of Lagos, defined as Lagos Island minus Ikoyi,
Iddo Island and Ebute-Metta. In 1908, when the Lagos Municipality
Board of Health was constituted, the limits of the municipality were
defined as in 1899. However, the first real development of local government came in 1917, when the Township Ordinance constituted Lagos
as the only first-class township in the country. The area of the township
included the earlier sanitary district of Lagos and covered a total of
52.62 square kilometers on both the island and the mainland.

However, the Lagos administration did not enjoy any autonomy
until 1941, when another ordinance was promulgated 'to make provisions for the constitution of and the appointments and elections of
members of the Lagos Town Council and to empower the council to
levy rates for township purposes'. Subsequently, Lagos obtained municipal status, with self-government and an entirely elected membership.
There was also provision for the post of Mayor, although this was

cancelled in 1953, when it was decided that the municipal government was to include traditional chiefs and to be headed by the Oba of Lagos as president.

Municipal councils all over the country were hindered in the execution of their duties by such factors as the quality of membership of the council and also by the general problem of manpower shortages. In Lagos, the inclusion of traditional rulers in the council has always been of very little use, since these people possess little or no competence in modern urban management. Modern democratic representation was a mixed blessing: while it broadened the base of authority, it has tended to encourage the election into office of the less educated and enlightened men who succeeded in partisan elections because of their ability to appeal to ethnic chauvinism rather than their administrative or professional expertise. This has meant a poor-quality urban management and also the council's inability to fully execute its programmes of taxation and other revenue-yielding activities.

In recent years, the Lagos municipal council has become one of six other councils that administer metropolitan Lagos. In many instances, such as refuse collection, sewage disposal and water and electricity supply, these councils have worked independently of one another, with little or no attempt at coordination. However, while there are certain activities that have to be performed at the local-government level, there are others that must be seen from a metropolitan point of view, and one consequence of the lack of coordination between local governments has been the poor supply of public facilities in such adjacent neighbourhoods as Apapa and Ajegunle; Surulere and Mushin; and Yaba and Shomolu-Bariga.

Today the provision of services in Lagos is in the hands not only of local government but also the state and Federal governments, functioning mainly through branches of the Ministries of Health, Works and Surveys, Agriculture and Natural Resources, the Governor's Office, the National Electric Power Authority, Nigerian Railways, Nigerian Airways, the police and the army. Since these organisations are responsible, in one form or another, for certain services, they significantly affect urban development. The serious functional and jurisdictional fragmentation between them further retards the effective and efficient administration and management of Lagos metropolitan area.

Other Institutional Problems

Although urban management in Lagos may be responsible for the perpetuation of many of the problems enumerated above, it must be accepted that there are some institutional problems that would make any urban management in the city less effective: in particular, the system of land tenure in the metropolitan area and the way that land is allocated for various uses. Mabogunje (1961) noted that the land on which metropolitan Lagos is situated belonged traditionally to the Awori, a subethnic group of the Yorubas. Before the arrival of the British, land was communally owned and all users of land had only the right to use the land but not to dispose of it in any other way. However, land acquisition by outright sale or other forms of alienation began in Lagos as early as the 1800s, and a Land Commission Court sat in Lagos between 1863 and 1865 to take evidence on all lands acquired between 1857 and 1861 (Mabogunje, 1961). Since then, the scramble for land has attained unimaginable proportions.

The problem with the land-tenure system arises in that the structure of the urban land market is burdened with customary land holdings which impede land transactions. Consequently, urban land prices have been generally inflated to an extent that only very few people can afford to own land. The need for rationalisation must be seen as a solution but, in a place where customary rights are still maintained, it is difficult to see how such a rationalisation would work. This was probably one reason why the Lagos State Council of Obas initially opposed the Land Use Decree of 1978, which vested all lands in the country to be held for the people by the government. Even today, in spite of the Land Use Decree, which is entrenched in the country's constitution, people still buy and sell land openly in Lagos. Consequently, the issue of land tenure must be seen as one important constraint on the rational allocation of land in Lagos.

Urban Planning in Lagos

The concern for urban planning in Lagos has its origins in the attempts of the colonial administration to protect European residents from the numerous endemic health hazards. As early as 1899, the governor of the Protectorate of Southern Nigeria set up a Lagos Municipal Health Board as an advisory body on the maintenance of a sanitary environment in the city. By 1909, the purely sanitary powers of the board were extended to give it jurisdiction over such items as sales by auctions and the licensing of spirits, dogs, markets and vehicles as a means of raising revenue. Even then, Lagos was not accorded the status of a municipality until another fifty years had passed, and the provision of such services as residences, water and the maintenance of a wholesome urban environment remained within the powers of the governor.

The legal basis of urban planning in Lagos, as in the country as a whole, is provided by two major statutes: the Township Ordinance promulgated by Lord Lugard (1919) in 1917; and the Town and Country Planning Act of Nigeria, 1946 (Nigeria, 1948). These two statutes are not only complementary but have also provided the rationale for the *modus operandi* of urban planning in the country, in spite of the fact that some of their rules and regulations are either outdated or do not really conform with Nigeria's cultural standards.

The Township Ordinance was promulgated to 'establish the broad principles of municipal responsibility, graduated according to importance of the community and the measure of its ability to accept and discharge satisfactorily independent and quasi-independent functions'. However, it also provided guidelines for the control and finance of urban land and the construction of buildings and roads.

The impact of the ordinance on urban planning in Lagos was twofold. First, either because of the concentration of the European population at that time in Lagos, or because of the growth in the export and import trade through Lagos, the city was made the only first-class township in the country. This meant that its boundaries were defined statutorily by the governor, and also that it enjoyed some form of government selected by the governor. This prime importance of place given to Lagos was the beginning of the priorities that the city has had over every other city in the country. Secondly, following Lugard's specifications about the laying-out of roads and streets and also the construction of buildings, much of the municipality of Lagos was laid out in a grid-iron pattern. However, the greatest impact of the Ordinance was felt in 1929, when the Lagos Executive Development Board (LEDB) was formed to clear slums that had developed in various parts of the city and, 'to make and execute town planning schemes with the general object of securing proper sanitary conditions and conveniences with the Township Area'. The immediate job of the LEDB was therefore to clear the slums in Oko Awo area of the city and to plan to resettle them elsewhere.

In later years, the LEDB undertook more slum-clearance schemes, especially in Central Lagos and the Marina in the 1950s, and resettled the displaced people in Surulere. In addition, the LEDB laid out residential districts in various parts of the city. In 1930, it set up the Yaba residential area to house the displaced people from Lagos Island and resuscitated settlement in Ebute-Metta, which was originally laid out by Governor Glover in 1900. Also in 1930, it gave physical expression to Lord Lugard's view that Europeans should be accommodated in separate residential districts, by founding and laying out Apapa. Hitherto, Europeans in Lagos had lived along the Marina, where they enjoyed the occasional sea breezes. For the next 15 or 20 years, Lugard's Ordinance was the legal basis of planning in Lagos.

The promulgation of the Town and Country Planning Act in 1946 coincided with the institution of major constitutional changes in the country and also the institution of a ten-year plan of development and welfare. Based on the 1932 Town and Country Planning Act of the United Kingdom, its major aim was to provide 'for the replanning, improvement and control of different parts of the country by means of planning schemes and planning authorities'. However, while its functions are similar to those of the Township Ordinance, the Act goes further in that it also makes provision for the preservation of places of natural interest or beauty, be they in urban or rural areas. Furthermore, this Act defines, up to the present time, the major policies on zoning and designation of land, land occupancy and tenure, building and architectural control, coordination of private and public investment of land and long-term development control.

In Lagos, the operation of this Act led to the creation within the Ministry of Works and Planning of a Department of Town and Country Planning. This Ministry collaborated with the LEDB both in the slum clearance schemes of the 1950s and in the creation of new residential estates at Ikoyi and Surulere and industrial estates at Apapa, Ebute-Metta and Iddo Island. Furthermore, the Act was instrumental in the creation of the Ikeja Area Town Planning Authority, which supervised the construction of residential estates at Ilupeju and Ikeja and industrial estates also at Ikeja, Mushin and Ilupeju. With the creation of states in 1967, and through some realisation of the complex problem of Lagos, the LEDB and the Ikeja Town Planning Authority merged to form the Lagos State Property Development Corporation (LSPDC).

The LSPDC, though formed to conceive and execute property development in the whole of Lagos State, has concentrated much of its efforts in planning or improving physical aspects of metropolitan Lagos. For instance, it has built modern 'model' markets, shopping centres and real estate in many parts of the metropolis, while it laid out plans recently for the development of five satellite towns around Lagos. One of these satellite towns, the Amuwo-Odofin new town has been completed on the Lagos-Badagri expressway and is being occupied by migrants moving out of congested Lagos. Furthermore, the LSPDC is developing high-rise residential apartments in other parts of the metropolis, especially in Ogba and Ogudu in the northern parts of the city.

Since the 1950s the Federal government has recognised the important role played by Lagos, not only as the national capital but also as the gateway into the country. In the early 1960s, there was a Federal Ministry of Lagos Affairs to oversee development in the Federal-capital territory, but this gave way to the creation of Lagos State in 1967. During these times, the Federal government had to develop Victoria Island as a high class residential area for the top echelon of its civil service and also for the ambassadors and high commissioners. However, there has also been much pressure on this government to provide housing for other categories of its staff. Between 1975 and 1977, the Federal government built Festac Town, used initially to house participants at the World Festival of the Arts and Culture held in Lagos in 1977. The buildings in this modest town had been turned over for use by residents in Lagos. The Federal government has also planned and executed further residential development on Victoria Island and a new office complex in Ikoyi.

Planning to contain the serious traffic congestions on the roads has been undertaken by both state and Federal governments. Thus while the Lagos State government has focussed attention on widening main roads and alleys in many parts of the metropolis, local governments have taken responsibility for minor roads, and the Federal government has invested heavily in the construction of major roads and bridges. For example, the Federal government has converted two roads (the Agege-Western Avenue motor road and the Ikorodu motor road) into dual carriageways for fast and efficient movement between the mainland, the rest of the country and Lagos Island. In addition, a system of ring roads, some of which were suspended above the Lagoon and the Atlantic, have been constructed, while an expressway now links Apapa on the southwest with Oworonsoki on the northeast as part of an outer ring road to Lagos Island (Figure 4.4). Furthermore, the Carter Bridge, the only link between the mainland and Lagos Island, has been replaced by two new bridges, the Eko bridge opened about 1972 and a New Carter Bridge opened in 1979, and a third bridge is under construction. A conservative estimate of Federal government investment on roads between 1975 and 1980 would be of the order of one billion Naira.

The effect of the 'Federal might' in urban planning in Lagos is undoubtedly more discernible than that of any other group of planners. However, these efforts have not solved, but only ameliorated, the problems of the metropolis. Furthermore, since the level of amelioration achieved by these efforts is still intolerable in many cases (traffic and housing congestion remain, and the provision of services and amenities is still unsatisfactory), the search for solutions continues. One outcome has been the decision of the Lagos State government to set up a master-plan project unit within the Ministry of Works and Planning. This unit, assisted by the United Nations Office for Technical Cooperation, is in the process of conducting studies and producing a master plan for orderly urban development in metropolitan Lagos. Its work is not yet complete, but it must be pointed out that the use of master plans for development in Lagos should be viewed with some caution. For instance, it is known that most master plans produced for cities in Nigeria, notably Kano and Kaduna, have played minimum roles in urban development, simply because they were out of date by the time they were produced; events had overtaken them. A further disadvantage is that, in the past, master-plan making in Nigeria has been seen as a single act rather than as a component of a cyclic planning process.

Today, Lagos is the most studied and perhaps the most planned urban area in the country. There is an awareness that the multidimensional problems of the metropolis arose because of the unique role it has played in the country's developmental efforts; and, equally, it is understood that state, local and Federal governments must all share the responsibility for planning the city and finding solutions to its problems. However, it is evident that success has continuously eluded attempts to solve these problems. A reexamination of the approaches utilised by the various planning organisations may lead to the development of a more satisfactory arrangement for tackling the problems of the metropolis.

Conclusion

It is obvious that the approach to urban planning adopted in Lagos is to react to problems as they arise. Such reactions are necessarily *ad hoc* and have succeeded only in ameliorating the situation. Thus, the numerous planning organisations react to the problems of inadequate housing and traffic congestion by creating new residential layouts and building dual-carriage expressways and a network of bridges and traffic exchanges, respectively. While these developments are not bad *per se*, their failure to actually solve the problems of the metropolis derives from their segmented or incremental approach to planning (Faludi, 1973).

Furthermore, the fact that they are responses to problems that have worked themselves out (Berry, 1973) means that they lack the essential mechanism for coping with future problems.

A major criticism of urban planning in Lagos, as in any other city in the country, is the partial approach adopted by planners in executing planning schemes. As a result of this lack of coordination of planners' activities, it is not unusual for beautifully executed housing schemes to be supplied with neither piped water or electricity. Furthermore, many schemes are conceived and executed without due consideration to their relationship to, and impact on, existing land uses. In Lagos, a classic example was a decision in 1974 to build high-rise blocks of office apartments on Ikoyi to accommodate the Federal civil service, even though it was generally agreed that Ikoyi and Lagos Island were already congested and that movement from the mainland to these islands was well-nigh impossible. Similar criticisms may be applied to the Amuwo Odofin new town, which had become engulfed within metropolitan expansion before it was completed. Undoubtedly many of these problems arise because of the poor coordination of planners' activities.

It must be understood that, while some of the problems of the metropolis can be solved by town planning, others have to be tackled within a regional planning perspective. The importance of the regional dimension to planning in Lagos is underlined when it is remembered that, as a result of the concentration of economic activities in the metropolis, and also because of its position as the national capital city, it is a destination for rural–urban migrants from all over the country. Undoubtedly, housing is in short supply, as also are job opportunities. Consequently, a decision to decongest activities from Lagos might be worthwhile. However, such a decision would be most beneficial from a regional-development-planning perspective. For instance, in 1975 it was decided that the functions of Lagos as a national capital would be removed to Abuja in the central part of the country, but this decentralisation alone will have only a marginal effect in alleviating the problems of housing and traffic congestion in Lagos (Ayeni, 1977). A more concerted effort at decentralising activities from Lagos might be worthwhile to supplement the removal of the Federal capital.

On the other hand, quite a number of the problems of Lagos could be solved by improved urban management and urban planning. For instance, in order to provide viable solutions to the problems of environmental deterioration, housing and the maintenance of urban services, urban management and urban planning must face squarely the problem of financial insolvency. Many revenue-generating avenues are being left untapped by the local councils that currently administer the city. Of course, it should be noted that some local councils do not collect these rates because of the high costs of collection, which could outstrip the revenues in some cases. Improved civic responsibility on the part of the residents, coupled with better systems of collection, may improve the situation.

Efforts to provide effective urban management in Lagos, as in other cities of Nigeria, have been intensified in the last few years. Recognising the unique problems of urban centres and metropolitan areas, the Federal government in 1976 promulgated a decree instituting a uniform local-government system in the country, and differentiated the form of urban governments from those of local councils in rural areas. Furthermore, it differentiated between the roles of the Federal, state and local government in the provision of services in cities and metropolitan areas. It was proposed that cities and metropolitan areas should operate a city-manager form of urban management, with a council of elected members, but the election of members on partisan grounds may impede progress in the future. Although the transfer of the Department of Town Planning from the state Ministries of Works, and Transport and Housing to the Ministry of Local Government may improve the performance of the city manager and his council, it is yet to be seen how these changes are manipulated to effect solutions to the problems of Lagos.

Bibliography

Ayeni, M.A.O., 'Spatial and Sectoral Changes in the Structure of Manufacturing Activities in Lagos, 1965-1972', *Nigerian Journal of Quantitative Economics*, vol. 2, no. 2 (1976), pp. 27-46
— 'Living Conditions of the Poor in Lagos', *Ekistics*, vol. 43, no. 255 (1977), pp. 77-80
— *Spatial Consequences of Political Decisions: An Impact Analysis of the Removal of Nigeria's Federal Capital from Lagos*, Development Series No. 10 (Centre for Development Studies, Institute of Urban and Regional Research, University of Iowa, Iowa, 1978)
Berry, B.J.L., *Human Consequences of Urbanization* (Macmillan, London, 1973)
Calaway, A., 'Nigeria's Indigeneous Education: The Apprentice System', *ODU*, vol. 1, no. 1 (1964), pp. 62-9
Doxiades Associates International, *Regional Plan for Lagos State: Existing Conditions* (Lagos, Nigeria, 1977)
Falae, O., 'Unemployment in Nigeria', *Nigerian Journal of Economic and Social Studies*, vol. 13 (1971), pp. 59-74
Faludi, A., *Planning Theory* (Pergamon, Oxford, 1973)
Fapohunda, O.J., 'The Workers of Lagos', Paper given at a Conference on Economic Development and Employment Generation in Nigeria (Nigerian Institute for Social and Economic Research, Ibadan, 1975)

Golan, T., 'From Abidjan to Lagos', *West Africa* (5 May 1975), pp. 505-7

Green, L. and Milone, V., *Urbanization in Nigeria: A Planning Commentary* (Ford Foundation, New York, 1972)

Koenigsberger, O. *et al., Metropolitan Lagos*, Report Prepared for the Government of Nigeria under the United Nations Programme of Technical Assistance (Lagos, 1964)

Lagos State Government, Ministry of Works and Planning, *Residential Densities in Metropolitan Lagos*, Master Plan Bulletin 3 (Ikeja, Lagos, Nigeria, 1977)

— *Provision of Physical Infrastructures in Metropolitan Lagos*, Master Plan Bulletin 4 (Ikeja, Lagos, Nigeria, 1978)

Lugard, F.D., *Political Memorandum: Revision of Instructions to Political Officers,* no. 11 (Frank Cass, London, 1919)

Mabogunje, A.L., 'Towards an Urban Policy in Nigeria', *Nigerian Journal of Economics and Social Studies*, vol. 16, no. 1 (1974), pp. 85-97

— *Lagos, A Study in Urban Geography*, Ph.D Thesis (University of London, 1961)

— 'The Evolution and Analysis of the Retail Structure of Lagos, Nigeria', *Economic Geography*, vol. 40, no. 4 (1964), pp. 304-23

— *Urbanization in Nigeria* (University of London Press, London, 1968)

Nigeria, 'Nigeria Town and Country Planning Ordinance, No. 4 of 1946' in *The Laws of Nigeria* (Lagos, Nigeria, 1948)

Schatzl, L., *Industrialization in Nigeria: A Spatial Analysis* (Munich-Ibadan, 1973)

University of Lagos, *Characteristics of the Unemployed in Lagos*, Bulletin 21003 (Human Resources Research Unit, Lagos, Nigeria, 1974)

5 TEHRAN

V.F. Costello

Many of Tehran's problems stem from the speed with which the city has grown, its present size and its likely rapid growth in the future. The city has grown from a population of just over half a million in 1940 to 1.7 million in 1956, 2.7 million in 1966 and 4.6 million in 1976, increasing at a rate of 5.7 per cent per annum between 1956 and 1966 and 5.3 per cent per annum from 1966 to 1976. It is thus one of the largest and fastest growing cities in the Third World and, to take a comparison with other countries in the Middle East, Iran's capital alone contains more people than Israel, Lebanon or Jordan. The population is likely to be about six million in 1981, and by 1991 between eight and ten million.

The physical expansion of the city has been equally rapid. Between 1940 and 1956 its area expanded by three times; in 1966 the total built up area was 180 km^2, and it was expected to cover some 400 km^2 by 1991. This expansion has been on a site where the physical environment imposes severe constraints. Greater Tehran is built at an average altitude of about 1200 m on a gentle slope running south from the Alburz mountains. The climate has marked seasonal contrasts, with a short spring and autumn separating a long and severely cold winter and a lengthy hot dry summer. But summer temperatures in the north close to the mountains are up to 7°C cooler than those in the south. The traditional core of Tehran is sited 20 km from the foot of the Alburz mountains on an east-west road, at a point where the road divides into two on either side of the foothills; this site provides ready access southwards to Qom and central Iran, and also commands the valleys leading northwards to the Caspian provinces. The advantage of potentially good communications is countered by the physical limitations of the site, which is some distance from either of the two principal rivers of the region — the Karaj and the Jaji Rud — and far enough from the mountains to be beyond the reach of perennial streams. From its inception, Tehran has always had to rely on artificial water supplies, initially through the use of gravity-fed underground canals, called *qanats*, the number of which increased throughout the nineteenth century. The inadequacy of the water supply to meet the needs of the expanding city is a continuing feature of Tehran's history, and there are

156

problems both in the provision of domestic water and in sewage disposal. The demand for water has consistently outstripped supply, and the city has only the beginnings of an integrated sewage system. At present, most human waste is discharged untreated into the ground or into water courses, greatly increasing potential hazards from disease.

Tehran's site, size and layout have also created other environmental problems. The transport network has become progressively less capable of dealing with the volumes of traffic generated by an increasing population and rising car-ownership rates. Many of those who are employed have two or more jobs, and congestion is aggravated by the extra vehicular movements which result. The accumulation of exhaust gases from the vehicles which crowd the streets — vehicles for which there are no emission-control regulations — produces severe air-pollution problems, comparable to Los Angeles before controls were introduced.

Urban growth out from the core has been much influenced by the environmental contrasts between north and south. The modern commercial centre, together with the suburbs where live the wealthier sections of the population, has developed northward from the old core towards the mountains, while the poorer suburbs have developed southwards towards the desert.

The contrast between the northern and southern suburbs of Tehran is illustrated in a number of quantifiable variables: in the mid-1960s population densities in the south were well in excess of 19,000 persons per km^2, while in some parts of the north they were less than a tenth of that figure; average monthly incomes showed a similar disparity (Connell, 1973). One park alone in the northern suburbs was over six times the size of the only substantial open space near the city centre (Bahrambeygui, 1977). While the old core is showing some signs of local population decline, with a corresponding increase in densities in the inner suburbs, Table 5.1 illustrates one important fact about the city: despite its physical expansion, mainly to the north, the amount of living space available per household is becoming smaller. In 1976 some 22,000 households were recorded as having seven or more persons living in one room.

The north-south contrast is one of the recurring themes of Tehran's social geography. It represents not simply a distinction in wealth and access to power between one class and another but a wider division in Iranian society between a westernised, technologically oriented elite and middle class and the tradition-oriented mass of the population.

In the wider national context, Tehran is of course considerably larger than any other Iranian city. Already by 1940 Tehran was over twice the

Table 5.1: Private Households by Size and Number of Rooms Occupied

| | Rooms per Household | | | |
	1	2-3	4-6	Over 6
Percentage of all Households				
1966[a]	6.96	41.2	41.6	9.8
1976[b]	31.1	40.42	23.9	3.97

Sources: a. Plan Organisation (1966), Vol. 10, *Tehran Shahrestan*. b. Plan and Budget Organisation (1976), *Five Per Cent Sample, Tehran Shahrestan.*

size of the next largest city (Tabriz); by 1966 some ten per cent of the country's total population was living in Tehran, and by 1976 this figure was 13.6 per cent. At this time the city was almost seven times the size of the next largest urban area, Isfahan. As the country's capital, and the business, cultural, educational and communications centre, it has attracted a large proportion of the country's resources: at least 40 per cent of large industrial firms, 70 per cent of industrial value added and 90 per cent of public and private decision-making centres are concentrated in the city. Here also are a large proportion of the country's social amenities: in 1964 one-third of Iran's doctors lived in the capital and more than half the country's telephones were installed there (Issawi, 1969).

Urban Growth

There has been a settlement on the site of Tehran since at least 1100 AD, though the city's importance dates only from 1786, when it was chosen by the founder of the Qajar dynasty, Muhammed Shah Qajar, as his capital. It then had a population of about 15,000. In the middle of the nineteenth century, the population was about 60,000, mostly living in closely packed residential quarters within the line of the old wall (dating from 1553).

By the turn of the century a distinctive number of features of Tehran's development were apparent: the city was, with about 250,000 inhabitants, by far the largest in Iran; the social geography of the city was already showing signs of marked differentiation on the grounds of wealth and power rather than tribe or religion; the physical difficulties of the site were revealed in regular summer shortages of water; and continued expansion was fuelled partly by royal patronage and central-government expenditure, to some extent at the expense of provincial Iran, since tribal and provincial leaders were forced to pay large sums to the Shah (Bahrambeygui, 1977).

The progressive concentration of administrative and commercial activity in Tehran was accelerated after Reza Shah Pahlavi seized power, and under his reign (1925–41) population increased to approximately 700,000. A number of ministries were built within the bounds of the palace complex and the University of Tehran was founded. Following a dangerous water shortage, a scheme was initiated to build a 52 km canal to bring water from the Karaj river, capable of delivering 1.3 m³/s, and a number of artesian wells were dug (Planhol, 1968). The water was distributed through the city by the traditional means of open channels, called *jubs*. The Shah was determined to reorder the city along lines similar to those of Haussmann in Paris. Lockhart (1939) describes the results:

> From being an Oriental city, without good communications and with but few modern amenities, it has been radically re-planned and re-built. Under the direction of H.I.M. the Shah, a most thorough and far-reaching town-planning scheme has been drawn up and put into execution. The ramparts and fosse surrounding the city have disappeared, and broad new avenues, intersecting each other at right-angles, have been cut through what were formerly squalid and congested parts. These new thoroughfares, which will remain as permanent records of an enlightened administration, are well designed and planned. At their points of intersection, attractive monuments and fountains have been placed, and along them are rising many new public and private buildings, whose style of architecture is in keeping with the Iranian national spirit.

The grid-iron pattern described here was subsequently extended to the rest of the city as it grew. Although this form of layout has a number of potential disadvantages with regard to modern traffic management, there were reasons for its use in Tehran other than a simple desire for order, as Planhol (1968) explains:

> the most desirable orientation for a house is east-west at right angles to the mountain breeze, which is essential for freshness in summer and must be allowed to pass freely through the dwelling at night. It is also preferable, on account of the winter cold, for the main facades of the house to face south. Building-plots must therefore be

oriented north-south, with the house built at the northern end facing the garden, which occupies the whole of the southern part. It follows that the roads should run from east to west (bordered on the south by the rear walls of houses and on the north by garden-gates), and be cut from north to south by the broad avenues that carry the principal irrigation channels. The orientation of the houses with regard to the winds, and the consequent shape of the plots, have thus confirmed the strict chequerboard pattern of the streets. Reza Shah's network, based originally on the limits of properties, which had been conditioned by natural circumstances, has therefore been extended with absolute regularity throughout all of the newer sectors of the city.

Off the main avenues which were driven through the southern districts, the alleyways remained as irregular as ever.

Reza Shah's reconstruction programme created thousands of new jobs, many of which were filled by migrants, who helped to swell the city's fast-growing population. While the proportion of Iran's population living in urban areas remained at about 21 per cent throughout the first 40 years of the twentieth century, Tehran appears to have grown at over twice the rate of other urban areas, so that by 1940 it was assuming a position of primacy over the rest of the urban system.

How far the city's population growth is due to migration and how far to other factors is uncertain, for a number of reasons: data on vital rates and on migration were unreliable before the First National Census of 1956; expansion of the city limits accounts for some growth, since Shemiran and Rey were incorporated only after the first census; and in any case migration and natural increase are not independent of one another. Migration of younger portions of the population from rural to urban areas may result in rapid urban growth with, a little later, a higher natural increase in the cities than the country as a whole, because of higher birth rates and lower death rates among the relatively youthful urban population, together with the effects of improved sanitation and health care. By the early 1960s the indications were that birth rates were at about 30 per thousand and death rates about seven per thousand, and it was calculated that, by 1966, natural increase was adding about 65,000 per annum to a total population of 2.7 million, while migration accounted for about as much again (Bahrambeygui, 1977).

Preliminary results of the 1976 National Census of Population and Housing, based on a five per cent sample, are compared with those

Table 5.2: Population of Tehran by Place of Birth, 1956, 1966, 1976, and by Sex Ratio

	1956	1966	1976	Sex ratio, 1976 (males per 100 females)
Born in Tehran (%)	50.0	51.1	54.8	103.3
Born in central province, but outside Tehran (%)	4.6	13.3	9.5	116.6
Born in other provinces (%)	43.9	34.6	33.9	123.8
Born in foreign country (%)	1.5	1.0	1.7	998.2
Total population	1,512,082	2,719,730	4,591,455	
Total sex ratio (males per 100 females)	112.2	110.3	111.1	

Sources: a. Plan Organisation (1966), Vol. 10, *Tehran Shahrestan.* b. Plan and Budget Organisation (1976), *Five Per Cent Sample, Tehran Shahrestan.*

from the earliest censuses in Table 5.2. A number of points should be noted. Firstly, some 45 per cent of the city's population, of all ages, was born outside the city; over one-third of the population was born in an Ostan, or province, other than the Central Province where Tehran is located; in absolute numbers, this is over 1.5 million people; among native-born Iranians there is a preponderance of males, particularly in the immigrant groups. The 1976 census also showed that some eight per cent of the resident male population of five years of age or more had migrated from other provinces to the city only within the previous five years.

A statistical study of nondependent migrants in Tehran between 1956 and 1966 indicated that 17 per cent were seeking a better job and 5.2 per cent came for education purposes, but that a total of 72 per cent were either searching for work or better work. Higher wages, more than double those of similar labourers in other parts of the country, were a strong incentive. Marriage was the motive for eleven per cent of the 235,000 migrants studied. Arranged marriages, where former migrants returned to Tehran with their wives after going to their home village or town to marry, were the most common (Bahrambeygui, 1977).

But not all those seeking work find it. The official census of 1976 gave an overall unemployment rate of three per cent of those

economically active. There are no unemployment benefits in Iran, so
there is little reason to register as unemployed, and a detailed study in
part of south Tehran in 1967 showed that, although the official figure
for Tehran was 4.1 per cent unemployed, real local unemployment
was about 14 per cent among males, and 51 per cent among females
(Bartsch, 1974).

Changes in the occupational and industrial structures of the
employed population of Tehran in the period 1966-76 are summarised
in Tables 5.3 and 5.4. A number of salient features may be noted.

**Table 5.3: Employed Population of Tehran by Major Occupational
Groups, 1966 and 1976**

	1966 [a]	1976[b]	1966[a]	1976[b]	1966[a]	1976[b]
	Male and Female	Male and Female	Male	Male	Female	Female
Total	755174	1302906	678172	1155581	76992	147325
Occupational group	(%)	(%)	(%)	(%)	(%)	(%)
1. Professional, technical and related workers	8.1	12.9	5.8	9.3	28.4	40.5
2. Administrative and managerial workers	0.9	1.2	1.0	2.1	0.3	0.8
3. Clerical and related workers	11.0	14.3	10.8	12.4	12.2	29.2
4. Sales workers	15.1	12.1	16.7	13.4	1.6	2.0
5. Service workers	15.4	10.0	12.7	9.0	41.9	16.4
6. Agricultural workers	1.2	1.3	1.3	1.5	0.2	0.0
7. Production workers	40.7	36.0	43.9	39.7	12.2	7.2
8. Workers not classifiable	7.6	11.5	8.1	12.4	3.0	3.7

Sources: a. Plan Organisation (1966), Vol. 10, *Tehran Shahrestan.* b. Plan and
Budget Organisation (1976), *Five Per Cent Sample, Tehran Shahrestan.*

There is a high proportion employed in the tertiary sector, significantly
higher than in urban Iran in general. Secondly, the rise in female
employment was much greater relative to male employment, and was
concentrated in the professional, technical and clerical occupation
group — those requiring education — rather than in services, much of
which was domestic service; this is clear evidence of the degree of
female emancipation taking place. It should be stressed that the

Table 5.4: Employed Population of Tehran, 1966 and 1976, and Urban Iran, 1976, by Major Industry Group

	Tehran		Urban Iran
	1966[a]	*1976*[b]	*1976*[c]
Total	755,174	1,302,906	4,103,231
Industry group	(%)	(%)	(%)
1. Agriculture, forestry, hunting, fishing	1.5	1.0	5.5
2. Mining and quarrying	0.1	0.9	1.4
3. Manufacturing	26.2	22.0	21.5
4. Construction	8.9	8.5	13.6
5. Electricity, gas, water, and sanitary services	2.2	1.4	1.3
6. Commerce	} 18.1	{ 14.0	13.0 }
7. Financial, insurance, real estate and business services		{ 4.0	2.3 }
8. Transport, storage, communications	7.8	8.6	8.2
9. Services	32.2	37.6	32.0
10. Activities not adequately described	3.0	2.1	1.7

Sources: a. Plan Organisation (1966), Vol. 10, *Tehran Shahrestan*. b. Plan and Budget Organisation (1976), *Five Per Cent Sample, Tehran Shahrestan*. c. Figures for settlements with a population of over 5,000 and *shahrestan* (county) centres from Plan and Budget Organisation (1976), *Five Per Cent Sample, Total Country*.

decline in manufacturing is a relative decline, since the numbers employed in manufacturing in Tehran increased by about 87,000 in the intercensal period. Expansion occurred both in the numbers of small-scale industrial enterprises found in central and southern Tehran and in the more highly capitalised factories to be found on the roads leading out of the built-up area, particularly westwards towards Karaj. Tehran benefitted from Iran's first phase of industrialisation, in the period up to 1970, which was based on food, agricultural and textile industries, building materials and import-substitute consumer goods. The city is also likely to benefit in the second phase, where the policy has been to develop heavy industry. This has taken place despite government efforts to restrict industry, which have often been circumvented by development on existing sites, and despite the limitations on production resulting from frequent water shortages. Tehran is at the centre of the communications network, is the decision-making centre and is by far the largest and wealthiest market in the country.

The physical expansion of the city which accompanied the rapid rise in population after World War II was at first subject to very little land-use planning control. Until 1951 any unused land on the periphery of the city was considered to be owned by whoever developed it. Much land around Tehran was seized by speculators, and enormous profits were realised as the land came into increasing demand. Legislation in 1951 placed such land in the hands of a government-controlled bank (Bahrambeygui, 1977). There was, however, no land-use planning as such, though there were a number of directives issued by the municipality. With a free market, the lower price of land at a distance from the city centre encouraged housing developments away from the edge of the built-up area, leaving unused sectors of various sizes to await development. There was relatively little outward expansion to the south of Tehran, where continued immigration resulted in increasing pressure on the housing stock, the subdivision of the larger houses which were once the homes of the wealthy in the older districts, with a steady rise in population densities per hectare and an increase in average household size. In the older neighbourhoods north of the bazaar, space also became exhausted. Rows of modest two- and three-storey houses were built to the east and west of the downtown area, while to the north, uphill towards the mountains beyond Reza Shah's Tehran, more spacious and expensive houses were built. The city had very few residential buildings of more than three or four storeys. The resort towns of Shemiran and Niavaran in the foothills gradually became commuter towns as rising car ownership among the wealthier middle classes freed them from living close to their work.

Government intervention in the process was confined largely to providing infrastructure facilities. The road network in the north was extended and improved, and the water supply increased. Attempts to improve the water supply were largely piecemeal until 1961, when a large dam was completed in the Karaj valley, with a capacity of 184 million m^3 per annum, and a further dam was completed on the Jaji river east of Tehran in 1967, to provide an extra 80 million m^3 per annum. Later, plans were laid to divert water from perennial streams which flow into the Caspian Sea southward under the Alburz mountains to the city.

Government participation in housing was relatively limited. The Construction Bank allocated plots for three major projects around the city. One, called Kuy-Ye-Narmak, was started on the Mazandaran Road in 1956; 400 hectares were divided into 8000 plots, ranging in size from 200 to 500 m², for one-storey houses with a mostly lower-middle-class population. A further 200 hectares were set aside on the site for administrative and service facilities. By 1966 the district had a population of 90,000. At Naziabad in the south west of the city a 300-hectare site was laid out close to the main industrial areas. Intended for a population of about 30,000 in the early 1960s, the site was divided into plot sizes as small as 80 m², and most of the housing units were two-room flats. The population rose to 63,000 by 1966 and was increasing rapidly. Both these schemes began as well-planned enterprises, but soon became surrounded by large numbers of small units built by private developers to benefit from the facilities provided. Despite its rapid growth, Tehran had comparatively few shanty settlements, though numbers of immigrants did occupy the extensive abandoned brickworks, living there as troglodytes. The inhabitants of one shanty and many of those living in the kilns were moved to a model show-piece community called Kuy-Nohom-Aban, where during 1965–6 some 3450 low-cost three-room housing units were built around a park, shops and public-service units. The former slum families were able to buy their new houses at cheap monthly rates over 15 years.

Attempts to develop a separate new town near Tehran were confined to Tehran-Pars, a district built in the desert 12 km east of central Tehran with capital largely from the Zoroastrian community. But the inhabitants had to rely largely on Tehran for shopping, and it became in effect a dormitory satellite rather than a separate community.

The Tehran Master Plan

The need for some form of comprehensive planning became increasingly apparent during the 1950s and early 1960s. In 1965 a High Council for City Planning was created, charged with guiding the preparation of master plans for Iranian cities. Most of the plans concentrated on physical planning, particularly the planning of new road networks. Among the problems experienced in the preparation of plans was (Plan Organisation, 1968):

> the limited number of specialized and experienced engineers in urban development, the lack of proper statistics and data concerning towns, the absence of concrete regional development policies at the national level, the failure to determine how to implement

comprehensive projects in the form of specific executive projects, and the lack of performance guarantees.

A master plan for Tehran was commissioned in 1966 from Victor Gruen Associates of Los Angeles and Abdul-Aziz Farman-Farmian of Tehran; it was completed in 1969 and adopted the following year. Comprehensive social, economic and physical studies of the city were carried out by the consultants before presenting their recommendations and, as requested, they wrote their own legislative proposals as to how the plan should be implemented. Among the fundamental assumptions made by the master plan was the explicit assumption that Tehran's population would rise to 12–16 millions by 1991, and also that the socio-political framework within which the future development of the city was to be directed would remain substantially unchanged in the future. Both these assumptions have been overtaken by events.

A variety of alternatives for the planned future growth of the city were evaluated, including the possibility of establishing a new nucleus to the west near Karadj, or the possibility of a radial expansion along the main routes leading into the city, with subcentres strung out on highway- and railway-oriented ribbons. The proposal chosen was a linear extension of the city largely to the west, but incorporating a number of satellite towns which would give local foci to the settlement pattern and relieve pressure on the present city. The effect would be to redirect Tehran's development from a north-south axis to an east-west axis between the Alburz foothills and the desert, guided by a new motorway and metro network (Figure 5.1).

The master plan also dealt with the sort of detailed design features which should be encouraged. The speed of the city's growth and the lack of all but infrastructure planning had resulted, despite Reza Shah's efforts, in a capital which was remarkably drab, lacking in monumental and architectural features of worth. Indeed Reza Shah must bear some blame for this, since he demolished many of the Qajar buildings in the old city. The plan made a series of recommendations for improving the appearance of landmarks, neighbourhoods and parks in the short term, and pointed to opportunities for good design in the long term.

The city development would be controlled by the establishment of a five-year service line. Special permission would be required for development outside the line, but the line would be moved outward every five years, until the outer limit of the city as envisaged was reached after twenty-five years. An interim development pattern for

Figure 5.1: Comprehensive Plan of Tehran

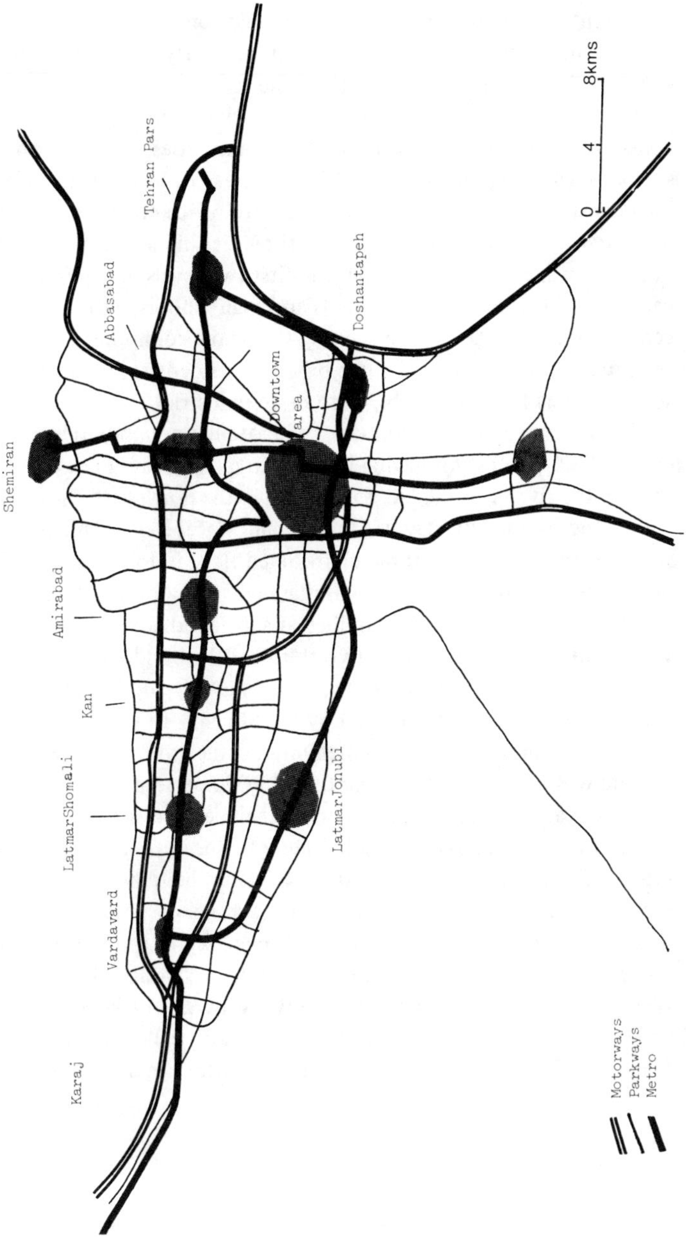

the city was proposed, with a series of fixed minima for plot sizes, ranging from 120 m^2 in and around Rey and in the southwest, and up to 350 m^2 in the northernmost suburbs. To consolidate administration of the continuously built-up area the municipality annexed the northern towns of Shemiran and Niavaran and the southern town of Rey.

The greater part of Tehran's residential development was to be concentrated in the proposed satellite communities, to avoid urban sprawl. Each community was to have a variety of low-, medium- and high-density housing, with its own areas for office employment, retailing, entertainment and recreation. A three-tier hierarchy of service provision was proposed for each, the first two levels being based on the catchment areas of primary schools and high schools, with a major centre, located on the metro, serving the whole community. Most of the satellites were intended to be basically residential in character; some, such as Latmar Jonubi, were more industrial.

Work was begun on a number of the satellite communities in the early 1970s, permission having been given in each case to develop outside the five-year line. At Kuy-e-Kan in the northwest a site was earmarked by the Ministry of Housing and Local Development. There were already some 1000 three-bedroomed flats, in four-storey buildings, on the site, but the expansion was planned to accommodate up to 475,000 people, mostly the families of subsidised government workers with medium incomes. About two-thirds of the buildings were planned as medium- to high-rise structures, the rest as low-rise for large families. A smaller enterprise was planned by the Ministry to the west at Lavizan. Intended primarily for low- to medium-income government workers, the site was planned to accommodate 45,000 persons. In contrast, south of Kan was Farahzad, named after the empress. It was promoted by the Pahlavi Foundation and privately financed. The scheme was intended to cater for nearly 55,000 people in the middle- and upper-income groups, some 20,000 at low density, nearly 25,000 at medium density and the rest at high density. Planned segregation of income groups was thus a feature even of those schemes designed for the relatively favoured government employees. By far the largest single project proposed, however, was that for an area called Abbasabad (Figures 5.2 and 5.3). This one was named after the Shah himself.

Case Study — Shahestan Pahlavi

The planning of Shahestan Pahlavi illustrates aspects of the socio-political milieu under the Shah, which was compounded of a mixture of private interest, public welfare and autocratic rule. The Fourth National Development Plan (1968) had called on the public, in this case the monied classes, to participate more fully in productive investments and social activities, while the central government was to be directed more to maintaining public order, establishing an infrastructure for economic activity, facilitating private initiative, protecting the rights of the

Figure 5.2: Land Use in Tehran, 1970

Agricultural/Gardens&Parks
Land Vacant or under Development
Residential Land Use
Government & Administrative buildings
Army Establishments
Industrial Land Use
E Educational Ests.
F Foreign
H Hospital   R Royal Palace
—·— Municipal Boundary   ···· CBD Boundary

individual, planning, determining overall policies, establishing standards and regulations and 'directing individual endeavours in the national interest' (Plan Organisation, 1968).

The Shahestan Pahlavi site was an almost empty tract of land some 554 hectares in extent, located only three kilometres to the north of the city centre. Most of the area had been acquired by the army, and some lots were sold off to individuals. The existence of this site, so close to the city centre, provided the planners with a unique series of

Figure 5.3: Location of the Abbasabad Site

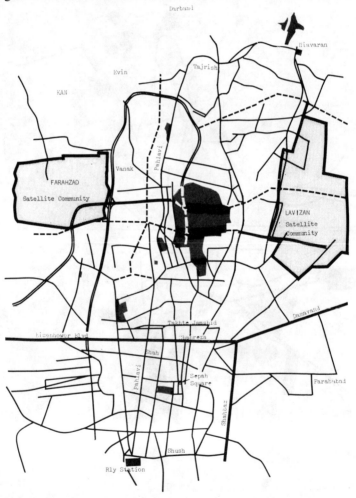

opportunities: to create a new national centre for government of high
design quality; to provide a coherent centre for the development of
northern Tehran; and to become a focus for the new transport network
which was to help deflect growth eastward and westward. It was first
necessary to clear the site: hundreds of houses were taken over by the
government under compulsory purchase orders (Bahrambeygui, 1977)
and demolished, the former owners being repaid in government stock.
Ownership of the land was vested in a public corporation which was to
oversee the joint private and public development of the project, while
the city was to exert planning control. Infrastructure was to be
provided by the corporation, the city, the national government and
public utility services. Proposals for overall planning schemes were
invited from international consultants, and the concept plan of
Llewelyn-Davies, Weeks, Forestier-Walker and Bor (1975) was adopted.

The concept plan provided for a central spine running north-south
along the length of the site. A boulevard system within a grid street
layout was to run along the spine, served by the new metro system and
lined with government and commercial offices, retail stores, hotels
and ancillary parking. Motorways would cross the site, but were located
within natural valleys, so reducing their visual impact. The focus of
the project during the day and after dark was to be Shah and Nation
square, a vast open space which would provide an appropriate setting
for public ceremonials, with monuments and fountains dedicated to
the monarch and his consort. The square was to be built over a motorway, at a location where the commercial, entertainment and tourist
zones of the site adjoined the cultural centre, which was to occupy the
high ground on the northern third of the site. The southern third of
the site was planned for a government and banking centre. A key
element in the plan was to be a number of large public open spaces,
intended to offset the lack of recreational space in the city as a whole.

The scale of the proposed development was remarkable. Government offices were to occupy 26 hectares, with 1.15 million m^2 of
built space, employing 153,333 people. Commercial offices were
allocated the same square meterage, but on 12 hectares of land
(Roberts, 1979). The high densities of land use allowed for large
amounts of landscaped open space on either side of the central area.
Some 81 hectares were allocated to residential land uses, of which
62 per cent were to be developed at medium density, 23 per cent at
medium to high density and the rest at high density. The projected
residential population was 50,000; the number employed on the site
was planned to be 200,000, which would make Shahestan Pahlavi

probably the biggest complex of tertiary activities and offices in the world — two and a half times the size of La Defense in Paris, and twice the size of the Houston Center.

Shahestan Pahlavi was to be a multi-use centre, which would bring together government, cultural and commercial functions in a monumental setting. The design brief given by the consultants was, in Robert's phrase 'a finely drawn combination of grandiose overview and minute attention to detail'. Elements of the 'capital image' characteristic of some of the major cities of the world such as Washington, London, Rome and Paris were examined in the original Tehran master plan. Following this, the Shahestan Pahlavi concept plan sought to combine the formal ordered and precise elements of design found in a number of European cities with Iran's own best examples of traditional urban design and layout. It was to be the Pahlavi equivalent of the Persepolis of the Achaemenian kings of ancient Iran, or the Isfahan of the Safavids. There is little doubt that, were the plan to be carried through, the results would be exciting, imaginative and truly splendid.

The intention of the revised concept plan was to implement development in three phases. The first was seen as lasting four years, 1976–80, during which most of the government and commercial development would be carried out. Housing, retailing, cultural and communal facilities would be built in 1981–5, or sometime after 1986 in the third phase. Work was going ahead when the Islamic revolution of 1979 called the project into question.

At an early stage in the planning process it was necessary to determine how much floor space would be needed in the private sector for offices, shopping facilities, hotels, recreation, entertainment and sports facilities. The massive private investments involved would be sparked off by the movement of national government and municipal offices to the site. To determine demand, the consultants carried out a series of investigations, and the resulting report provides insights into the way they envisaged the project taking shape and the assumptions necessary to forecast ultimate demand (Llewelyn-Davies, 1975).

Forecasts for the growth of Tehran, on the basis of projections calculated from past trends, put the population of Greater Tehran at 4.6 million in late 1975, between 5.5 and 6.4 million by 1981, and by 1991 at between eight and 10.5 million. Forecasting the rate of national economic growth was more difficult, however, given the volatile state of Iran's economy after the 1973 rise in oil revenues. The revised fifth national plan forecast an increase in GNP of 26 per cent per annum at constant prices, with 15 per cent per annum for the period up to 1985.

Private income and expenditure were expected to rise by a similar amount. Government policy, however, was ostensibly aimed at some redistribution of income, with lower-class incomes rising faster than upper-class incomes. There was some concern whether Shahestan Pahlavi, designed for middle- and upper-income groups, would suffer if this policy ever became effective. The consultants' calculations, however, were that, even with some relative redistribution of wealth, GNP was rising so rapidly that the future wealth of their customers seemed enough to be able to afford the scheme.

A further set of assumptions was made in regard to the availability of resources in the building industry. It was expected that Iran's rapid development would lead to strong competition for finance, labour and material inputs to building projects. Foremost among these projects were the satellite communities of Kan, Lavizan and Farahzad, which would compete for private-sector management skills and physical resources, and for government financial assistance to supply their basic infrastructure. In this respect it was assumed that Shahestan Pahlavi's national importance, and the fact that its government connections were at the highest, that is imperial, level, would give the project a significant advantage. Taken together, it can be seen that these various building projects were undertaken in a context of capitalist competition not just between individual firms but between the consortia building the new towns. There were also considerable vested interests in the bazaar and the old downtown centre of the city. Worries expressed that Shahestan Pahlavi would lead to a relative decline of the old centre were partially allayed by restricting the allocation of future demand for privately built land to 50 per cent. Throughout their feasibility studies, the planners stressed the logic of growth and development in the capital, though published government policy was to halt or slow the physical expansion of the city and check population growth. Despite the possibility, indeed the likelihood, that Shahestan Pahlavi would lead to an acceleration of the capital's growth and so exacerbate Tehran's internal problems and its problems in relation to the rest of Iran, Shahestan Pahlavi was claimed to be a special case, to which published policies need not apply even if they applied to other projects. Under the Shah, the conflict between what was perceived as being in the best interests of the country — that is, restriction on the capital's growth — and the desire of the dominant groups to enjoy the fruits of growth was nearly always resolved in favour of growth.

Case Study – The Planning of Transport

The pace of growth and development may outstrip the ability of
government to analyse what is happening and mobilise the resources
necessary to cope. The problems of gathering information, choosing
appropriate methods of analysis, evaluating alternatives and mobilising
the resources necessary to implement policy are well illustrated in the
efforts made to improve transport in Tehran. The master plan made
some general provisions for transport, but in 1971 the Municipality
of Tehran commissioned a firm of consultants, the *Société Francaise
d'Études et de Réalisation de Transports Urbains* (SOFRETU), to
prepare a series of comprehensive transportation studies and a plan,
which was published in 1973. Their reports pointed to a series of
problems which were likely to get worse if no action was taken. The
road system had a number of deficiencies: many major roads were
discontinuous one with another; poor traffic control at junctions and
the inadequacy of the roads serving, in particular, the old centre of the
city led to severe congestion. The rate of car ownership, however, was
relatively low, calculated in 1971 as 33 cars per 1000 inhabitants. A
population of 3.6 million was estimated to make 5.5 million vehicular
trips daily, 2.3 million by private transport and 3.2 million in buses
and taxis. The public transport system was inadequate to deal with the
demands placed upon it.

Tehran was served by 18 bus companies until 1956, when they were
amalgamated into the United Bus Company, policy control of which
was taken over by the municipality in 1967. There were some 1800
large buses in 1970, including many double deckers, and 500 minibuses,
but of these only 60–70 per cent were operative at any one time
because of the lack of maintenance. The 90 bus routes were each in the
charge of a head of route, who was chosen more for his toughness and
ability to deal with awkward bus drivers than for his literacy (Thomson,
1977). The bus fare was very cheap, and charged at a flat rate for any
distance. An attempt to increase revenue by raising the fare led to
popular demonstrations in 1970 and the Shah ordered the restoration
of the old rate. In addition to the buses, Tehran was served by some
12,000 taxis operating on a share-taxi system, whereby the driver may
pick up passengers additional to those already carried if the prospective
passenger is going in the same direction. It may well be that the relative
cheapness of public transport has encouraged urban sprawl.

It became apparent in the SOFRETU studies that the master-plan
estimates regarding future population would have to be revised;

SOFRETU projected a growth instead from 3.6 million inhabitants in 1971 to 5.5 million in 1981 and eight million in 1991. The active population was expected to increase from 870,000 in 1966 to 1.8 million in 1981, and to 2.9 million by 1991. In fact, it had already reached 1.3 million by 1976. Expected increases in the female economic-activity rate and a decline in the percentage of the young population led SOFRETU to predict a change in the activity rate in 1971–91 from a low 29 per cent to 36 per cent. In the event, it reached 39 per cent by 1976, clearly indicating a much more rapid change than expected. During the same period of 1971–91 SOFRETU estimated that per capita income would rise by 1.9 times in the first decade and by 3.2 times overall, and the rate of car ownership was expected to rise from 33 per 1000 inhabitants to 134 in 1991, corresponding with the forecasts of the master plan. This implies a ninefold increase in the numbers of cars. Despite the marked differences between SOFRETU and the master plan on projected future population size, the transportation plan kept its recommendations within the main objectives of the master plan regarding the limits of the built-up area, which was to be 714 km^2 by 1991, the development of satellite communities and the concentration of secondary-sector employment in the south west. Whether the consultants retained these objectives from conviction or from a requirement of the original terms of reference is unclear.

An evaluation of alternative transportation schemes by SOFRETU was made in the light of the need to accommodate an estimated 17.7 million daily vehicular trips by 1991. A scheme which gave priority to the private car, with an extensive expressway road network and a dense bus network to take suburban residents to metro stations, was rejected on the grounds that the projected number of journeys could not be accommodated without extending the road system so far that it would destroy the urban fabric of central Tehran. One point which should be made here is that the decision to go ahead with some form of metro had already been taken even before these detailed transportation studies, just as the decision to go ahead and build on the grand scale in Shahestan Pahlavi had been taken before detailed demand studies. They were both political decisions, where the desire for projects worthy of the capital of Iran was uppermost in the minds of these governing the state.

SOFRETU's final recommendation was for a mixed transportation system with only a fraction of the expressways of the first alternative, 139 km of freeways and expressways, 133 km of roads 'of regional interest' and no inner ring road. Three rapid-transit railway lines were proposed, two north-south and one east-west. Implementation of part of the system was already underway by 1972, before SOFRETU produced their final report, when the fifth national plan assigned monies for the construction of an east-west and a north-south line and the purchase of 1600 extra buses. A final recommendation of SOFRETU was to establish a Regional Land Agency, able to purchase land and prevent speculation on land necessary for public use, with a regional authority to coordinate traffic and public transport, while developing and implementing urban improvement policies.

Within a year of the publication of the SOFRETU plan a critical appraisal was carried out by a team under contract with the ministry responsible for preparing and implementing Iran's national development plans, called Plan Organisation, later Plan and Budget Organisation. The appraisal claimed to identify major deficiencies in every aspect of the SOFRETU analysis and plan, of sufficient magnitude to cast suspicion on the investment strategy proposed (Kain, *et al.*, 1974). Fundamental to the SOFRETU analysis was the assumption, based on European and North American experience, that provision of a rail rapid-transit system can shape the growth of cities. This the Plan Organisation team rejected, but they also rejected the detailed population and employment estimates of the earlier study, where an increase of 4.5 million in Tehran's population in 1971–91 would be accompanied by a threefold increase in the per capita income of residents, to reach levels found in the major West European cities during the 1960s. Adhering to the physical objectives of the master plan and allowing only limited geographical expansion of the city would result in an increase in Tehran's gross population density from 102 persons per hectare to 137 by 1981, which appears improbably high, given the expected levels of car ownership and income. The appraisal team's own figures suggest levels of between 61 and 66 persons per hectare, and further rises in per capita income and vehicle ownership would lead to even lower densities by 1991. Again, while SOFRETU projected large increases in central-area employment and the development of Shahestan Pahlavi, the appraisal team expected central-area populations to decline substantially, with most new residential development at the periphery being at low densities. Total central-area employment growth was expected to be modest, with even a possible decline in the older centre – a possible problem anticipated by the Shahestan Pahlavi demand study. It was also felt that much of the transportation plan was based on the unrealistic assumption that 30 per cent of all trips by Tehran residents would be made on the 60 km of metro expected to be ready by 1981.

A high-performance rail rapid-transit system was seen by SOFRETU as an easily controllable instrument to shape Tehran's future development. Tehran would develop its own versions of the 'Metroland' of suburban London or Paris. However, the parallel sought between Tehran and European and North American examples, where a dense central core was served by rail rapid-transit systems, appears misguided. The examples selected were cities shaped by the provision of intercity rail and intracity electric railways, using the technology of the late nineteenth and early twentieth centuries. More extensive road transport, rising incomes and the availability of motor-truck and private-automobile transport have given industry and private residents much greater freedom to locate. Writing in 1974, when oil still appeared plentiful and cheap and Iran's own reserves far from depletion, the appraisal team thought that planned improvements in the road network would help diminish the influence on urban form which can be wielded by a metro or any other rapid-transit system. It was concluded that SOFRETU's enthusiasm for a metro led them through a series of small biases in the technical procedures chosen, in the transportation models and the evaluation techniques chosen, to produce a conclusion in favour of a metro. This was thought unlikely to be the result of a deliberate or conscious effort to bias the results.

Nevertheless, as with so much else, events overturned assumptions. The current fashion is against the private car and more in favour of urban public transport, which in nearly every city must be subsidised if it is to operate effectively. Congestion in central Tehran has been decreased in recent years by imposing bans on private cars at certain times of the day, and plans for the metro are proceeding. At the time of writing, however, it seems unlikely that a rapid and massive extension of the metro will be possible without the absorption as in so many of Tehran's prestige projects, of a disproportionate share of the nation's resources.

The Current Situation

The perceived need to make revisions to the Tehran master plan was part of a wider reappraisal of planning in Iran which was under way by the mid-1970s, and it should be seen in the general context of Iranian planning philosophy, organisation and effectiveness. It will be apparent from the above case studies that there were serious weaknesses in many aspects of Iranian urban planning. Under the Shah, the most common interpretation of the source of those weaknesses pointed to the inefficiency of bureaucratic control, which could be cured by reforms and by greater effort. More fundamental interpretations came from some Islamic thinkers, who ascribed the faults to a general moral turpitude, and from radical authors, notably Halliday, who regarded the problems as almost inevitable, given the structure of the state. That structure was defined as capitalist, with a developing form of capitalism; a dictatorial state which was monarchist in form and in a certain sense dependent on the advanced capitalist countries (Halliday, 1978). Iranian planning combined entrepreneurial corporate and private planning, industrial and real-estate development, with the public entrepreneur acting at the behest of private interests. The requirements of capitalist interests for short-term gain worked against long-term planning; oil revenues were spent not on developing the economy but on consumption or speculative housing. The lack of a proper planning machine stemmed partly from the monarchical nature of the state, or as Halliday (1978) put it: 'the only kind of planning in Iran is what the Shah wants'. This radical criticism argues that Iran's failure to benefit from oil, despite its plans and propaganda, was a result of the regime's misspending of oil revenues, a policy derived from its class character. Certainly the plans and the propaganda were well mixed, as in the fourth national development plan: 'In the new social order of Iran different groups and classes are striding towards common ideals and objectives under the banner of unity and harmony and in a spirit of cooperation and mutual assistance'. There was much talk of a 'Great Civilisation' emerging. The reality in the case of Tehran was the diversion of resources to the middle- and upper-income groups. The significance of speculative development is illustrated by estimates that over 100,000 housing units were standing empty in the capital in 1976 because new tax laws made owners reluctant to rent property, so causing great resentment to those without accommodation (Clark, 1980).

The ineffectiveness of planning was already being criticised from within the regime before its collapse. The main framework of Iranian planning was a series of national development plans, the drawing-up and implementation of which were the responsibility of what came to be called Plan and Budget Organisation. Up to and including the fourth plan (1968–72) there was a marked preference for the economic and quantitative aspects of planning, with little reference to physical and spatial aspects, or to social aspects, with the exception of the kind of rodomontade quoted above. The allocation of responsibilities within every ministry and within Plan and Budget Organisation was based on sectoral divisions with, as a result, only poor control over problems of geographical or intersectoral coordination. Many of the reports of foreign planning consultants did more or less point out these deficiencies, and there was a continuous cry for more effective bureaucratic control of planning and of the land market.

Some progress was made by the fifth national development plan (1973-8), which stressed that broader social and economic objectives should be taken into account, and showed a desire to integrate urban planning into a broader regional and national strategy (Clark, 1980). Among the problems which may be identified here was the lack of coordination between those responsible for urban physical growth — the municipalities and the Ministry of Housing and Town Planning — and those responsible for economic development; for example, Iran's largest housing developer, the army, did not come under municipal control. It was apparent also that some form of regional authority would be necessary to oversee Tehran's development.

The declared good intentions of the fifth plan were overtaken by the rise in post-1973 oil revenues. A revised plan was prepared, allowing a doubling of investment targets, but the spatial consequences were hardly considered. The tendency to measure the effects of decisions purely in monetary terms, ignoring qualitative aspects, may be partly a result of the ready availability of quantitative techniques, and one later government-sponsored report pointed out that techniques and criteria relating to monetary profitability lead to preference for short- or medium-term solutions (SCET IRAN, 1976), and it advocated a longer-term view. It might be argued, however, that the largely capitalist nature of the state made such techniques and their outcomes inevitable.

In response to criticism, Plan and Budget Organisation established a centre for national spatial planning, with powers to formulate planning policy, train planning personnel and conduct research; it also set up a high council for spatial planning. A series of reports were commissioned from the organisation SCET IRAN, which provided a perceptive diagnosis of Iran's planning ills and a series of imaginative proposals for dealing with them, called the national spatial strategy plan. The plan provided first a summary of the main trends and problems facing the country and then a series of specific measures designed to cope with and in most cases reverse the trends or mitigate unwanted effects. Whatever government becomes established in power in Iran, these problems will have to be tackled, or they will get worse.

Firstly, gaps in real income between socio-economic groups, between urban and rural areas and within urban areas have been widening for many years. Oil revenues have not been used in such a way as to change the situation. The sixfold increase in oil revenues between 1973 and 1975 resulted in a tripling of imports, congestion on roads, in ports and in customs clearance, a breakdown in the supply of construction material and a high rate of inflation.

Secondly, changes in the number and spatial distribution of the Iranian population in the past 40 years have been immense. The increase in rural population has, in absolute terms, been much greater than urban population. The years 1955–75 saw a shift towards more extensive, capital-intensive farming, with an overexploitation of limited reserves of water and usable agricultural land, the widespread upset of ecological systems and the overpopulation of rural areas (Costello, 1977). Rural emigration is likely to increase further, leading, possibly within one or two generations, to an absolute decline in rural population. Urban growth rates, fuelled by immigration, have been nearly five per cent per annum overall. The concentration of population in the big cities, and especially in Tehran, may have been favourable or even essential to the modernisation of the economy and society, if that is what is desired, but it is apparent that there are large sections of Iranian society who do not desire it. The harmful effects which Tehran's growth has had on the quality of life and the environment in the city, and on the vitality of regions away from the city, are now beginning to appear elsewhere also, notably in Isfahan.

Public investment has been concentrated in smaller areas in response to the concentration of population and resources in these areas and, as Tehran was the first to demonstrate, space is becoming as scarce a resource as water and agricultural land always have been. Accompanying these changes, vast areas of the country are becoming relatively marginal in economic and physical terms. Planning policy has done little to narrow the gap between them and the developed areas. Tehran's water-supply problems in the future, for example, can only be solved at the expense of rural communities to the north. If water is abstracted from Alburz rivers it cannot be used for existing agriculture. Enterprises like Shahestan Pahlavi show that the main focus of government interest has been on the capital. The preference for large-scale projects, not just in building but also in industry and agriculture, has likewise helped promote centralisation in the economy. The small-scale labour-intensive industrial enterprises which were among the principal employers in traditional urban life have benefitted only marginally

from growths in GNP. The rift between modern and traditional sectors
of the economy which SCET IRAN noticed in 1976 was seen as likely
to become the outstanding economic problem of the coming decade.
Furthermore, while a large proportion of the active urban population
who are unskilled or semiskilled can be found jobs in the early phases
of industrialisation, it will become much harder to employ them as
industry becomes more technologically sophisticated. SCET IRAN
(Vol. 1, 1976) was fully aware that the desire for growth threatened
the nation's cultural and environmental heritage, and of the possible
social dangers: 'so far the existing social structures have been sufficiently
flexible to absorb this mass of migrants relatively satisfactorily into the
urban way of life. But there is a delicate balance which is threatened
by the increase in the size of the towns, especially the new towns,
even without any increase in the rate of population growth'. It was
proposed to slow Tehran's growth rate and, above all, to seriously
curtail the Shahestan Pahlavi project.

The social geography of Tehran and its planning problems at present
are the inheritance of the Pahlavi era. Data relating to socio-economic
differences within the city were collected by SOFRETU and Llewelyn-
Davies *et al.* (1975) for use in the preparation of transportation and
other plans; some are given in Table 5.5. Figure 5.4 illustrates the
sectors devised by SOFRETU. The use of such large zones tends to
obscure detailed differences within the city. Tehran Pars, for instance,
has a higher average income than the inner suburbs, which are grouped
together with it in sector six. It can however be seen that the southern
suburbs, sectors three, four and five, have a total population of about
1.8 million, and that average household incomes are less than one-
third those of the northern suburbs, while figures for households owning
at least one vehicle show a disparity of one to twelve with the north.

The central sector, sector one, has been divided into a northern
and southern zone approximately along the line of the bazaar's
northern boundary. The bazaar zone, 00, in the old core of the city has
characteristics of household income and vehicle ownership similar to
those of the southern suburbs, while the northern central zone —
essentially Reza Shah's Tehran — is similar to its neighbours upslope.
Taken together, zones 05, one and seven contain about 20 per cent of
the city's population, and this includes of course many of the domestics
and other servants of the wealthier classes, while 52 per cent live in the
south. The eastern and western suburbs grouped together by SOFRETU
are intermediate in characteristics between north and south. In general,
populations of the inner portions of these sectors have lower incomes

Table 5.5: Household Revenue, Car Ownership and Population of Tehran, by Sector

Sector number and designation	Average household income, 1973[a] (thousand rials per month)	Percentage of households with at least one vehicle, 1973[a]	Estimated population, 1975[b] (thousands)	Projected population (thousands) 1981[b]	Projected population (thousands) 1991[b]	Projected change 1975–91[b] %
00 Centre south	11.1	7.2	} 598	522	475	−20.6
05 Centre north	20.7	31.6				
1 Northern contiguous suburb	28.2	47.4	295.5	368	478	+61.8
2 Northwestern contiguous suburb	15.0	23.4	529	842	840	+58.8
3 Southwestern contiguous suburb	8.1	4.1	851	790	810	−4.8
4 Southern suburb	7.5	5.6	571	620	750	+31.1
5 Southeastern suburb	7.7	5.9	377.5	410	500	+33.2
6 Northeastern suburb	11.4	15.0	984.5	958	1305	+32.6
7 Northern peripheral suburb	23.5	37.4	359	505	865	+140.9
8 Western peripheral suburb	18.2	29.4	} 34.5	310	855	} +5630
9 New western satellite communities	—	—		175	1122	

Sources: a. SOFRETU (1973). b. Llewelyn-Davies *et al.* (1975), assuming a total population of 5.5 million in 1981 and eight million in 1991.

Figure 5.4: SOFRETU Socio-economic Sectors of Tehran

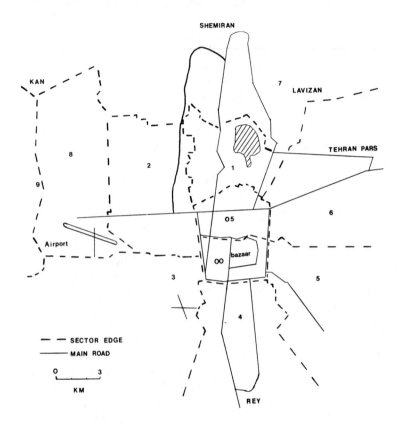

and live at higher densities than the outer areas, and in the western peripheral suburb, which is sectored separately, the figures available suggest a socio-economic profile similar to the northern peripheral suburbs. In addition, therefore, to the north-south contrast Tehran shows the spatial ordering of socio-economic groups which is to be expected in a predominantly capitalist society, with many of the wealthy living at a distance from the city centre. Predictions of future shifts in population made in the mid-1970s showed what would happen if the socio-economic forces which operated up to then were to continue into the future, guided to some extent by the planners. The Llewelyn-Davies data projected a decline in the population of the northern and peripheral suburbs and in the more distant satellite communities of the west, as Tehran's urban structure was reshaped along the lines set out originally in the master plan. Whether a deep-rooted change in the political philosophy of the Iranian government will have different effects on the ground remains to be seen.

The division between the westernised, cosmopolitan classes who ran the country under the Shahs and the intensely traditional Islamic masses is clearly visible on the ground. In a sense, the effect of the Islamic revolution was to shift the initiative for social change away from north Tehran towards the south. North Tehran is an area where the lifestyle is modern, with a population which was once a mixture of Iranians and foreigners, though now with very few foreigners. Much of it is newly built, with four-storey apartment blocks and large houses. In the northernmost districts, served by the new motorway network, there is a cluster of high-rise buildings, including the Hilton Hotel. Mosques are almost absent. The main north-south avenues were occupied by rows of shops, social clubs, bars and restaurants serving foreign cuisine; alcohol was freely available; and women wore western dress, until the revolution. South of Avenue Takhte Jamshid (Figure 5.3), but including it, is the modern central business district, where finance offices, numerous headquarters of national and international companies, hotels, doctors' and dentists' surgeries and the major airline's bureaux are located. Most of the avenues were laid out by Shah Reza, and here at least mature trees provide shade for pedestrians. Here also, in an area around Avenue Lalehzar, south of Avenue Shah Reza, was one area frequented by prostitutes. A 'reserved quarter' had also been set aside by the municipality in an area west of the old city where provincial travellers first arrived in Tehran (Vielle and Mohseni, 1969). These activities were ruthlessly suppressed by the Islamic revolution.

Southern Tehran begins at the bazaar, which is still at the centre of the city's major concentration of retail and service establishments. There are numerous mosques, tea houses, kebab restaurants and religious libraries. In contrast to the modern athletic facilities found in the north, the traditional Iranian sports are practised in 'houses of strength'. Women all wear *chadors* (a plain garment which shrouds the body from head to toe) in public, and always have done so here. The main streets are thronged with people, and noisy with the cry of hawkers. The city is, as one hostile observer reported in 1980, 'run down and dirty, and marked by long queues for food and public executions'. It is certainly dirty. The southern districts are at the foot of the slope coming down from the mountains; all the litter and filth thrown into the open waterways which are meant to irrigate the trees uphill is carried southwards. Mounds of rotting garbage were sometimes to be seen before the revolution, but the general move towards disorder which accompanies many political upheavals has meant in some instances a worsening of standards of public health. In any case, tuberculosis, not found elsewhere in the country, has been common in southern Tehran for many years, and its spread is aided by overcrowding.

It is perhaps this overcrowding, resulting from a shortage of housing, which is the single most important problem facing urban planners. The policy of the prerevolutionary administration was to provide credits for housing (and there was an increase in cooperative housing ventures in the later years), but to favour building for government employees. The fifth national plan (1973-8) projected only 21,000 units to be built by the public sector in Tehran, out of a total of 221,000. Priority in the public sector was to be given to replacing buildings in old and insanitary areas with large low-cost apartment blocks. Nearly all of the 200,000 private-sector housing units were to be built for the creditworthy, as we have seen in the plans for the satellite communities. Tehran shares these characteristics with other Third World cities: 'private sector activity in the Third World is generally capital-intensive and geared to the maintenance of economic growth rates rather than the distribution of such growth. The shelter needs of the poor cannot be met within the constraints of such mechanisms, since their lack of credit-worthiness makes it difficult for them to afford conventional housing' (Payne, 1977).

Iran has apparently moved away from the capitalist philosophy of the Imperial era, which wholeheartedly embraced western technology and institutions, and for which the guiding principle has seemed to be 'Enrich yourselves', towards a form of Islamic fundamentalism. Whether that will lead towards socially redistributive policies remains to be seen. At present it ostentatiously rejects 'westernisation'. It must be said, though, that the atavism of some elements in the Islamic regime is not, and may not be, conducive to the rational ordering of the city.

Bibliography

Bahrambeygui, H. *Tehran: An Urban Analysis* (Tehran, 1977)

Bartsch, W.H. 'Unemployment in Less Developed Countries: A Case Study of a Poor District of Tehran' in D.J. Dwyer (ed.), *The City in the Third World* (London, 1974)

Clark, B.D. 'Urban Planning Problems' in G.H. Blake and R.I. Lawless (eds.), *The Changing Middle Eastern City* (London, 1980).

Clark, B.D. and Costello, V.F. 'The Urban System and Social Patterns in Iranian

Cities' *Transactions of the Institute of British Geographers*, Vol. 59 (1973), pp. 99-128

Connell, J. *Tehran: Urbanisation and Development*, Institute of Development Studies Discussion Paper 32 (Sussex, 1973)

Costello, V.F. *Urbanization in the Middle East* (Cambridge, 1977)

Gruen, V. and Farman-Farmian, A.A. *Master Plan for Tehran* (Tehran, 1979) (in Persian)

Halliday, F. *Iran: Dictatorship and Development* (Penguin, Harmondsworth, 1979)

Issawi, C. 'Economic Change and Urbanization in the Middle East' in I.M. Lapidus (ed.), *Middle Eastern Cities* (Berkeley-Los Angeles, 1969)

Kain, J.F., Fauth, G.R. and Beesley, M.E. *Transport Planning for Tehran: An Evaluation of the SOFRETU Study* (Plan Organisation, Tehran, 1974)

Llewelyn-Davies, Weeks, Forestier-Walker and Bor *Demand Report: The Feasibility of Private Sector Development in Shahestan Pahlavi* (Tehran, 1975)

Lockhart, L. *Famous Cities of Iran* (Brentford, Middlesex, 1939)

Payne, G. *Urban Housing in the Third World* (London, 1977)

Planhol, X. de. 'Geography of Settlement', in W.B. Fisher (ed.), *The Cambridge History of Iran*, vol. I, *The Land of Iran* (London, 1968)

Plan Organisation *National Census of Population and Housing* (1966)

— *Fourth National Development Plan 1968-1972* (Tehran, 1968)

Plan and Budget Organisation *National Census of Population and Housing* (1976)

Roberts, H. *An Urban Profile of the Middle East* (London, 1979)

SCET IRAN *National Spatial Strategy Plan, Third Quarterly Report* (1976)

SOFRETU *(Société Francaise d'Etudes et de Realisation de Transports Urbains) Tehran, Transportation Plan. Final Report, Summary and Conclusions* (Tehran, 1973)

Thomson, J.M. *Great Cities and Their Traffic* (London, 1977)

Vielle, P. and Mohseni, K. 'Écologie Culturelle d'une Ville Islamique: Tehran' *Revue Geographique de l'Est*, vol. 9, no. 3-4 (1969), pp. 315-59

6 BOMBAY

C.D. Deshpande and B. Arunachalam

The modern metropolis of Bombay began as a group of seven islands off
the mainland of North Konkan on the west coast of India. As a consequence of the British East India Company's trading activities, the
population grew, reaching 60,000 by 1675, and over the course of two
centuries the seven islands were interconnected by means of causeways
and the intervening depressions were reclaimed. The 'native' town
grew up to the north of the factory-cum-European town. In the second
half of the nineteenth century, Bombay's commercial growth, which
was sponsored mainly by Gujerati and Parsi financiers, was encouraged
by the American civil war and the import of cotton from the rich tracts
of the Gujerat, Maharashtra and Karnataka regions, which promoted
the city's textile industry. This industry continues to be important,
but Bombay's economic base has been diversified and strengthened
during the post-Independence period, through the further concentration of port activity, transport, commerce and governmental and
nongovernmental administration and managerial functions in the city.

Bombay's industrial and commercial growth has been accompanied
by a steep increase in population, from 0.9 million in 1901, to 1.8
million in 1941 and 5.9 million in 1971, with an estimated 1980
population of more than eight million (Table 6.1). This phenomenal
demographic expansion, especially in the last three decades, is reflected
in the vast urban sprawl of Greater Bombay (Figure 6.1). For administrative and planning purposes, the original seven islands have been
combined to form the Bombay City Island, which is separated by the
Mahim Creek from the suburban Salsette Island. Except for a small
northern portion of Salsette, which is part of Thane district, these two
districts form the municipal unit of Greater Bombay (Figure 6.1). The
Bombay metropolitan region, of which Greater Bombay is a part,
extends onto the mainland beyond the Ulhas estuary and the Thane
creek, including the embryonic New Bombay. This region is defined for
planning purposes only, however; New Bombay is administered, in its
present phase of development, by the City and Industrial Development
Corporation (CIDCO) (BMRBP, 1974).

Table 6.1: Population in Greater Bombay, Bombay City, Suburbs and Extended Suburbs, 1901–71 (thousands)

Year	Greater Bombay			Bombay City			Suburbs[a]			Extended Suburbs[a]		
	Total	Male	Female	Total	Male	Female	Total	Male	Female	Total	Male	Female
1901[b]	928	562	366	776	480	290	71	41	31	80	42	38
1911[b]	1149	732	417	979	640	339	82	47	36	87	45	42
1921[b]	1380	884	496	1176	771	405	118	68	50	86	45	42
1931[b]	1398	878	520	1161	747	414	141	81	60	95	49	46
1941[b]	1801	1115	686	1490	942	547	205	118	88	106	55	51
1951	2994	1868	1126	2329	1480	849	510	300	211	155	89	66
1961	4152	2496	1656	2772	1705	1067	1037	597	439	344	194	149
1971	5970	3478	2492	3070	1838	1232	2167	1229	938	733	411	322

a. Suburbs denote areas annexed in 1950, including present-day wards H, K, L and M, while extended suburbs are areas annexed in 1956, including wards P, R, N and T. All the suburbs are located in Salsette Island.
b. The pre-1951 population figures are adjusted to ward and section boundaries.

Figure 6.1: Bombay: The Regional Setting

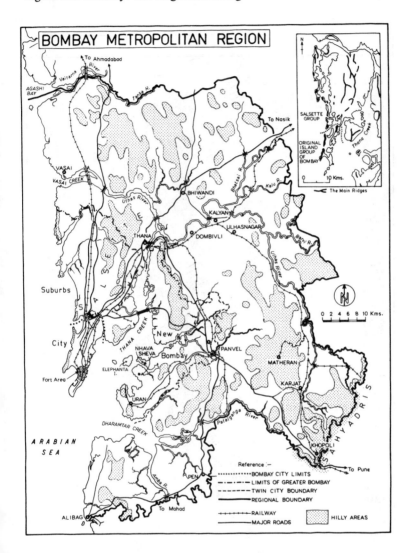

The Physical and Urban Setting

Geomorphologically, Salsette and Bombay Islands have developed over an erosional relic of a basaltic landscape with two parallel ridges running north-south, enclosing valley depressions and fringed by belts of tidal

Figure 6.2: Morphogenetic Regions of Bombay

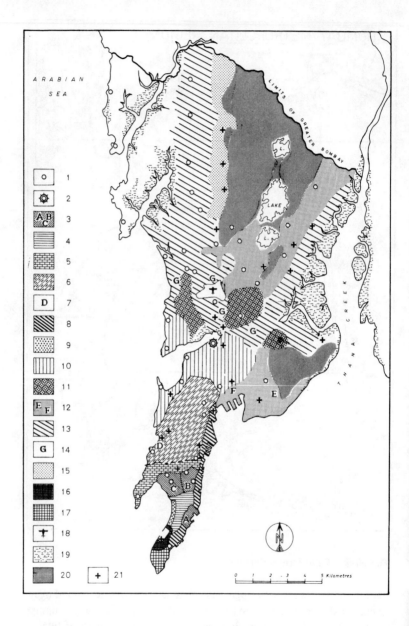

Key

(1) Precolonial settlement nuclei (fishing and farming); (2) twelfth- to thirteenth-century fortified Hindu township of Mahikavati; (3) colonial period: European town and native quarters: (A) European town and factories with a Parsee bazaar sector within fort; (B) Muslim quarters and shopping area; (C) native Hindu township; (4) area in between 3A, 3B and 3C: open ground and esplanade; (5) eighteenth-century extensions for European quarters (better-class) and Governor's residence and commercial zone; (6) mid-eighteenth to mid-nineteenth century reclamation; ground developed by joining the seven islands, followed by roads on reclamation embankments; late nineteenth-century mills and industrial labour tenements (chawls); (7) the last breach, Hornby Vellard and the adjoining racecourse; (8) late nineteenth- and early twentieth-century portside reclamations; docks and dockside functions; (9) early-twentieth-century (up to 1930), Back Bay reclamation; 'Queen's Necklace' and five-storey 'matchbox'-type upper-middle-class flats; (10) 1930 to 1950: lower- and middle-income residential area; early suburbs; (11) post-1950 residential 'dormitory' suburbs; (12) post-1960 industrial expansion: (E) protected industrial area; (F) newer reclamations and dock extensions; (13) post-1970 residential suburban expansion; (14) extensions of older suburbs away from rail corridor towards sea and new reclamation; (15) post-1970 industrial expansion in the outer western suburbs; ((16) post-1970 Back Bay reclamation: new skyscraper complex, partly offices, partly upper-class residences; (17) defence area; (18) airport; (19) marshes and salt pans; (20) hills; (21) major slums.

swamps and marshes.[1] The lakes formed by the impounded valley tracts of the hills of Salsette initially provided Bombay's water supply, but at present act as balancing reservoirs, drawing larger supplies (over 97 per cent) from the impounded water of mainland rivers of the adjoining Thana district. The north-south stretch of the two islands and their relief provide the basic orientation to the growth of Bombay, its suburban extensions and its pattern of transport and commuting. The growing intensity of urban land use, however, has caused significant changes in the local relief (Figure 6.2). In the south, land for intensive urban use in the form of an emerging alternative central business district (CBD) in a skyscraper complex is being reclaimed from the sea;[2] the central part of Bombay, which constitutes the industrial heart of the city, lies mostly on eighteenth- and nineteenth-century reclamations; in the north, the first 'suburbs' of Bombay in Mahim, Matunga and later Sion developed over the reclaimed marshes and salt pans to house low- and middle-income 'service-seeking' in-migrants. The margins of Mahim Creek house the large slum area of Dharavi and the tannery works. Farther beyond, the post-Independence suburban growth in Salsette initiated along the rail corridors is steadily pushing itself into the tidal marshes along the creeks, which are being steadily reclaimed for low- and middle-income residential flats, while the industrial landscape is skirting and probing into the central hill complex and the horseshoe valley of the lakeside in between. Many low hill ranges have been levelled down, either to make Bombay Airport safer or to provide material for building and for dumping into the shallow sea and creek areas under reclamation.

These man-made changes in relief have not been made without environmental backlash. Land reclamation seems to have entailed greater erosive action in the Back Bay in the south and Versova in the north (along the western seafront), where measures to protect valuable urban land from sea erosion are underway. Reclamation of lowlands has meant severely modified and derelict natural drainage, and this too has raised problems of recurrent flooding and sewage management. One has to only go round the city on a very wet monsoonal day to see the contours of the original seven islands separated by flooded streets. Thus, while technology has enabled urban Bombay to reclaim land and to construct modern high-rise buildings in the south and along the western shores, it has introduced other environmental problems — principally problems of urban water supply and drainage on the one hand, and the ever-present threat of epidemics of water-borne diseases such as infectious hepatitis and typhoid on the other (Koshy, 1978).

Urban Demography

Of the total population of 5.96 millions of Greater Bombay (1971), 52 per cent reside in Bombay Island, 26 per cent in the inner and 22 per cent in the outer (or extended) suburbs.[3] The highest densities (over 2000 persons per hectare) are recorded in the crowded central parts of Bombay, in the original native quarters outside the Fort (parts of B and C wards) (Figure 6.2). Away from the city centre, densities progressively decrease towards the north and north-west, though relatively denser concentrations exist around the major sub-urban railway stations. The density gradient from the city centre in the south towards the northern fringe now simulates the typical gradient of a western city, in that the Fort and the adjoining area of the CBD or city centre has a low residential population (125 per hectare). The most recent tendency in the city centre is towards 'infilling' of these low-density areas, both by rich residential communities and their domestic servants and by hotels.

The most significant aspect of Bombay's population is its linguistic and cultural diversity, caused by a century-old in-migration from other districts of Maharashtra as well as from other states of the Union. Further strong infusion took place in the troubled post-Partition years (1947–9), when Sindhi and Punjabi migrants from Pakistan came into

the city. Later the spurt in industrial and commercial growth during
the plan periods of independent India brought in large streams of jobseekers from all parts of the country. Thus, in-migration accounts for
63 per cent of Greater Bombay's population. Of the migrants, 42 per
cent were drawn from other districts of Maharashtra, particularly the
Konkan coastal region, the hill sections of Satara-Sangli and the drought-
prone areas of the plateau Maharashtra (the Desh). Among the migrants
from the other states, Gujaratis (17.6 per cent) are the largest in
number, evidently as a legacy of the period when Bombay was the
administrative capital of the Presidency, which comprised parts of
Gujarat, Maharashtra and Karnataka. These migrants are mostly engaged
in banking, finance and wholesale and retail trading. Migrants from
other states, too, show marked preferences in their occupations: those
from Uttar Pradesh (12 per cent) specialise in perishables and milk
supply, and public-transport services, the stream from Punjab-Haryana
in taxi services, auto-garages and engineering units, and those from
Rajasthan in shopping; labour for building and road construction hails
from Andhra (2.2 per cent) and Karnataka (2.2 per cent); white-collar
service seekers from Tamil Nadu (2.6 per cent), Goa (1.0 per cent) and
Kerala (2.2 per cent); and those who have settled down from Sind
(2.6 per cent) specialise in retail trading and construction work (Census
of India, 1973). This strong migrant element lends a colourful and
polyglot character to the city, and gives expression to the various parts
of the social landscape of Greater Bombay.

Residential Land Use in Greater Bombay

The residential areas of Bombay reveal a stratification based on income
levels as well as social and ethnic segregation, creating a distinctive
spatial pattern, an oriental mosaic that differs greatly from the patterns
seen in western urban models (Figures 6.2 and 6.3). The city centre and
the commercial core are fringed by upper-class residential zones, except
in the highly congested old cores of the 'colonial native' town, where
progressive intrusion of high-intensity, high-rental land use, coupled
with urban renewal, is pushing the lower-middle-class service population
out into the suburbs. Farther north, in the central parts of the city, the
industrial zone and its accompanying low-income single room tenements
of industrial workers are anachronistically found. The north of the city
island, and the ever-expanding suburban rings mostly accommodate the
lower- and middle-income groups, although between suburbs an income-

Figure 6.3: Functional and Social Areas of Bombay City

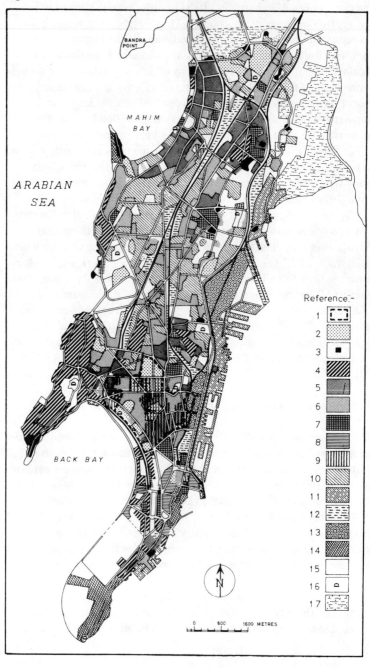

Key
(1) old buildings inside city area and bazaar zone; intense mixture of functional and social ranks; areal segregation on traditional lines of religion and language; (2) slums within core areas and Zopadpattis (strong segregation); (3) old village nuclei; social deterioration; (4) residential: upper-class and upper-middle-class 'Churchgate flats'-type and 'Malabar Hills'-type; colonial bungalows being replaced by skyscrapers in urban renewal; (5) middle-class colonies (up to World War II), segregation following language, religion, regional descent (Matunga-type). Later mixed cooperative-society flats; older middle-class areas; Mahim schemes of new colonies and old bungalows; (6) lower-class industrial tenements; (7) public institutions (government, educational, medical); (8) big business houses: pure or dominantly commercial function; (9) bazaar zone (wholesale, retail, small-scale); markets and small-scale industries within bazaar zone with strong religious, linguistic segregation; (10) factory zone; (11) harbour and fishing docks; (12) rail lines; yards and bus depots; (13) storage *godowns*; (14) restricted areas (military installations); (15) parks, garden, recreational areas and open land; (16) cemetery and burning *ghats*; (17) swamp and salt pans.
Source: Adapted from Nissel (1977).

level differentiation is apparent. Thus, in this Indian city, it is the low- and middle-income service employees who commute the most and the longest. Another interesting aspect is the repeated change in location of the upper-class residential areas, presently situated on the hills in the west away from the harbour, bazaar and industrial zone, as well as in the western suburbs on the newer reclamations (Figure 6.2).

Interspersed and intermingling even with the high-class apartment houses of the city's elites are the hutments that spring up almost overnight, and create pockets of urban blight throughout the urban fabric. Numbering about 500, these slum areas account for almost 20 per cent of the resident population in Greater Bombay.

Characterisation of Social Areas

Superimposed on the general matrix of the Maharashtrian Hindu (Marathi-speaking) population spread over the entire Greater Bombay area (accounting for 42 per cent of the population) are strong pockets and nuclei of other linguistic and religious groups, recreating in miniature their home 'social' environments in different parts of the city. Thus, of the dominant minorities, the Urdu-speaking Muslims form a strong nucleus in the commercial functional zone of B ward and adjoining parts of C and E wards (i.e. the Masjid, Dongri, Mazagaon, Market and Umarkhadi areas), with smaller pockets in Mahim and Kurla; these constitute some of the most densely populated sections of Bombay (Figure 6.4). The Hindu Vaishnav sect and Jain Gujaratis live

Figure 6.4: Greater Bombay: Place Locations

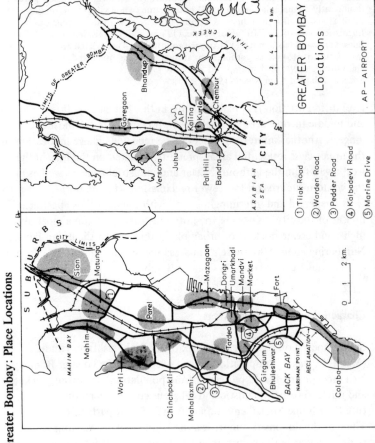

GREATER BOMBAY
Locations

AP – AIRPORT

① Tilak Road
② Warden Road
③ Pedder Road
④ Kalbadevi Road
⑤ Marine Drive

in dense clusters, close to the wholesale and retailing zones of Bhuleshwar (C ward) and in the western suburbs. The industrial centre of Bombay, drawing its semiskilled and unskilled labour supplies from the Konkan districts and hill zone of Maharashtra, is predominantly Maharashtrian Hindu in character. Pockets of Tamil-, Telugu- and Malayalam-speaking populations congregate in the north of the city and in specific suburbs like Chembur, Bhandup and Goregaon. The Uttar Bharativa from Uttar Pradesh and Bihar are found mainly in the outer western suburbs, while the small but rich community of Parsis live in well-knit pockets around the old city core in Colaba, Tardeo and Grant Road.

While the characterisation of social areas is dominantly seen in the low-income residential zones and in the slum and shanty-town zones (reaching its limits in the formation of *samaj* and *sangh*, i.e., associations, at the home village level), the middle- and upper-class residential zones, such as those of Malabar Hill, Worli, Matunga-Sion, Bandra and others, and the more recently emerging State Housing Board and private co-operative-sector apartments and flats have a much more mixed, cosmopolitan character. Here, however, there is evidence of an altogether different form of stratification, based on occupation and service; for example, film people congregate in the smart apartments of Bandra-Pali Hill and Juhu Reclamation, businessmen in Pedder and Warden Road colonies, and civil servants in Marine Drive flats and Housing Board colonies.

The migrant character of Greater Bombay also manifests itself in the abnormal age and sex structure of its population. The preponderance of males over females (650 females for every 1000 males), especially in the working age groups of 15 to 59 and the bulbous one-sided shape of the age-pyramid of the city population clearly demonstrate the sex- and age-selective nature of in-migration. The suburban population shows a greater parity between sexes; the working-class areas of central Bombay display the worst imbalance, indicating that the older in-migrant labour class from Konkan and nearby districts mainly consists of the male stream (returning 'home' a couple of times during the year for farm work and festivities) and that the newer, later migrants colonising the suburbs are moving in as families. Of the out-of-state migrants, the Sindhi and Gujarati population show a more balanced sex structure, while the Uttar Bharatiya reveal the most abnormal sex ratio.

Literacy in Greater Bombay as a whole stands at 64 per cent but is higher in males (71 per cent) than in females (52 per cent). As other social indicators would suggest, it is lowest in industrial central Bombay and in the slums, and highest in the mixed middle- and upper-class residential zones.

Functional and Spatial Changes

The functional landscape of colonial Bombay was almost a replica of other colonial cities of the British Empire, such as Calcutta, Madras or Singapore: the Factory-cum-Fort with its dominating Anglican Church, the docks on the eastern waterfront and a moated wall on the other three sides with 'Gates' connecting the Fort with the rest of the small urban area outside. While the southern parts of the island site were progressively occupied by civil and military administration, the eastern waterfront saw the construction of a succession of docks, and the interior behind it was filled with railway termini, storage yards and wholesale and retail markets. Beyond, to the north and west, lay the residential quarters, with a fair amount of segregation of the Europeans on the Malabar Hill, the Maharashtrians in Girgaum, the Gujaratis in Kalbadevi, the Muslims in Pydhonie and Mandvi and the Goans in Mazagaon (Figure 6.4).

The location of the modern textile industry in the second half of the nineteenth century in the Parel-Chinchpokli-Mahalakshmi-Tardeo area, then on the outskirts of the city, introduced new and important elements to the functional landscape of the colonial trading town. This industrial zone continued to grow throughout the next 100 years on the low-lying reclamation ground in the heart of the island, strengthening the earlier transportation and commercial functions and laying the foundations for suburban development along the two railways. This took place initially in the northern end of Bombay Island, followed later by the growth of suburbs on Salsette Island. World War II gave further stimulus to industry, but in the post-war period the rate of industrial development has been phenomenal, with two marked features: (a) the location of new housing units in the Salsette suburbs and Trombay and on the mainland fringe; (b) a partial shift of the older textile industry from central Bombay to the mainland fringe and its substitution by many small-scale units of engineering industry (mostly producing components) and consumer products in the compounds of the old textile mills (Figure 6.2). This shift, mainly the result of intense pressure on the limited land in the city, but also induced by government policy, has been only partial, however, and many mills, through inertia, still persist in their old locations. There has been a significant diversification in factory industry, with a greater stress on oil refineries and associated products, engineering (light, medium and heavy), consumer industries and chemical and pharmaceutical factories, most of which are sited outside the city island. Spatially, this diversification has brought in its wake a wider diffusion of the industrial areas, the newer ones being mainly in the suburbs along the rail corridors and in the 'lake' zone.

The Central Business District

A significant element in the city's growth is the commercial-cum-administrative city centre on the site of the original colonial fortified 'factory' town. This core of the city, initially multifunctional, has undergone a gradual transformation, until today it is dominated by tertiary and quaternary functions. It has a heavy concentration of banking, financial and insurance institutions, big-business houses in the Ballard Estate area, theatres, upper-class hotels and higher educational institutions, and is dotted with innumerable mail-box firms in the upper floors and interior streets; 'city industries', such as stationery stores and printing and publishing houses, also cluster within this area. The main roads contain the typical city shops with western features like display windows.

This CBD is bounded roughly by the two suburban rail terminals in the north and the adjoining wholesale-cum-retail markets, the docks in the east, the 'esplanade' maidans and upper- to middle-income residential apartment houses and an emergent skyscraper complex housing tertiary functions along the western waterfront. In the south, the CBD grades into the fashionable shopping area of Colaba causeway. With about one-third of the job potentials of the urban complex concentrated within it, the CBD is characterised by a daily morning ingress and evening exodus of over a million commuters, converging on it through the suburban rail and road arteries.

Successive expansions of the city northwards from the eccentrically located CBD (in the south of the city island) has brought a broad concentric pattern of land uses in the city, with the older residential and commercial (wholesaling and retailing) areas clinging to the CBD; an upper-class residential area to the west; an industrial-cum-labour tenement area further out; middle-class residential zones still farther north; and the harbour and its associated functions to the east.

The Bazaar Area

The bazaar area is sharply divided from the CBD to the south along the Tilak Road and Phyle market complex just north of the Victoria Terminus rail terminal, and lies to the east of the Western Railway. The eastern part of it — Masjid, Mandvi, Dongri, Pydhonie — is predominantly Muslim, and the western half Hindu and Jain Gujarati. Bazaar streets and markets are the dominant elements in this zone, which is better aligned and planned in the eastern sections. Within the bazaar area, services, tertiary functions, residence, retail trade, whole-saling and 'backyard' small industries all freely intermingle, even within single buildings, producing a combination of intensive and diverse land-use functions, and a typically Indian economic landscape, not readily found in western urban counterparts. In spite of this intensive economic use of space, the bazaar zone records the highest population densities of Bombay.

A distinctive feature of the bazaar zone of Bombay is its spatial organisation not only on economic lines, but more particularly on the basis of socio-cultural linkages. While wholesaling and warehousing dominate the eastern parts of the bazaar zone adjoining the central railway, wholesaling, retailing and *godowns* (storehouses) are more readily mixed in the western parts. Street and area specialisations in commodities and services are discernible, but there is an undercurrent of social and cultural linkages due to the family inheritance of pro-fessions: Muslims in metal and furniture works, tools, bakery and butchery, coir inlay work and perfume markets; Marwaris in money-lending and petty jewellery; Gujarati Hindus and Jains in textile and cloth and yarn markets; Sikhs in transport services, auto-parts and forwarding agencies; Southern Indians in restaurants and coffee shops and the like. The commercial function is most distinct in the south and centre of the zone. The main streets are dominated by retail shops and craftsmen producing high-value goods like jewellery, watches and electrical appliances, with outlets for handicrafts and small-scale industrial goods in the side streets and backyards. Shop owners typically live above their shops, and employees live either in the shops themselves or on the pavements. Within the bazaar zone, residential areas are essentially mosaics of community neighbourhoods, based on language, religion, caste or even place of origin.

The expansion of industrial and tertiary activities in Greater Bombay has had its impact on the other functional activities: for example, zones of transport, storage and commerce have become more intensive in both spatial and functional terms. In the concomitant growth of residential areas, five spatial patterns are to be seen. These are: (a) new residential structures consisting mainly of high-rise apartments, developed in suburban ribbons expanding outwards along the rail corridors; (b) skyscrapers and high-rise buildings on Bombay Island constructed either on newly reclaimed land or as part of an urban-renewal programme, and designed mainly to house business, offices and 'elite' residences; (c) temporary sprawling structures arising in the suburbs either as strip shopping bazaars or as low- and middle-class tenements; (d) the steady intrusion of 'high-rent' retailing outlets and smaller offices from the main commercial complex adjoining the city centre into the main arterial corridors of the older residential zones close to the city core, initially in the ground level and steadily ingressing to the upper floors, thereby pushing the residential function outwards into the suburbs; and (e) slums – the *zopadpattis* – principally in the ill-drained marshy areas and road and railway margins, but with a ubiquitous interstitial spread practically all over Greater Bombay, on open land adjacent to already built-up apartment areas.

Urban Renewal and Its Social Implications

A major part of the city proper and the older cores of practically every suburb are in the throes of urban renewal. Two opposing forces are at work. The first is the 'urban force', in the form of pressure for more space permitted by the higher floor-space index in the city core.[4] This pressure demands demolition of older structures and the erection of high-rent, high-rise buildings that cater for more intensive urban land uses, thus pushing the residential areas outwards. Secondly, there is the social force represented by the Rent Control Act and the responsibilities of the Housing Repairs Board, which seeks to protect tenants from eviction and rack-renting by landlords. The Rent Control Act, in operation since 1940 (and revised in 1959), protects tenants by freezing rents at the pre-war level, and preventing eviction except under special circumstances. This Act also seeks to standardise the rents of new buildings, and may be regarded as having broadly similar objectives as UK 'fair-rent' legislation. Unfortunately, the general result has been the gross neglect and lack of maintenance of existing buildings till they literally collapse, accompanied by the unhealthy practices of illegal and excessive deposits for rented quarters and 'overnight' arrivals of squatter colonies and shanty-towns. In partial response to this, a

Housing Repairs Board was set up as a Corporation, to ensure repairs when the landlords refused to carry them out, but the bureaucratic delays and 'utter state of neglect' of buildings cause many house collapses every year.[5]

The overall result of these two largely ineffective measures has been to create a bizarre differentiation in the urban landscape. High-rise modern buildings jostle with low rickety structures, while hutments proliferate and squeeze in where there is space. Generally speaking, behind the new buildings along the main roads of Bombay the old Bombay lies crumbling and dilapidated. The social implications of this structural change are profound. Apart from pushing the poorer older low-income residents out into the suburbs in search of quarters suitable to their income levels, these incursions into purely residential areas bring in ribbons of higher-intensity land uses, like retailing and office functions, and introduces a more 'mixed' middle- or upper-middle-income residential white-collar service-seeking population into areas that were formerly socially homogeneous. This creates social tensions, and new demands for amenities not previously available in the area, as has happened, for example, in the Tardeo area of the city and in Bandra-Khar in the suburbs.

In a new high-rise building, the ground floor might be claimed, typically, by retail shops, and the upper floors by a hotel and a suite of administrative offices or small warehouses; or the whole building might be given over to a set of managerial houses, as in South and West Bengal. Normally, if the building lies on a main road, be it on the Island or in the suburbs, retail shops will claim the ground floor and residential flats the rest; if it is situated away from main roads, the whole building will be turned over to residential flats. In this process of transformation, the rich push out the middle class, and the middle class push out the poor, although the Rent Act resists eviction and protects tenants of weaker economic status. The overall result of these trends has been to further complicate Bombay's social pattern, making the various areas more blurred and more difficult to demarcate than they were 50 years ago.

The Social Zones in Transition

About 50 years ago, it was possible to identify fairly well the distinct social zones of Bombay city (Nissel, 1977), with each enclave dominated by Maharashtrians, Gujaratis, Parsis, Muslims, Goan Christians and

Europeans. During the early phase of suburbanisation, Hindu and Parsi 'colonies' of Matunga and Mahim found new neighbours in the Southern Indians and Goan Christians respectively. The suburban process in the Salsette Island also produced areas of marked Maharashtrian, Gujarati, Goan Christian and Uttar Bharatiya concentrations. The rapid post-war suburbanisation which spread over Salsette, on the other hand, infused new and vigorous elements through clusters of Sindhi and Punjabi immigrants in Khar, Bandra and Chembur; as the newer out-of-state migrants and immigrants from elsewhere in the state have settled in the suburbs, so the earlier social groupings have grown more indistinct. Almost everywhere, social patterning is being confused and obliterated by new industrial locations, by the sporadic rise of slums and by the newer suburban apartment-house schemes provided by the government under town-planning schemes. In such schemes, the state-organised Housing Board allots flats on the basis of income levels and the drawing of lots, thus cutting across all socio-cultural strands. Company and city improvement trust schemes, as well as banks promoting residential quarters for their employees, have also promoted cosmopolitan ways of living. In addition, private cooperative housing societies promoted earlier by individual communities for their own neighbourhood are also on the wane; the newer cooperatively built residential areas have a better mix of the cosmopolitan population of the city.

These changs away from social patterning on religious, linguistic or cultural grounds and towards a socio-economic division of the city raise the question of how far the urban communities of Bombay tend to group together on the basis of a common economic status, as in a western city. A recent study by Nissel (1977), though rather inconclusive, does show that some parts of the larger social zones tend to acquire 'higher' or 'lower' middle-class status. This is apparent in the markedly richer class concentration along the western waterfront from the south to the north of Greater Bombay. At the other end of the scale, the lower-class residential areas and slums, strewn practically all over the city, show an internal patterning that strongly reflects affinities of language, cultural traits of the residents' home region and caste or profession (Chavan, 1976). These areas form villages within the city, in each of which socio-cultural groups congregate within the overall framework of poverty, being forced by economic and spatial necessity to live side by side, but striving to maintain their individuality of status by recreating in miniature their 'native' cultural environments within the larger urban mix of the city.

The Urban Economic Base

The economic base of the city is dominantly industrial, but is under-going a rapid transformation. Table 6.2 shows the extent of rapid

Table 6.2: (a) Growth of Industrial Units and Workers in Greater Bombay, 1901-70

	1901[a]	1931[a]	1951[b]	1970[b]
Units	138	432	3064	4933
Industrial workers (thousands)	108	166	384	569
Textile workers (thousands)	102	95	212	235
Textile workers as a fraction of all industrial workers (%)	94.4	57.2	55.4	41.3

a. Figures for the city only. b. Figures for the whole of Greater Bombay.

(b) Industrial Composition of Greater Bombay, 1970

Type of industry	Units	Workers
Textiles	603	235.3
Chemicals	368	37.7
Printing	436	19.7
Non-metallic	207	18.2
Basic metals	217	14.9
Metals	710	39.9
Electrical machinery	296	29.9
Machinery	461	33.0
Transport equipment	166	54.9
Miscellaneous	1469	85.0
Total	4933	568.5

growth of the factory industry since 1901, the job opportunities which it offers, and its growing diversification: the relative importance of the textile industry is declining as other industrial horizons are expanding. Nearly 22 per cent of the work force is engaged in trade and commerce, eleven per cent in transport and communications and 20 per cent in services. Over the last three decades, the proportion of population engaged in services has been on the decline (Table 6.3), not because of an absolute decline in service employment or its outmigration, but because the growth of the industrial sector has been much faster, especially in the suburbs, where new industrial nuclei have been developing and growing at a spectacular rate. A related trend is the steady concentration of the 'office' (service) function in the CBD, which has been further stimulated by the emerging multistorey skyscraper complex at the Nariman Point, just adjoining the CBD (Figure 6.4).

Table 6.3: Percentage of Total Workforce Engaged in Different Urban Occupations, 1951–71

Occupation	1951	1961	1971
Manufacturing	35.0	40.8	42.3
Trade	24.3	18.0	22.4
Transport	8.4	11.2	10.8
Service	31.6	25.4	20.2

Bombay derives the force of its commercial function from its port activities. About one-third of the sea-borne trade of India converges on Bombay, though imports exceed exports almost in the proportion of 5:2 in terms of tonnage.

In terms of physical assets, the growth of the port function has meant a steady extension of docks and storage houses, of refineries and oil-storage capacity, of additional railway tracks, improved roads with flyovers and telecommunication, and a manifold increase in railway and bus frequencies. Altogether, Bombay is estimated to contribute about one-third of the country's industrial production. It is highly debatable whether Bombay, as a node of economic production, is serving the nation and its poor or only the richer section, which practically monopolises production and takes advantage of low labour costs to promote its export efficiency.

The Main Issues

Bombay shares with most other cities of the world urban problems such as inadequate parking facilities, traffic congestion, particularly at peak times, limited open space, urban crime, inadequate housing and poverty. Some of these problems have assumed alarming proportions, because the urban administrative agencies and other public agencies have been unable to cope with the rapidly growing population of the city and its suburbs.

Housing

With the city's continuous spatial and demographic growth, the demand for housing has been increasing. Prior to World War II, housing supply generally kept pace with demand. The sudden influx of a huge refugee population and a spontaneous spurt in the industrial and commercial functions of the city in the post-war period brought in its wake an unprecedented, and critical, shortage of housing. Rents were frozen at their pre-war levels under the Rent Restriction Act (1939); as noted above, this provoked a lack of maintenance of buildings, leading to house collapses, illegal high rentals and a lack of initiative and incentive on the part of the private builders to commence new housing. Rising land prices, together with a shortage, and greatly increased costs, of building materials and labour, added a further dimension to the problem. The Housing Repairs Board, constituted with the specific intention of avoiding house collapses and carrying out repairs to buildings in utter neglect, has not been able to make any significant headway. At state level, the Maharashtra Housing Board is engaged in providing industrial housing for low- and middle-income groups. Many state and private employers also build their own quarters for their staff. In addition, with the aid of state and other public-sector loans, private cooperative housing societies have taken the lead in the suburban areas. The average number of tenements constructed per annum by the Maharashtra Housing Board, municipal authorities, state and central government, statutory bodies and private societies are 4200, 1800, 1650, 250 and 9700, respectively. (It may also be noted that the state policy in permitting housing schemes favours cosmopolitan societies and frowns upon community segregation.) In spite of such measures, the present estimate of housing deficiency in the city is about 600,000 tenements, and this gap is widening with time.

The direct result of this serious shortage of housing is that an increasing proportion of the population resorts to individual, informal provision of shelter, resulting in urban blight, with the spontaneous growth of hutments and slums on public land, roadsides and quarry sites and on land under reclamation. About 500 hutment areas have been identified, mostly occupied by those who have no better housing facilities 'within reach'. The only solution to the housing shortage seems to lie in gigantic housing schemes undertaken on a 'war footing', in conjunction with a serious attempt at the planned progressive dispersal of the population, and decongestion of the city.

Traffic

Coordination of traffic is one of the major problems of the metropolis. Six rail corridors and a network of arterial roads serve the city's needs. The north-south elongation of the city island (now almost a peninsula), its insularity, and the two causeways guarding the entry into the city from the suburbs impose severe physical constraints, and regulate the traffic flow mainly in a north-south orientation. Since the city centre lies at the southern extreme of the island, and even today two-thirds of the job opportunities are concentrated in the city (one-third in the CBD and its immediate surroundings alone), there are strong daily movements of commuters through the island, into and out of the city; over one million people converge on the city rail terminals in the peak rush hours (9.00–11.30 a.m.).

Table 6.4: Modes of Commuting in Greater Bombay

Type of transportation	(%)	Pattern of commuting	(%)
Suburban rail	39	Intracity	23.6
Public bus	39	Intrasuburbs	13.0
Private vehicles	10.6	City to suburbs	22.8
Taxi service	9.3	Suburb to city	22.9
Others	2.1	City to beyond city	4.6
		Beyond city to city	4.6
		Suburbs to beyond city	2.5
		Beyond city to suburbs	2.4

As Table 6.4 shows, suburban rail services and public transport on the roads contribute the lion's share to the traffic flows. In 1960–1, the road mileage per km^2 was 1.99, or 0.2105 per 1000 population; the corresponding figures for 1970–1 were 2.37 and 0.1736, respectively. While the population per private car, taxi and motor cycle has decreased (suggesting their greater claim on road space), population per public bus service has increased from 3710 in 1960 to 4160 in 1975 (Keswani, 1977). The narrow streets in the city centre offer little scope for road-widening, and there is steadily increasing congestion on the arterial roads. Bottlenecks in the traffic flows arise at the two causeways and at the major intersections between the east-west cross flows and the main north-south streams; attempts to relieve the pressure are being made, with the construction of flyovers at vital crossroads.

Commuter traffic by rail has increased from 60 million in 1941-2 to 43 million in 1971, a compound annual growth rate of over ten per cent (Malhotra, 1975). Laying additional track, increasing the number of rail compartments and scheduling trains at higher frequency have helped to an extent, but rail commuting has almost reached saturation point, with little scope for further improvement.

The earlier one-way commuting pattern between the suburbs and the city (from suburban homes to city workplaces in the morning, and back in the evening) is changing, with the growth of factory industry in the suburbs, to a two-way movement over most of the day. Bombay's transport systems, though evidencing, unlike the equivalent systems in Delhi or Calcutta, good coordination between road and rail traffic, are now showing signs of strain. There are plans for a metro and a harbour-side ferry service, though how far these measures will succeed under present conditions is an open question.

Urban Services

Other major problems in Bombay are the difficulties in maintaining supplies of water and electric power, and the spatial mismatch between the location of civic and social services and the areas of population growth.

Though Bombay can call upon a fairly large supply of water from six different sources, this is not enough to meet the city's needs, and the supply has to be monitored and regulated. The present level of demand is expected to double in the next two decades, and a search for fresh sources of supply is now underway, but there is an inevitable clash of interests here between the city itself and the surrounding region, which can only supply more water to urban Bombay at some cost to itself. Electricity consumption in Bombay has trebled over the last twenty years, and now accounts for more than half of the power generated in the state. Nevertheless, there are still acute seasonal shortages, which impose severe restrictions on industrial productivity. Reconciling the needs of the city and the larger region is again a problem here.

Civic and social amenities such as hospitals, institutions of higher education, major markets and recreation facilities, which in the colonial era were concentrated in the city centre, have already begun to disperse to the north of the city and into the suburbs; the balance remains heavily loaded in favour of the CBD, however, which produces a serious bias in the level of service provision throughout the city, while also adding to the commuting problem. These services not only have a lopsided distribution, but have been quite unable to match the growth in population, despite the efforts of public and other agencies; in this, Bombay resembles most other Third World cities caught in the throes of explosive growth.

Environmental Problems

Seasonal flooding during the heavy wet spells of the monsoon is an annual occurrence in Bombay, causing traffic dislocations, house collapses and electrical short-circuits. Although the high intensity of tropical monsoon rains is the primary cause of such flooding, the contribution of Bombay's bowl-like topography and its situation on low-lying (at or just above sea level) land reclaimed from the sea is certainly not small. For example, the repeated choking of the railways during the heavy rains may be attributed to the siting of the rail corridors along the keel of the elongated depressions.

The man-made terrain of Bombay poses a severe challenge so far as the management of sewage and storm-water drainage is concerned (Arunachalam, 1979). A large part of the old city interior is on reclaimed ground, at or near to sea level, which renders gravity flow of sewage into the sea almost impossible; pumping is invariably required. The drainage system is thoroughly unsatisfactory in as much as the level of the main drain is below the level of the low-water spring tides. If a wet spell of high-intensity rains coincides with a spring high tide, characterised by rough seas and swell waves striking the shores, not only is drainage outflow impossible, but it is also necessary to check the reversed inflow of the tidal waters into the land; sewage surfacing in the industrial heart of the city, which lies in a low bowl, means that water-borne diseases like infectious hepatitis and enteric fever are endemic in the city.

Water and air pollution constitutes yet another of Bombay's environmental problems. In the anthropogenic landforms of Bombay and its suburbs, natural outlets of drainage flow have all become derelict. Mahim Creek, which separates the city at its northern end from the suburbs, was famous forty years ago for its oyster beds and marsh-bird sanctuary, but is now notable for black oil sludge and industrial waste, disappearing marsh vegetation, encroaching buildings and an increase in mosquitoes. Thana Creek, which forms the head of the harbour bay, was once bristling with many fishing hamlets, but now receives large quantities of industrial and domestic waste. Sediment samples indicate a marked increase in mercury concentration from the harbour bay to Thana Creek (Zingde and Desai, 1980). The refineries, thermal station and fertiliser complex of Trombay throw out air so foul with gas and carbon that the neighbourhood has been nicknamed 'the gas chamber'. About 1000 tonnes of pollutants a day (38.4 per cent carbon mon-oxide, 34.4 per cent sulphur dioxide; the balance is suspended particulate matter) are released into the air by the city's industries, in addition to 260 tonnes of carbon monoxide a day from automobile exhaust fumes (Desai, 1980). The average concentration levels for trace elements observed in Bombay are the highest for any Indian city, and are comparable with the world's most polluted cities, such as Tokyo (Gopalakrishnan *et al.*, 1980). The northeast of the city (Sion-Chembar area) and the industrial city centre are the most polluted areas. Attempts are underway to control air and water pollution through NERI (the National Environmental Research Institute), municipal agencies and the newly established Maharashtra Prevention of Water Pollution Board, by imposing legal restraints on industry and providing better regulations and controls.

It is no overstatement to say that 'socio-cultural' pollution of this highly man-made environment is no less distressing. Modern technology and styles of living have led to a diminution of sociability and civic consciousness in cities throughout the world, but their impact on Third World cities seems to have been the most severe. Bombay conforms to the general features noted by McGee (1967). In Bombay, inequalities in income have appreciably widened since Independence; the opulence in the rich residential areas of the south and west of Bombay has a stark neighbourhood contrast to the slums that often fringe the sky-scrapers. Slum and pavement dwellers add to crowding and environ-mental disorder, and the very process of crowding and interstitial hutment development has led to unsociability, loss of identity, isolation, antisocial attitudes and growing urban crime. Life in Bombay today is a highly competitive rat race; residents are far too occupied in day-to-day living to cultivate the finer shades of civic life. Leisure is a privilege only of the rich few. A recent study revealed that a slum dweller's perception of Bombay consisted of his residence, his place of work and the route connecting the two!

Overview

All these aspects of the urban environment raise some basic issues which might best be understood from a comparative study of the tropical cities of the Third World. The present metropolis does not conform to any of the conventional land-use models of Hoyt, Burgess, Ullman and Harris, nor even that of Smailes (1969). Nor does it represent an evolution of the indigenous Indian city. Can it be that the metropolitan city of the Third World is evolving a model of its own, out of its economic and social environment? Such cities pose important questions for planners and administrators. Do large-scale economic production and modern urban engineering and technology unleash an urban expansion with a snowball effect aggravating the imbalances between the city and the countryside? Can a city's requirements for the natural resources of water supply and timber be commandeered from the surrounding countryside without impoverishing it? Are metropolitan areas in a national economy that is either free or 'mixed' (i.e., part socialised) to be regarded as gigantic machines of economic production, yielding benefits that go predominantly to the rich and trickle down to the vast urban poor only indirectly, through government expenditure. What ultimately, is the significance in terms of social values of a metropolitan city in a developing country?

It cannot be said that Bombay provides the answer. It is extremely difficult to project, as has been done for Canberra, for instance, a picture of Bombay in 2000 AD in conditions where diversion of the in-migration process to other regions (following the successful example of Greater London) is impossible, and where available resources are limited, competing claims are many and urban engineering technology is outpaced by incoming numbers.

The Urban Sprawl and Development Plans for the City and Its Region

Ever since the city of Bombay developed a strong industrial character, with the rise of the cotton textile industry, the municipal authorities have been engaged, through the specially instituted Improvement Trusts, in constructing cheap single-room tenement chawls for industrial workers around the industrial areas. This activity practically came to an end in the 1920s, when, following the first Town Planning Act of 1914, town-planning schemes were floated for the development of new residential suburbs in the north of the city. The Shivaji Park and Mahim schemes in the late 1930s and 1940s and the Khar model suburb in the 1940s belong to this category (Figure 6.2). However, these schemes, with their limited objective of developing new residential areas, could not solve the city's more general problems. A special committee was appointed by the state government to plan the post-war development of Bombay. This committee stressed the need to include a larger area within the urban limits of Bombay, so as to provide space for further expansion of the city, and also recommended that a

master plan be prepared to control the development of urban functions
and future spatial growth. Accordingly, the outlines of a master plan
were formulated by Albert Meyer-Modak in 1947. Though not a complete master plan in itself, it provided guidelines for the detailed
planning of areas designated for different purposes. It also indicated
lines along which further city growth was to be regulated, and new
suburbs and satellite towns planned.

The Mayer-Modak plan could not take effect till 1957, when the
Maharashtra Town Planning Act of 1954 came into force and gave the
requisite powers to the Corporation. By the early 1960s, however, the
city had changed considerably, and the Corporation set about preparing
a fresh master plan (1964), taking into consideration the recommendations of the earlier plan (1947), the S.G. Barve Study Committee's
recommendations (1958) and the more recent trends in spatial and
functional urban growth.

The new (1964) master plan has the following main objectives:
(1) the protection of the existing character of Bombay, and the gradual
reorganisation of its structure by promoting the development of areas
on a neighbourhood basis, with internal self-sufficiency and a sense of
healthy interdependence; (2) the establishment of optimal residential
densities in its wards; (3) the gradual dispersal of the city population
over a larger suburban zone; (4) the decentralisation of commerce and
industry from the city through the reservation of areas in the suburbs;
(5) a comprehensive programme of slum clearance; and (6) a regulated
and coordinated comprehensive development of urban infrastructure.

In keeping with the recommendations of the state government's
special committee, the administrative area of Bombay was enlarged
during the 1950s; whereas before the expansion the city included only
Bombay Island itself (a total area of 69 km^2), today it covers a major
part of Salsette Island, and the total urban area extends over 603 km^2.
A regional plan for the wider metropolitan region over the period
1970–91 has also been prepared (BMRPB, 1974). It was realised that the
Corporation's jurisdiction over the Greater Bombay urban area would
help in projecting development within the urban area only if a regional
plan for a larger metropolitan region was considered simultaneously. The
industrial spill-over from urban Bombay had already started to complicate the situation. The Gadgil Committee recommended the formulation
of a metropolitan regional plan, and accordingly the state enacted the
Maharashtra Regional and Town Planning Act, replacing the earlier
Town Planning Act of 1954. This Act provided for the constitution of
the Bombay Metropolitan Regional Board to formulate a metropolitan-

region plan. The state was also empowered to designate any area
reserved in the regional plan as a site for a new town, and to constitute
a separate development authority for its implementation. Accordingly,
a metropolitan region of 4000 km² was delineated, extending over the
mainland up to the Ghats, and including the natural commuting and
perishable-service hinterland, through which the main rail corridors
run (Figure 6.1).

Furthermore in establishing the development authority to undertake
the creation of a new Metropolitan centre, the government broke new
ground by setting up the City and Industrial Development Corporation
(CIDCO), which is now engaged in establishing the new town of New
Bombay on mainland Maharashtra (CIDCO, 1973).

New Bombay

This latest plan to relieve the pressure on Greater Bombay is a part of
the larger proposal to plan the Bombay metropolitan region (Figure
6.1). It seeks to develop a new counter-magnet to Bombay on the
mainland, presently joined by the Trombay-Vashi Bridge across Thana
Creek. It will consist of administrative, industrial, commercial and
residential sectors. New Bombay is planned to house about two million
residents. An important adjunct to New Bombay would be the construction of the Nhava-Sheva port to relieve the pressure on the old
Bombay port, which still handles a lion's share of the national imports
and exports.

The new urban complex of New Bombay will be flanked on one side
by the existing and growing industrial complex of Kalva-Belapur, and
on the other by a proposed residential area. The existing Thana-Belapur
road and a proposed road along the western flanks of the creek will
form a circuit of expressways within which the entire residential and
commercial areas will be accommodated. The Bombay-Poona highway
via the new bridge across Thana Creek runs west-east through the heart
of this township. The residential area is split into a number of planning
districts and sectors. Each sector would possess the necessary social
infrastructure and community facilities; and a group of three to four
sectors would have a common district centre. The township runs north-
south over a length of 20 km. It is proposed to develop three commercial zones: one in the north; another in the middle, close to the entry
from Bombay; and the third in the south, integrating the trans-Thana
development with the emerging Uran-Nheva-Sheva-Panvel urban complex.

Major recreational areas and parks are proposed in the intervening green belt, so as to provide an open area of 1.5 hectares for every 1000 people. The area of the whole stretch is about 5000 hectares, and sectoral population densities of about 125 per hectare are envisaged for the complex as a whole.

New Bombay, supported by the new port at Nhava-Sheva, will have direct access to the Bombay-Konkan highway as well as to the Diva-Panvel railway. For all practical purposes, the new city will be independent of Bombay, yet part of the urban complex of the Bombay region. It is proposed to shift the administrative functions of Bombay to the new metropolitan centre. The occupational structure and social composition of the new centre are yet to be assessed, but it is expected that the new city will carry the same cosmopolitan ingredients as old Bombay.

All that exists at present is a small residential township — Vashi — close to the entrance to the mainland from the city of Bombay, apart from an administrative complex (the Konkan Bhavan) and an older industrial area. The proposed port is yet to take shape, although the national government recently approved the project. Unfortunately, the developing residential township is situated athwart the thorough-fare from Bombay to Poona and has not been able to sustain itself as an independent neighbourhood in the absence of a local commercial zone and an administrative zone. Many of the township's residents now commute to the city, while employees of the administrative unit commute from Bombay, adding further to the problems of the area. As such, the development of New Bombay is very much in its infancy.

The choice of New Bombay has been criticised on several grounds. For example, the residential sector is exposed to air and water pollution as a result of its location between the earlier established Thana-Belapur chemical and pharmaceutical units and the Trombay refinery and petrochemical plants. It has also been argued that, far from relieving the pressure on old Bombay, its proximity means that it will further aggravate the urban situation and its urban sprawl will entail heavy claims on the water and power resources of the Sahyadries. On the other hand, the continuing reclamation of land in the Back Bay region in the south of the city and the rapid emergence of a huge multistorey skyscraper complex to accommodate commercial and administrative expansion is leading steadily to a further concentration of urban functions in the already congested southern end of the city, and in this context it is highly doubtful whether the contemplated objectives in the creation of New Bombay, namely decongestion of the urban functions, would materialise at all! These apprehensions appear to be valid, but the possibility of metropolitan expansion as a pseudo-megalopolitan growth cannot be ruled out, for Bombay's metropolitan influence, through its goods and commuting traffic, reaches as far as Surat, Nasik and Pune. The Nhava-Sheva port and the proposed Kalyan-Bhiwandi rail-junction complex and Konkan railway are likely to shift the urban gravity of the city to the mainland.

The greatest obstacle for the development plan, however, concerns the sources of finance. The funding of the New Bombay project to a large extent depends upon resources drawn from World Bank aid and other international agencies, apart from the central government, much less being drawn from the state itself. Greater Bombay does not contribute to this development. Since these funds are not readily forthcoming and the cost of the project runs into several hundred millions, the project has been suffocated practically at its inception. In practice, the development plan is being ignored, and unregulated growth continues in Bombay. A major problem would seem to be that the existing authorities are incapable of ensuring balanced and coordinated development of the city and surrounding region: there are four different local bodies which share responsibility for the areas concerned, and antagonisms between them are common.[6] It is becoming increasingly apparent that the establishment of a new town authority to develop a particular area is no solution to the overall regional problem. The establishment of a single metropolitan regional development authority, with adequate powers and finances, is essential if the development of the city is to be checked before it reaches a state of total disorder and chaos![7]

Notes

1. The central depression of the city island is mostly reclamation ground at about the mean sea-level, reclaimed since the 1670s, and even today is liable to flooding during the heavy rains. However, the north-middle sections of suburban Salsette are a tangle of hills rising to over 500 m, with an enclosed horseshoe valley opening southwards towards the Mahim Bay, now occupied by three lake reservoirs, and a derelict Mahim River.

2. The Back Bay reclamation scheme, which is still underway, was conceived in the latter part of the last century and begun early in this century. Today, the older parts of this reclamation area have five-storey residential structures along the 'Queen's Necklace' (Marine Drive), while the newer post-1950 reclamations have multistorey skyscraper complexes that are commercial-cum-administrative, promoting an emergent new CBD area that is replacing the older one along the docks on the eastern waterfront.

3. In the last two decades, demographic growth has been more rapid in the

suburbs than in the city, where, overall, the growth rate is slowing down; close to the city centre, the population is even declining (Arunachalam, 1978).

4. The floor-space index is the ratio of the built-up area to the area of the block on which the buildings stand. It is used as an indicator to show the amount of set-off area around the building which is to be left unbuilt for use by the building's residents. The FSI varies according to the area of the city. Its value is about 3.5 in the heart of the city and declines to 0.5 in the suburbs. It acts in favour of villa-type houses in the suburbs and skyscrapers in the city centre.

5. According to the municipal census, over 9000 houses in the city have outlived their usefulness and need to be demolished. See Bombay Civic Trust (1970).

6. The four authorities sharing responsibility for the New Bombay project area: the local district authorities of the two districts in which New Bombay lies; the Bombay metropolitan region; and the City Industrial Development Corporation. Land acquisition is essentially in the hands of the CIDCO; links between the four authorities are weak and no clear-cut jurisdiction has yet been worked out between the various authorities; hence the problem.

7. The authors are most grateful to their colleagues in the Department of Geography, University of Bombay, for their kind assistance and valuable comments. They are particularly thankful to Shri Vijay Rao, the cartographer of the Department, for his assistance in preparing the final maps.

Bibliography

Arunachalam, B. 'Bombay: An Exploding Metropolis' in R.P. Misra (ed.), *The Million Cities of India* (Vikas, Delhi, 1978)
—— 'Seasonal Flooding and Its Impacts on Urban Bombay: A Crisis of Urban Environment' in *Proceedings of UEC Seminar on Ecosystems* (Waltair, 1979)
Bam, S. *Water Resources of Greater Bombay*, Unpublished MA Dissertation, (University of Bombay, 1978)
BMC *Report on the Development Plan for Greater Bombay* (Bombay, 1964)
BMRPB (Bombay Metropolitan Regional Planning Board) *A Regional Plan for Bombay Metropolitan Region, 1970-1991*, Report of the Committee Appointed for Regional Plans for Bombay-Panvel and Poona Regions (Government of Mharashtra, 1974)
Bombay Civic Trust *Bombay's Development and Master Plan – A Twenty Years' Perspective* (Bombay, 1970)
Bulsaram, J.F. *Patterns of Social Life in Metropolitan Areas (With Particular Reference to Greater Bombay)* (Bombay, 1970)
Census of India *1961 Census*, vol. X, *Maharashtra*, part X-1b, *Greater Bombay Census Tables* (New Delhi, 1966)
—— *1971 Census: Greater Bombay Census Handbook, Primary Census Abstract* (Bombay, 1973)
Chavan, V.R. *Slums of Kalina*, Unpublished MA Dissertation (University of Bombay, 1976)
CIDCO *New Bombay – Draft Development Plan* (Bombay, 1973)
Desai, A.R. and Pillai, D.S. *Slums and Urbanisation* (Popular Prakashan, Bombay, 1970)
Desai, V.D. 'Problems of Bombay City' in *Proceedings of International Symposium on Management of the Environment* (Bombay, 1980)
Edwardes, S.M. *The Rise of Bombay: A Retrospect* (Bombay, 1902)
Gopalakrishnan, S., Negi, B.S. and Mishra, G.C. 'Trace element concentration in

the urban environment in India' in *Proceedings of International Symposium on Management of the Environment* (Bombay, 1980)

Gore, M.S. *Immigrants and Neighbourhoods – Two Aspects of Life in a Metropolitan Society*, TISS 21 (1970)

Government of Bombay *Report of the Panels Appointed by the Study Group for Greater Bombay* (Barve Committee Report) (Bombay, 1973)

Institute of Town Planners, India (eds.) *Selected Papers in Urban and Regional Planning* (Blackie, Bombay, 1977)

Keswani, K.S. 'Traffic and Transportation Problems of the Bombay Metropolitan Area. in Institute of Town Planners (eds.), *Selected Papers in Urban and Regional Planning* (Blackie, Bombay, 1977)

Koshy, M. *The Spatial and Temporal Variations of the Incidence of Infectious Hepatitis and Enteric Fever in Greater Bombay*, Unpublished MA Dissertation (University of Bombay, 1978)

Malhotra, S.K. *Suburban Commuting along the Western Railway*, Unpublished MA Dissertation (University of Bombay, 1975)

McGee, T.G. *The Southeast Asian City* (Bell, London, 1967)

Narain, V. and Jain, M.K. 'Metropolitan City Structure – An Indian Study' in J.V. Ferriera and S.S. Jha (eds.), *The Outlook Tower* (Popular Prakashan, Bombay, 1976)

Nissel, H. *Bombay: A Sociogeographical Study in Structure and Dynamics of an Indian Metropolis* (Institut für Geographie, Technische Universität Berlin, 1977)

Smailes, A.E. 'The Indian City: A Descriptive Model' *Geographische Zeitschrift*, vol. 57 (1969)

Smith, W. *et. al. Bombay Traffic and Transportation Study* (Bombay, 1963)

Visaria, P. 'Level and Pattern of Work Participation in Greater Bombay' in J.V. Ferriera and S.S. Jha (eds.) *The Outlook Tower* (Popular Prakashan, Bombay, 1976)

Zingde, M.D. and Desai, B.N. 'Mercury Pollution in Thana Creek in *Proceedings of International Symposium on Management of the Environment* (Bombay, 1980)

7 SINGAPORE

L.H. Wang and T.H. Tan

The Republic of Singapore is the smallest state in Southeast Asia, covering an area of about 616.3 km^2; its population is 2.3 million, giving a gross density of 3800 persons per km^2.

The British occupied Singapore in 1819, as a means of establishing a bridgehead for colonial expansion in the region, and the growth of the city in the early days was related to the development of international trade. The city's economic activities attracted thousands of immigrants each year, mainly from China and the Indian subcontinent, and a multiracial society was formed, with Chinese in the dominance from the beginning (Puthucheary, 1960). Ideally situated at the cross roads of the Straits of Malacca, the South China Sea and the Java Sea, Singapore prospered. Its port grew rapidly, as did its urban population. It became a million city in the early 1950s and the fourth largest port in the world a decade later (Table 7.1).

Table 7.1: Population Growth in Singapore

Census year	Population (thousands)	Rate of increase (%)	Population density (persons/km^2)
1901	227.6	2.3	391
1911	303.3	2.9	522
1921	418.3	3.3	719
1931	557.7	2.9	959
1947	938.7	3.3	1613
1957	1445.9	4.4	2487
1970	2074.5	2.8	3538
1980	2400.0[a]	1.5	3750[a]

a. Estimated figures.
Source: Saw (1980).

Despite the prosperity of the colonial city, which was a world centre for tin and rubber, it suffered serious urban problems, many of which were caused by a lack of proper administration and planning: urban sprawl was unchecked and physical conditions deteriorated. The congestion in the downtown area due to high-density shop-house

218

development was exacerbated by the radial design of the island's transportation network and the continual extension of the sectoral land-use pattern. The colonial administration's piecemeal response to urban-transport problems left Singapore, like many other Third World cities, with serious traffic congestion. The public-transport system, for example, was handled by not less than ten bus companies, each of which competed with the others. A statutory master plan for the city did not appear until the late 1950s, when the urban population was well over 1.5 million.

The period after World War II witnessed the most rapid deterioration of the shop-houses in the central area, as a result of overcrowding; the arrival of large numbers of immigrants dramatically increased the density in these shop-houses. With the inability of the central area to absorb the rapid population expansion, new squatters' settlements with temporary structures began to emerge at the fringe of the city. These mushroomed rapidly, especially during and immediately after World War II when control was obviously lacking. These areas later became the seedbed of social and political unrest, as the living environment and the level of general economic opportunity for their inhabitants were far from satisfactory.

The housing conditions in other parts of the city were also deteriorating at an astonishing speed, as a result of the rapid population increase (Teh, 1969). Congestion was a prominent feature, especially in the so-called Chinatown area of the city, where most of the oldest buildings were concentrated. Of the city's 938,000 inhabitants, 72 per cent lived in the central area, creating a density of 25,000 persons per hectare. New private-housing development projects were rare, as the general per capita income level was not high enough to generate demand. Although the Singapore Improvement Trust (SIT) was established as early as 1924 and in 1927 started functioning as a public agency to improve physical living conditions, developments in public housing were negligible. The inadequate public-utility facilities available compounded the problems of the poor living conditions.

As the central area continued to deteriorate, the rich and the Europeans began to move to the suburbs, leaving their premises for the chief tenants to subdivide and sublet. Basic amenities and the physical conditions of the premises were difficult to maintain in such an overcrowded situation. Even so, the demand for these low-quality premises was highly inelastic, because of the immobility of the poor. By 1968, about two-thirds of the households in the central area were living in substandard dwelling units (Tan, 1972).

The above discussion illustrates the important fact that urban growth is a social process, in which the magnitude and the direction of growth of a city are determined, on the one hand, by the politico-economic forces in operation and, on the other, by the level of adaptation and adjustment its dwellers are able to achieve under an evolutionary environment. It was due to the efforts and the military support of the British colonial government that Singapore emerged as a key seaport of the region. It was also the lack of concern on the part of the authority for the environment in general, and the level of urban congestion and physical decay in particular, that helped to cause the subsequent social unrest. Public intervention was considered to be costly, both politically and financially. Controls were exercised very selectively, with the focus mainly on maintaining the minimum viable conditions for the entrepôt trades. This liberal policy prevailed up to the beginning of the 1960s.

Post-war Development

Most of the major changes in the island have taken place since the present government was elected to power, in 1959. Massive development projects have been designed and implemented during the last two decades, leading to a rapid transformation of the urban landscape, both spatially and structurally. Partly as a result of political commitments made during the election campaign preceding self-government in 1959, and partly in view of the rapid deterioration in the urban environment, public-housing development schemes were top on the priority list of national development, followed by an industrialisation programme aimed at solving the unemployment problem. The implementation of these programmes became more urgent after Singapore had withdrawn from the Federation of Malaysia[1] to become an independent state in 1965, and again after the British decision to withdraw its military forces from east of Suez in 1968. Large-scale urban-redevelopment projects were initiated in 1974, after the full-employment target had been achieved, and a second industrial-development programme aiming at the medium-technology industries was launched recently, when Singapore began to experience a labour shortage and severe competition from other developing countries in international markets for labour-intensive manufacturing products.

Public Housing

The first major urban-development project undertaken was in public housing. With ineffective legislative powers, token financial backing and a lack of implementation ability, the SIT failed to ease the over-crowding in the city. A reorganisation of the SIT into the Housing and Development Board (HDB) with statutory powers was instituted in 1960 (Garner, 1972; Yeung, 1972).

During its earlier years, the HDB was faced with the task of providing basic housing facilities for one-quarter of a million people living in badly degenerated slums in rent-controlled premises in the inner-city areas and another one-third of a million in squatter areas. It had not only to tackle the deficit of housing, but also to provide for housing demand due to population increase (running at about three per cent per year). Based on the experience of the SIT, the HDB has been ambitious since its formation (Table 7.2). Nevertheless, although over 400,000 flats of various sizes have been built, demand for public housing continues.[2]

Table 7.2: Public-housing Development Plans under the SIT and HDB

Development plan		Dwelling units		Approximate proportion of population in public housing (%)
		Target	Completion	
SIT:	1927–59		20,907	8.8
HDB:	first, 1960–5	51,031	54,430	25
	second, 1966–70	62,120	64,114	35
	third, 1971–5	100,000	113,819	45
	fourth, 1976–80	125,000–150,000	155,000	67
	fifth 1981–5	90,000–105,000	–	70[a]

a. Estimated figure.
Sources: Yeung (1972); HDB (1980).

Public-housing development under the HDB is carried out in two distinct localities, i.e. housing estates and residential new towns. Housing estates are concentrations of high-rise residential buildings on small lots of land scattered over the island. Residential new towns are generally larger in size and more comprehensive in design and land-use allocation. Notwithstanding these differences, the overall residential

Table 7.3: Floor Area and Breakdown Cost of Different HDB Flat Types

Floor area and breakdown cost	Flat type, defined by number of rooms				
	One	Two	Three	Four	Five
Internal floor area (m²)	33	45	60–69	97–100	127
Circulation floor area (m²)	18	20	13–20	16–17	17–22
Covered floor area (m²)	51	65	73–89	113–7	144–9
Net dwelling density (units per hectare)	250	250	200	175	150
Construction cost (excluding land) per unit as at 1980 ($)[a]	11,910	15,609	20,457–23,800	29,816–30,900	41,300–44,800
Service and conservancy charge per month ($)[a]	14	17	20	25	30
Selling price ($)[a]: new town	3800	9200	13,600–18,200	27,100	40,300
suburban area	3800	11,000	15,600–20,200	30,500	44,600
urban area	–	12,700	20,200–22,500	35,700	53,900
Rental per month ($)[a]: new town	26	50	82.50–110	165	–
suburban area	33	61	82.50–110	165	–
urban area	–	75	121	–	–
Total dwelling units under HDB management	69,846	46,049	152,093	49,059	16,587
Total dwelling units sold	1212	4017	130,761	45,696	16,524
Total dwelling units rented	68,634	41,978	21,435	1654	56

a. All monetary units are in Singapore dollars: US $1= S $2.10.
Source: HDB (1980).

density is uniformly high, regardless of the type of flat (Table 7.3).
Generally speaking, a good mix of flats of different sizes is attempted,
giving rise to an overall average density of about 220 dwelling units per
hectare. Given the assumption of five persons per unit, the net residential density is 925 persons per hectare. As more and more larger flats
will be built in the future, the corresponding density figures will
eventually decrease. Interesting enough, despite the high density level,
some of the open spaces within the new towns are found to be under-
utilised (Wang, 1979), partly as a result of the suboptimal spatial
arrangement of high-rise buildings and its cooling effect on the micro-
climatic conditions, and partly because these communities are generally
new, and hence sufficient social and cultural interaction among residents
is yet to be established.

The location of public-housing estates and new towns forms part of
the comprehensive island land-use master plan, to be discussed later.
The residential new towns are linked to the overall transportation
network, and the town centres form a hierarchical system of service
centres, also serving the non-public-housing area surrounding them. The
new towns are planned to be self-contained in services (Liu and Tan,
1979).

A neighbourhood principle was initially adopted in planning the new
towns. Each neighbourhood consists of 4000 to 6000 units, together
with a neighbourhood centre which contains a market, a hawker centre,
shops, playgrounds, schools and a kindergarten within walking distance.
Where there are three or more neighbourhoods close to each other, a
town centre is provided. Facilities such as banking services, post office,
library, creche, cinema, transportation terminal and shopping centre are
located at the centre. The plan is functional; the scene, however, is
rather monotonous, with limited variety in different housing estates and
residential new towns. A recent attempt has been made to introduce the
precinct concept of planning to the latest new towns, with the hope of
creating an individual identity and character for each precinct. Under
the precinct concept, approximately 600 to 1000 dwelling units are
grouped around a landscaped square provided with social and recreational facilities. This also encourages more social interaction among residents,
which is lacking in the neighbourhoods. In order to discourage
unnecessary travel to work, about 20-5 per cent of the land is reserved
for industrial purposes. However, the lack of a positive employment
policy in the new towns and the depopulation of the central area as a
result of public-housing programmes have created more commuting
problems than expected.

The high-rise public-housing strategy adopted by the HDB, which differs from the SIT policy, does not go unchallenged. Lim (1975) and others argue that a similar residential density level could be achieved with low-rise buildings. Although the direct effects of high-rise living on the physical and mental health of the dwellers are not clear, most of the residents are conscious of the immediate improvement in their physical environment (Yeung, 1972). The cordial and friendly relationship among residents that was once common in the slums and squatter areas is lacking in some of the estates, however. An experimental project on low-rise public housing is now underway, based on the concept of a condominium living environment, which is a common feature in private apartment areas in the city.

One of the major problems facing public-housing projects in many countries is the maintenance and upkeep of the living environment by the tenants after the erection of the buildings (Freedman, 1969; Yeh and Laquian, 1979). This, in turn, has led to serious social and management problems. The problem, however, can be at least partially solved by the introduction of home ownership. The advantages of home ownership include the nurturing of pride and a sense of belonging among home owners, which in turn discourages unnecessary intra-urban migration and improves social stability; and recovery of the capital outlay within a shorter time than otherwise, thereby lightening the financial and administrative burdens on the part of the supplier. In line with the highly subsidised rental programme, the flats sold under the home-ownership programme introduced in 1964, have been offered at well below the market price (Table 7.3). The programme has been most successful in the middle-income group. While more than 98 per cent of the one-room flats are occupied by tenants, the corresponding figure for two-room flats is only nine per cent and 93 per cent of the four-room flats and almost all the five-room flats are sold. The demand for the relatively more spacious large flats has been increasing over the years as the economy improves.

Public-housing development in Singapore has more important implications for the city-state than the immediate objective of providing the needed shelter. It is a programme that has prompted a series of changes and adjustments in urban society. The clearing-up of the slums and squatter areas and the relocation of their inhabitants in various newly established housing estates and new towns have led to a reorganisation of the social structure. Spatial concentrations based on social status and ethnic or dialect groups have begun to disappear gradually, giving way steadily to a carefully organised community.

Redistribution of the population has helped to eliminate the once-considerable political, racial and social unrest, while the demolition of the slums, squatters' areas and some rural villages at the urban fringe has removed the physical source of the turbulence.

In addition to this political dimension, public-housing development has also contributed to economic development. Wang (1979) has argued that public-housing schemes have helped to transform social attitudes from a slum-type mentality to an attitude oriented towards industrial employment and a consumer society. In other words, public-housing development in Singapore has provided a foundation for the economic transformation of society.

Another reason for the selection of public housing as the first phase of a series of development programmes can be related to the input-output multiplier effects provided by the construction industry. The early 1960s saw a severe decline in the urban economy, mainly due to the Indonesian confrontation over the dispute on the formation of the Federation of Malaysia. Trade was affected, and new investments were rare. The massive construction industry thus served as a needed stimulus to the economy. Public housing is not considered as a liability, but rather as an asset to the overall development programmes of the city-state. It not only solves housing shortage, but has had a significant impact on development in other sectors. It is generally valid to conclude, in the case of Singapore, that without the public-housing programme, most other sectors might not have developed so fast.

Urban Renewal

In close conjunction with public-housing development, urban renewal has been undertaken in the central area of the city. Located to the north and south of the Singapore River, the central area covers about 800 hectares; this figure does not include 300 hectares of reclaimed land nor the further reclamation of another 300 hectares for the proposed Marine City located to the east of the city (Figure 7.1). The central area was once the zone of population concentration. Today, it accommodates only about 210,000 people, slightly less than ten per cent of the island total. It remains a centre for employment opportunities, however, providing 32 per cent of the 720,000 jobs in the city-state in 1977 (Tan, 1979).

Problems associated with the downtown area of Singapore are rather similar in kind and magnitude to those in most major cities in

Figure 7.1: Development Plan for the Central Area

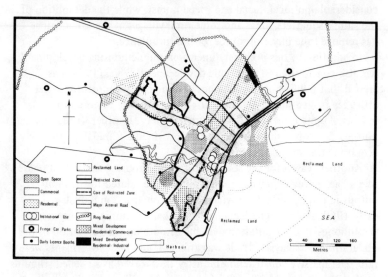

Southeast Asia. The overcrowded and deteriorated housing conditions
have greatly affected the normal expansion of the urban economy. It
was estimated that the residential density reached 2500 persons per
hectare or, in terms of dwelling space, as little as 5-8 m² per person.
Physical decay was accelerated by the practice of rent control
introduced in 1947, in addition to rapid natural population increase
and in-migration. As well as the overcrowded living conditions, there
was a worsening of the traffic-flow system, with an average attainable
speed of only 18 km/hr. The congested streets were further blocked by
an increasing number of street hawkers. The informal sector expanded
rapidly in the earlier years, as a result of the decaying state of the urban
economy, but its increase in recent years has been due to the high
marginal profit level attainable in this sector as the economy improved.
It was estimated that in 1975 there existed a total of 15,000 vendors in
the central area, causing serious traffic-congestion problems to the city.
Another serious problem in downtown Singapore was the fragmentation of land ownership. The introduction of a liberal policy of urban-
land subdivision during the colonial era had generated a situation in
which the land-owner density was over 100 persons per hectare. Their
central location ensured a high demand for these fragmented plots,
resulting in a sharp increase in land costs for development. The process
of redevelopment was slow in the 1960s, when slum clearance was in

the hands of the urban-renewal department of HDB, and remained so until 1974 when responsibility was handed over to the newly founded Urban Redevelopment Authority (URA), an agency with statutory powers dedicated to slum clearance and revitalisation in the central area. The URA is empowered to designate urban-redevelopment areas, where private owners are required to develop according to its guidelines within three years, failing which the properties may face acquisition. Other than redevelopment, URA is also responsible for the approval of car-parking plans and the management of public car parks. Like other statutory boards, the authority finances its development projects by obtaining government loans. However it is currently self-financing, without public subsidies.

In approaching the complex problems of urban redevelopment, Singapore acknowledged the importance of a comprehensive approach to land use and transportation planning, as well as coordination in implementation, especially between public housing and urban redevelopment and the provision in advance of infrastructure facilities, such as sewers, gas, water, electricity and telephones. The long-term land-use plan for Singapore adopts a strong-centre strategy, with the flexibility of incorporating an underground subway mass-rapid-transit (MRT) system, and a traffic-restraint/management approach prior to the implementation of the proposed MRT system. As planning and development within the central area have an impact on the development of the whole island, the planning and implementation is coordinated through URA's representatives in the pan-island master-plan committee and the development-control committee.

As well as observing the principles of comprehensive planning, the implementation of development projects is undertaken on a large-scale precinct basis. Each precinct comprises a balanced mix of land use, involving public and private housing, schools, open spaces, preservation, commercial and entertainment development and resettlement centres. Two pilot precincts of this kind have been completed, and have successfully achieved the main objectives of urban redevelopment, that is, slum clearance, revitalisation of the city centre, improvement of housing, traffic circulation and the environment, increase of tax base, the provision of opportunities for private participation, increase in employment opportunities and the sustaining of the central area as a specialised employment centre of the city-state.

Redevelopment, however, is not without its difficulties. One of the most difficult tasks in any redevelopment scheme is the amalgamation of land. Land banking is possible only when the implementing agency is entrusted with legislative powers to assemble rent-controlled and fragmented properties, with proper compensation. The URA maintains a land bank which keeps a stock level for at least three years of projected demand, obtained through legalised acquisition. Land acquisition is imposed when private owners are not in a position to assemble lands themselves.

Another difficulty in urban redevelopment is related to slum clearance, which is a tedious process. Relocation disrupts the traditional operation of small shops and the lifestyle of the residents. A redevelopment project can only obtain the sympathy of the residents affected if disruptions are minimised. In addition, an improvement in the living environment, together with better employment opportunities and higher incomes, should be provided for the affected shops and families after their relocation. In the case of the URA, the locations of resettlement centres are carefully selected. High-quality specialised centres are being built to accommodate similar and complementary commercial activities under one roof, thereby achieving internal economies of scale as well as increasing the convenience of shoppers. In order to help keep down excessive rentals in private centres, resettlement centres are also allowed to accommodate firms which are not affected by relocation or slum clearance. To date, over 113 hectares of slum land have been cleared for redevelopment purposes (Tan, 1979), affecting 784 resettlement cases, of which 75 per cent are residential and 25 per cent commercial (URA, 1980). Some of the acquired land has also been sold to private developers.

One major task is to sustain the size of the residential population in the central area. The older parts of the city are heavily overcrowded. Although the current overall density is about 25,000 persons/km^2, certain areas of the old city have a density as high as 100,000 persons/km^2. In some selected areas, the net space ratio of 8 m^2 per person compares with 15 m^2 per person in a HDB three-room improved flat, while the house-sharing ratio can reach five households per census house. To clear one hectare of land, as many as 300 households need to be resettled. Working on a proposed density of 250 dwelling units per hectare in new public-housing projects, it is clear that redevelopment can often mean a loss of housing units. To achieve a target of 10,000 units over a five-year period, eight hectares of land must be cleared annually. The existing housing stock must be more than doubled to sustain the same number of people by the year 1990. In areas not urgently required for redevelopment, there is potential for rehabilitation to prolong the life of these buildings and to upgrade their standards. To date, 16,000 public-housing units have been completed in the central area.

The successful public-housing programmes have paved the way for the smooth implementation of urban redevelopment in the central area, not only relieving the excessive overcrowding in the shop-houses but also providing resettlement facilities to make slum clearance possible. A depopulation process occurred, as more and more urban dwellers moved out to the suburban public-housing estates and residential new towns. This, in turn, has affected the active night life which the central area once enjoyed. Ironically, one of the objectives of URA at present is to induce in-migration into the depopulated central area, a situation which the city had tried desperately to avoid only two decades ago (Tan, 1979).

In order to attract an inflow of residents into the central area, the environment must be further up-graded; existing conditions are generally not conducive to residential development. On smaller sites, vertical segregation of commercial and residential use has been attempted. For larger sites, however, horizontal segregation of uses provides better opportunities for creating a traffic-free pedestrianised environment, with better provision of open spaces. The existing overall central-area open-space standard is about 0.36 hectare per 1000 residents. The central-area open-space plan conceptualises a hierarchical system of connected open spaces and walkways. The environment around existing buildings could also be further upgraded by pedestrianisation.

Urban-redevelopment programmes have transformed the landscape of the central area considerably, with several positive effects on the urban economy. First, better utilisation of the valuable and strategically located land is made possible, resulting in an increase in the volume of floor space and the enhancement of public utilities and safety. The total commercial floor space has increased fourfold during the last decade, to 2.3 million m^2 in 1980, of which about two-thirds are for office use and one-third for shopping space. The central area is becoming a more attractive place as a result of redevelopment. Land value, however, has increased drastically, partly because of redevelopment and partly because of land speculation. Secondly, redevelopment has reduced the social costs of slums. Together with an increase in property tax due to the enhancement of land value in the central area, the reduction in the social costs of slums has strengthened the fiscal position of the public sector. Thirdly, urban-renewal projects have helped to improve the investment and employment opportunities. An efficient downtown is attractive to investors, and the growth in the construction industry provides jobs, especially at times when the threat of unemployment is high. For example, the announcement of the British military withdrawal led to the speeding up of the HDB and URS projects. Although the capital-output ratio of 3:4 in the Singapore construction industry is much higher than an average ratio of 1:4 for all other forms of investment (Oshima, 1967), the provision of a well-organised infrastructure is essential to any future development.

Notwithstanding the fact that urban redevelopment is an appropriate strategy to adopt, the transformation of land uses has not been free from difficulties. In some cases, for example, the lack of careful and accurate planning has caused an oversupply of amenities in certain localities. The rapid expansion of the construction industry also led to an overdemand for building materials and skilled building personnel, causing a tremendous increase in construction cost and an inflated property market. The situation was further worsened by the international energy crisis and the resultant world-wide inflation of the early 1970s. The increase in floor space in the central area has also, inevitably, generated further traffic congestion there, even after most of the vendors were properly relocated at newly designed hawker centres. The number of street hawkers remaining in the central area today, estimated at 4200 persons, is half of the 1975 figure. Depopulation in the central area, on the other hand, remains acute, as the response of the private-housing supply sector has been sluggish.

Furthermore, urban redevelopment has extensively reorganised the spatial distribution of shops, and hence has considerably affected the shopping behaviour of consumers. The traditional low-rise shop-houses are being replaced by modern high-rise buildings and large shopping complexes. The high rentals for the new premises inevitably forced the small retailers to give way to large departmental stores and emporiums. With the improvement in the overall economy, a Westernised consumer society is gradually emerging. Other things being equal, the correlation between urban redevelopment and inflation may not just be a coincidence.

Environmental Control

The HDB and URA programmes have provided the city with a base for environmental control, as most of the old and dilapidated houses have been torn down to give way to high-rise buildings. In order to help the residents to become acquainted with high-rise living, related educational programmes have been constantly launched through the mass media and elsewhere, together with legislative regulations to ensure that the city is kept clean. Strict regulations and monitoring are employed to cope with noise pollution from residential areas and air pollution from industries and automobiles, as well as cultural pollution from literal and pictorial publications. The resettlement of street hawkers into permanent structures since 1972 has also contributed to the improvement of public health. In addition, various health-education campaigns have been launched. Urban landscaping and pedestrianisation programmes are incorporated under a garden-city concept, to create a pleasant living environment and the image of one of the cleanest cities on Earth. Trees, flowering plants and shrubs by the millions have been grown, and a plan to construct a total of 38 km of walkways and malls for pedestrians is underway.

The number of street hawkers has decreased from 15,000 in 1975 to 6200 in 1979. To date, there are about 27,000 hawkers in Singapore of which only 23 per cent are still on the streets. Of these remaining hawkers, 60 per cent are within the central area. A programme is being carried out to clear all street hawkers by 1984 (Tan, 1979). Getting the hawkers off the streets and into permanent structures has not only improved sanitary standards, but has enabled the authorities to have a better estimate of their turnover for tax purposes. Street hawkers have been regarded as a source of urban problems in many Asian cities, although the service that they provide is of immense significance in urban life. Singapore's success in regrouping the hawkers is at least partly attributable to the HDB public-housing development. The concentration of a large population in the residential new towns provides instant markets with lucrative marginal profit levels. Many of the hawkers in the HDB new towns and housing estates no longer belong to the lower-income group. Specifically, the regrouping process has transformed this informal sector into a formal sector: the hawkers now have to function like any other retailers. The elimination of the informal sector seems to be part of the national policy in moulding a Westernised urban society.

Population Control

The rapid increase in urban population after World War II has been partly due to in-migration and partly due to natural domestic increase. In order to cope with the high unemployment rate and the associated social expenditures, such as education, health and housing, a policy to control population growth was implemented in the early 1960s. As a result, the annual population growth rate dropped from 4.4 per cent in 1957 to 2.8 per cent in 1970 and 1.5 per cent in 1980. Based on this trend, Saw (1980) estimates that zero population growth will be attained in the year 2040.

Various programmes have been introduced to reduce the birth rate. These include family-planning education, induced abortion, liberalised sterilisation and control of international marriage. A series of incentive and disincentive measures with varying degrees of severity and effectiveness has become an integral part of the population-control programme. An accouchement fee is charged to large families. Small families are encouraged by means of higher income-tax reduction, short waiting time for public-housing allocation, and priority for schooling allocation. As the population becomes more urbanised and the society more industrialised, these programmes will eventually come to be seen as socially acceptable rather than as regulatory measures to maintain a small family size.

Zero population growth has significant implications for the future development of the city-state, since, in the long term, there will be proportionally fewer school-aged children and more senior citizens. It is estimated, for example, that fifty years from now only 20.2 per cent of the population will be under the age of 14, while 22.2 per cent will be aged 60 and above. The respective figures for 1980 are 28.3 per cent and 7.2 per cent (Saw, 1980). Gradual social adjustments are needed. The aging of the labour force, together with a zero population growth, will cause a further shortage of labour in many sectors of the economy. Restructuring of the urban economy, with greater emphasis on automation and computerisation, seems to be inevitable.

Urban Transport

A direct reflection of the land-use efficiency of a city is provided by its traffic-flow system. Careful land-use planning avoids excessive traffic generation and travel demand. Ironically, however, traffic congestion is today a common phenomenon in almost all the large cities in the world, despite the widespread application of land-use planning. Traffic congestion arises as a result of several factors, including a badly designed road network, growth in car ownership, the misallocation of residential and employment activities and an inefficient public-transport system. Singapore is no exception in terms of traffic congestion, especially in the downtown area during peak hours.

The existing road system comprises a radial network of highways focusing on the central area. Almost all of the traffic flow from one end of the island to the other has no alternative but to pass through the central area. In addition to the vast volume of trips to the central area due to its concentration of economic and employment opportunities, this through traffic has further aggravated the flow problems. Ong (1977) has estimated that about one-third of the downtown land area is taken up by roads, and more than 50 hectares of building space is being reserved for car parking.

The provision of wider roads and more parking space in the central area is made possible by the urban-redevelopment and decentralisation programmes. Paradoxically, these programmes seem to have intensified the existing traffic-congestion situation. The removal of the dense population from the central area has given rise to new office buildings and, as a consequence, more employment opportunities there. The people rehoused in the residential new towns now have to travel a longer distance daily into the central area for work, shopping and other recreational and social purposes. The lack of an employment policy during the early stage of public-housing development, which was mainly designed to clear the huge backlog of housing demand, has resulted in serious traffic congestion. On the other hand, the enlarged road capacity of the downtown area improves its relative accessibility and induces more incoming trips. The problem is further compounded by a continuous increase in car ownership. Hence, the urban-transport problem of Singapore is, to a great extent, caused by a lack of co-ordination in land-use and transportation planning during the early stages of development. Theoretically at least, planning of traffic flows is easier in Singapore than in many other cities, since the future land-use pattern of the city is well under control, and there is little danger of unpredictable urban sprawl.

Solutions to the traffic problems are many, and attempts are constantly being made to improve the flow system, such as a progressive traffic-restraint policy to reduce car ownership and unnecessary movement, an areal licensing scheme (ALS) to discourage unnecessary trips into downtown during peak hours, the building of a pan-island expressway network and the proposal for a possible MRT system (Smith *et al.*, 1974), plus the reorganisation of the bus system to provide a better service to both the captive and casual passengers (Figure 7.2). The first stage of the expressway network has just been completed, and the

Figure 7.2: Future Transportation Network

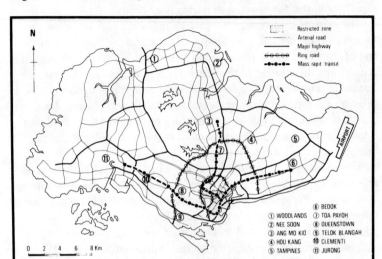

MRT project is under serious consideration. Although there is room for further improvement in the bus service, the performance of the major public-transport undertaking, Singapore Bus Services (SBS), has been encouraging since its constitution in 1973, after the merger of three bus companies, which, in turn, were amalgamated from eleven smaller companies in 1971. A park-and-ride scheme served by 15 fringe car parks located outside the city centre operated without success. Regulations introduced under the traffic-restraint policy, among others, include a periodic increase in import duty on cars, road tax, new vehicle-registration fees, taxes on petrol and parking charges (Watson and Holland, 1976, 1978a; Ton, 1977). This policy of restraint through a higher cost of car ownership, however, is offset to a great extent by the rapid increase in wages and in disposable income.

The primary objective of the ALS·was to alleviate congestion through a reduction of the total traffic volume in the central area by 25 to 30 per cent during peak hours (Lim, 1975), to be accomplished by a 50 per cent reduction in the total number of motor vehicles in the city-state. The ALS, implemented in 1975, is the first and only one of its kind in the world, and hence its performance is of significance to future traffic control in other cities.

The ALS requires all vehicles, except for certain exempted categories, to possess and display a special licence while entering a designated restricted zone, which coincides roughly with the central area, during the morning peak hours. The exempted categories include public service and military vehicles, goods vehicles, motorcycles and buses with a seating capacity of twelve or more; taxis were included at first. Two ring roads (Figures 7.1 and 7.2) are provided outside the restricted zone to cater for bypass traffic. The restricted hours were first defined from 7.30 a.m. to 9.30 a.m. inclusive and later extended to 10.15 a.m. The ALS has altered considerably the traffic flow and the modal-split choice patterns during the morning peak hours, with a sharp increase in captive ridership (Table 7.4). The effect of restriction was strongly felt immediately after the scheme was introduced, though a recovering trend has appeared in recent years (Table 7.5). Congestion during the evening peak hours, however, remains unchanged, as the bypass traffic through the central area is not checked. A bypass express-way, the East Coast Parkway, is now under construction, with a view to easing the flow, especially in the evening. Although the ALS has provided a short-term solution to the traffic problem, its actual effects on the business activities and the urban economy, in general, and the trip behaviour of the commuters, in particular, are not clearly known. Partly because of the possible negative effects on the economy and partly because it is inconsistent with the policy of revitalising the city's night life, the ALS is not introduced during the evening peak hours.

Table 7.4: Changes in Modal Split for Work Trips in the Restricted Zone

Mode	inbound home-to-work trips (%)		outbound work-to-home trips (%)	
	Before ALS	After ALS	Before ALS	After ALS
Bus	33	46	36	48
Car	56	46	53	43
car driver	32	20	35	23
car pool	8	19	5	12
car passenger	16	7	13	8
Motorcycle	7	6	7	6
Others	4	2	4	3

Source: Yee (1980).

In addition to licensing, a measure on staggered working hours and car pooling was also implemented under the ALS. To encourage car pooling, saloon cars, station wagons and mini buses carrying four or more passengers are allowed to enter the restricted zone freely.

Table 7.5: Inbound Traffic Flow to the Restricted Zone

Month	Private cars			Other vehicles			Total vehicles		
	07.00 – 07.30 a.m.	07.30 – 10.15 a.m.	10.15 – 10.45 a.m.	07.00 – 07.30 a.m.	07.30 – 10.15 a.m.	10.15 – 10.45 a.m.	07.00 – 07.30 a.m.	07.30 – 10.15 a.m.	10.15 – 10.45 a.m.
March 1975	5,348	42,790	n.a.	4,416	31,224	n.a.	9,800	74,014	n.a.
August 1975[a]	7,078 (+32.3)	11,130 (−74.0)	7,375	5,009 (+13.4)	31,767 (+1.7)	7,784	12,087 (+23.3)	42,897 (−42.0)	15,159
May 1977[a]	6,488 (20.5)	10,350 (−75.8)	6,636 (−10.0)	5,001 (+10.0)	33,968 (+8.9)	7,169 (−7.9)	11,489 (+17.2)	44,318 (−40.1)	13,805 (−8.9)
May 1980[a]	7,147 (+32.7)	13,844 (−67.6)	6,284 (−14.8)	5,663 (+28.2)	40,908 (+31.0)	8,817 (+13.3)	12,810 (+30.7)	54,752 (−26.0)	15,101 (−0.4)

a. The figures in parentheses represent percentage changes relative to March 1975, except for the period after 10.15 a.m., in which the figures are relative to August 1975.
Source: Yee (1980).

Paradoxically, car pooling has led to a sharp increase in the number of motor vehicles entering the restricted zone, counterbalancing the effect of the ALS. Not all the car passengers are car owners; in fact, many of them were captive public-transport passengers before car pooling. Hence, car pooling in Singapore has achieved the optimal utilisation of cars, at the expense of road-space utilisation. On the other hand, it is also valid to argue that by turning some captive riders away from public transport, car pooling has helped in relieving the burden on the bus system. The extent to which car pooling has prompted a resurgence of illegal private taxis is not known.

It is important to note here that regulations and controls are only short-term measures for dealing with the urban-transport problem. As the urban economy improves, the demand for a more efficient and comfortable transport system will inevitably increase. The long-term solution lies in the provision of an efficient, equitable and inexpensive public-transport system, supported by a reorganisation of the land-use pattern within the framework of a viable urban economy.

Restructuring the Urban Economy

The diversification of the urban economy began almost at the same time as the public-housing programme. The unemployment rate in 1960 was estimated at 13.5 per cent of the total workforce (Pang and Seow, 1979). A regional shift of trade patterns had been occurring for some time, as countries in the region began to bypass Singapore in their international trade. The political confrontation with Indonesia over the formation of Malaysia worsened the situation.

Industrialisation was chosen as the key instrument for the diversification programme. As expected, labour-intensive, import-substitution industrialisation was adopted in the initial stage, with a low-wage policy to absorb unemployment. In 1965, a large industrial estate was built, with the necessary infrastructure, on reclaimed swampy land in Jurong at the southwest corner of Singapore Island, four years after the establishment of the Economic Development Board (EDB), a statutory agency involved in the promotion of industrial investment. As the import-substitution industries were at full force, a policy aimed at the creation of a labour-intensive but export-oriented manufacturing sector was introduced, to attract foreign investment. A new statutory body, the Jurong Town Corporation (JTC), was formed in 1968 to take charge of the Jurong Industrial Estate and the development and maintenance of other industrial estates on the island. Full employment was achieved in 1972, followed by a relaxation of immigration controls to permit the employment of guest workers as a means of sustaining industrial expansion, especially in the manufacturing and construction sectors.

Rapid industrial expansion was made possible by a combination of several factors. As an entrepôt port, Singapore already possessed some of the requisite economic infrastructure, such as port, communications and transport facilities, public utilities and banking and business expertise, and thus had a locational advantage over other cities in the region. A large pool of labour, the provision of tax holidays and concessions, the free repatriation of profits and other liberal policies towards foreign investments were all conducive to the rapid growth of the manufacturing sector. Furthermore industrialisation in Singapore began at a time when many multinational corporations were at their third production cycle (Vernon, 1971) and were keen to establish labour-intensive branch plants in the developing countries, in order to reduce production costs.

In addition, planning agencies like the EDB and JTC have been quick to respond to changes in economic climate. The city-state embarked on a new phase of industrial development in 1970, when the unemployment problem had been brought under control, transferring emphasis to higher technology and skills. Recently, a new high-wage policy was adopted, with the aim of developing high-technology industries, in order to avoid an acute labour shortage and direct competition for international markets with other industrial economies in Asia, such as South Korea, Taiwan and Hong Kong, where labour supply is still inexpensive and abundant.

The importance of the manufacturing sector in the urban economy of Singapore lies in its increasing contribution to gross domestic product and employment share. As well as industrialisation, the restructuring of the urban economy includes efforts to promote the city as the financial, professional services, shopping, tourist and convention centre of the region. These policies provide major inputs to the redevelopment programmes in the central area of the city. Changes in the urban economy over the last two decades are summarised in Table 7.6.

An interesting issue related to the massive structural reorganisation of the urban economy is its impact on income distribution in terms of equity and equality. Although the per capita gross domestic product has substantially increased, a calculation of the Gini concentration ratio of income distribution (Lee *et al.*, 1978) reveals that the inequality level has in fact increased from 1966 to 1976. The

Table 7.6: Changes in Some Economic Parameters, 1960–79

	1960	1970	1979
Output as percent of gross domestic product (GDP):			
manufacturing	11.7	19.3	27.2
construction	3.6	7.1	6.1
wholesale and retail trade, restaurants and hotels	31.9	24.5	36.1
transport, storage and communication	35.3	29.6	13.2
finance, insurance, real estate and business service	11.1	13.9	13.7
other sectors	6.5	5.5	3.7
GDP at current market prices ($ million)	2018.4	5804.9	19,589.7
Percent of annual change of GDP at 1968 factor cost	8.7	9.4	9.3
Per capita capital formation at 1968 prices ($)	134	825	1518
Reexport as percent of total trade	43	24	18
Index of industrial production (1974 = 100)	–	58	155
Land area (km²)	581.5	586.4	616.3
Built-up area (%)	31	33	43.2

Source: Department of Statistics (1980).

distribution pattern is such that tax payers have been pushed up the income ladder since the restructuring of the urban economy, leading to a sharp increase in the middle- and upper-income groups in terms of both the absolute number and percentage of income received.

Planning Philosophy of the State

Planning is subject to the ideological constraints of the state. Singapore has had an open economy since the establishment of the colonial port. Hence, foreign investment and international trade have been two important sources of development input. An open economy of this kind is clearly opposed to any form of protectionism that could hinder its access to the world market. It is argued that, in terms of domestic affairs, however, a certain degree of control is required. For a developing country with limited resources, the unrestrained operations of the free-enterprise system can result in uneven development, which would upset social priorities and harm the wider interests of the community. Therefore, in order to ensure a smooth implementation of development policies, active state participation supported by legislative powers is deemed necessary. Statutory boards are thus established to take charge of various development issues. Private companies are formed in some cases by the government as its agencies to compete with and to complement the private sector. These agencies cover a wide range of business activities, from banking, international trading, air and ocean transport to publishing. Each agency is expected to be financially independent after a certain period of operation. Governmental departments are expected to be cost effective as well. Welfare statism is generally discouraged, as 'nothing is for free' in the city. State subsidies are given very selectively, normally after thorough scrutiny, to development sectors that are considered of high priority in the overall national development framework, such as public housing and education. Efficiency and effectiveness thus become the prerequisite of success for the various bureaucrats in charge of these agencies. Administration is business-like, highly meritocratic and mechanically efficient.

An efficient system is required to be able to respond quickly to changing conditions. It is felt that, in order to be realistic, policies must be as flexible as possible, in the sense that new rules and regulations should be introduced whenever they are needed, normally with immediate effect. In short, reactions to change are oriented towards problem-solving. The danger of adopting a myopic solution does exist. Development planning in Singapore, although highly dynamic and progressive in nature, is occasionally a cyclical process of trial and error. Bureaucrats are expected to provide quick solutions to problems of a complicated nature. Diagnoses, though not circumambulatory, are inevitably circumstantial in many cases. However, it is important to note that the public system is built with a fast-feedback mechanism. Mistakes and side effects are identified and ratified rather quickly throughout the course of project implementation. Public objections to the frequent changes of regulations in, and approaches to, policy implementation are kept to a minimum through careful mass-education programmes.

Hence, planning in Singapore is basically a top-down process. Development goals are set at the top of the political hierarchy, and plans are designed to meet predefined objectives. Development is thus policy-oriented; planning serves as an operation device. The overall approach can be best examplified in the following statement by the First Deputy Prime Minister in 1975:

> Actually when we first won the elections in 1959 we had no plans at all. We produced a formal document called the *First Four Year Plan* in 1960 only because the World Bank wanted a plan. We cooked it up during a long weekend. I have very little confidence in economic planning. Planning as we know it has limited value. Economic policy is more important.

The theoretical foundation of Singapore's development strategies is the belief that a strong, wise and far-sighted government will lead. The importance of public participation in decision-making is recognised, but not unduly emphasised. The debate as to whether planning should be a top-down or bottom-up process is confined to the classroom. It is under this condition that the various statutory bodies are able to carry out their respective development strategies effectively and efficiently. The key issue in many developing economies is not so much the theoretical consistency of a plan, but rather the operational ability of the agencies that carry out such a plan. In the city-state, a workable plan is considered a good plan.

Much current thinking on urban planning regards public participation in the development process as desirable if not essential. In the context of Singapore's top-down approach to planning, public participation is viewed basically as a process of mass education, the aim of which is to familiarise the public with the programmes in hand,

and to motivate public support for their implementation. Mass education is necessary in order to mould the people into a self-disciplined force, without which the smooth implementation of development plans and policies would inevitably meet with endless obstacles. The introduction of a policy or programme follows a series of well-designed campaigns intended to inform the public of the seriousness and importance of a particular issue. The discussion of different ideas is encouraged if such debates would assist the policy-makers to strengthen their decisions at a higher level of certainty and accuracy. This strategy helps to dissipate much of the expected friction in the course of development. In several instances, this mass-education process has even miraculously led the citizens to feel that the introduction of a designed policy is a result of their positive participation.

The policy makers' pragmatic approach over the past two decades has helped to create an efficient administrative city-state. The planning laws so far introduced are progressive in terms of their problem-solving capacities. Conceivably, strong government has made the implementation of certain unpopular but practical policies possible.

Development Plans

The future growth of the city is outlined in its development plans. Basically, there are two separate but interrelated development plans in Singapore. The first is the statutory master plan (SMP), which was first designed under the colonial government: the second is the Singapore concept plan (SCP) proposed in the late 1960s.

The SMP, as proposed, was a comprehensive physical plan for the whole island, aiming at the regulation of public development through zoning and at the reservation of land for public purposes. The plan was initially designed to cover a 20 year period from 1953 to 1972. The basic planning strategies spelled out in the SMP are rather conservative by today's standards. Major proposals included a green belt to arrest the further expansion of the central area, together with inducements to reduce its population in order to overcome congestion in the downtown area. Three self-contained new towns were to be built under a decentralisation policy of urbanisation to absorb future urban population growth. Generally speaking, the drawback of the SMP was in its basic strategies for controlling growth and limiting development, in the face of the traditional entrepôt trades and a rapid expansion in population.

In order to cope with the serious deterioration of the urban environment and its economy, public development since the 1960s has been freed from the inflexibility of the legal restrictions of the SMP through the establishment of the various statutory agencies, such as the HDB and the EDB. The initial planning assumptions and urban-restraint strategies of the SMP were replaced by a solution-oriented policy to cope with the increasing demand in housing and employment. The deviation from the conservative development policy of the SMP began to lead the city-state into a process of massive spatial reorganisation.

In addition, a new planning concept was sought. With the assistance of the United Nations Development Programme, the Singapore concept plan was introduced in 1967. This is a long-range land-use plan, with a transport plan as an integral component. A close look at some of the assumptions of the SCP and its basic features is necessary in order to appreciate the development trend of the city and to assess its performance.

Like the SMP, the SCP was constrained in its conceptualisation by the geographical layout of the island's physical and economic features. It also incorporated some of the fundamental planning concepts of the SMP, such as the building of satellite towns and the favouring of a decentralisation programme. Nevertheless, the SCP was based on a principle of flexibility in optimising objective functions rather than on simple restriction of growth. It is argued that such an approach would provide the city with the necessary capacity to cope with rapid growth and at the same time allow room for manoeuvre and adjustments to cope with any unexpected changes in the urban economy. Thus, by definition, the SCP is an expression of principles and policies of land-space utilisation, rather than a collection of detailed proposals. As such, the SCP is treated as if it is a dynamic organic system, which is constantly vitalised through an in-built feedback mechanism. In other words, the SCP is constantly under review, in order to maintain its flexibility in staging, growth and land utilisation.

The major argument of the SCP can be summarised under ten basic headings, as illustrated in Figure 7.3. For example, future urban expansions are expected to sprawl outwards from the city centre, linking the major economic areas of the island (Plan 1). As these areas are potential employment sources, the major traffic corridors that link them would provide the ideal 'spines' on which high-density public-housing estates and new towns could be located. The development pattern so derived comprises two interrelated linear systems, i.e., the southern belt linking Jurong with Changi through the city centre, and the supporting ring around the central water-catchment area (Plans 2

Figure 7.3: Singapore Concept Plan (SCP)

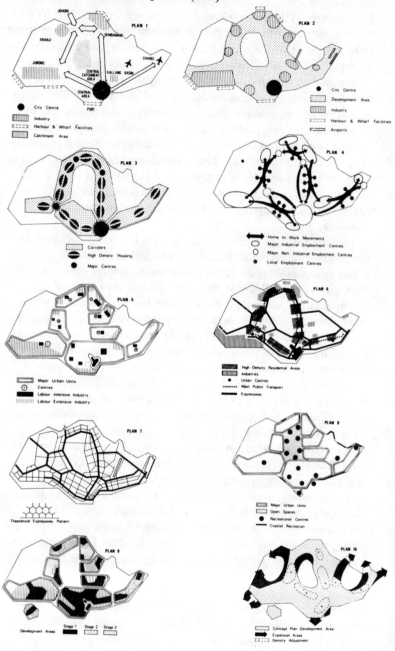

and 3). Low- and medium-density private-housing development is placed beside the corridors, to supplement the major public-housing nuclei. This concept of locating residential areas away from and between major potential employment centres implies a heavy demand on the traffic system in the future for various travel purposes along the corridors. Further, it implicitly suggests that the residential new towns so developed should no longer be independently self-contained. This is in contradiction to the concept initially introduced in the SMP. A wide choice of small local employment centres, however, is still available near the residential areas (Plan 4). According to the SCP, seven large new-town districts, each with a population varying from 200,000 to 350,000, will be established outside the city area. Most of the central-type functions will remain in the central area (Plan 5). However, because of their special locations, Woodlands and Jurong will also accommodate some of these functions, serving as regional centres.

In order to meet the high interdistrict transport demand resulting from the above-mentioned land-use arrangement, a transportation system comprising a pan-island expressway network and an MRT system will be needed to link all the major districts with the city centre (Plan 6). The expressway-network system is made up of a series of modified hexagons with three-way junctions. The arterial system, however, is based on a single grid pattern. The international airport will be further shifted away to Changi in the east on reclaimed land (Plan 7).

Open spaces are reserved at standards related to residential population for parks and recreation (Plan 8). The central water-catchment area is an ideal natural open space, as are some of the less inhabited outer islands. In order to reduce air pollution, open spaces are kept as buffers between major industrial and housing centres. While major industrial estates are located away from prime open spaces, large housing estates are separated by open spaces or institutional areas, with further landscaped buffers to screen them from expressways.

Development as outlined in the SCP will be implemented at different stages (Plan 9). One of the long-term development goals of the plan is to provide a viable habitat for a designated population of four million people. Future expansion beyond the SCP horizon year of 1992 will then be made possible through internal adjustments and on further reclaimed land. Plan 10 in Figure 7.3 highlights the potential areas of adjustment and the possible directions of future expansion, based on the land-use structure outlined in the SCP. Should the future urban expansion follow the directions indicated, a multiring-cum-linear pattern of development will eventually emerge from the basic ring-cum-linear pattern advocated in the SCP (Figure 7.4).

On the basis of the concepts outlined above, the SCP is adopting a strong-centre strategy, with an emphasis on the revitalisation of the central area. This strategy suggests a direction of development opposite to that of the SMP. This change in development strategy appears to be a natural consequence of the state's growth-oriented philosophy under a new set of politico-economic conditions.

Figure 7.4: Future Land-use Structure

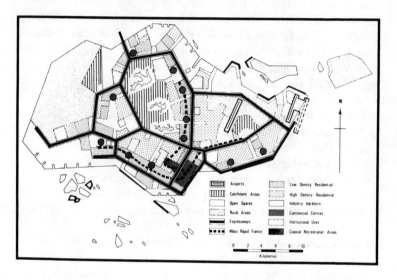

It is important to note that, although the present development strategies of the city are based on the SCP, the original SMP has not been totally abandoned. Instead, the SMP has been reviewed once every five years, to incorporate the various developments that have already taken place, or are expected, as a result of implementing the SCP. Although, from the operational point of view, the SMP is passive and inflexible in the face of the rapidly changing urban environment, it is retained because of its implications for the regulation and control of urban land values. In addition, it provides a statutory basis for development control, as well as a source of revenue from development charges.

While the SCP serves as a general guide, the SMP has been legislated, with statutory powers of enforcement. Hence, the two plans today complement one another in terms of development functions. For example, the structural plans prepared by the various statutory boards, such as the URA, HDB and the JTC, are designed according to the principles outlined in the SCP, but an approval from the planning department according to the regulations stated in the SMP is required. This process ensures the autonomous status of the various agencies in plan implementation, with central coordination of the overall development pattern.

Conclusions

Considering the role of the SCP in the past ten years, the outlook for the future growth of the city could have the following features. First, there will be a readjustment of the density and intensity of public housing and industrial development. As most of the residential new towns will soon be completed, such a readjustment would be carried out through renewal. For example, old housing estates could be upgraded, and old industrial estates decongested, with the elimination or relocation of those factories which give rise to environmental problems. Secondly, a structural readjustment of the SCP seems necessary. The location of new airports and seaports, the construction of a new causeway to link with the Malay Peninsula in the north and the sea link with the adjacent Indonesian Islands to the south will all call for rethinking of the land-space utilisation concept in the future. Thirdly, in addition to a rearrangement of the settlement distribution pattern so as to lay emphasis on public-housing development in the west, as a counterbalance to the over concentration in the east, a reorganisation of the employment capacity of existing residential new towns in the direction of economic diversification will be needed. This will permit acceleration of the decentralisation programme. Fourthly, the land consumption rate will be further increased as urbanisation gathers momentum. As a consequence, any future enlargement of space for commercial and residential uses must look largely to reclaimed land and the conversion of existing agricultural land. More intensive use of the sea floor around the island for recreational and even residential and employment purposes in the not-too-distant future does not seem to belong only to the realm of speculation; proposals for a project of this kind, in fact, already exist.

Lastly, a more important issue relates to how the higher expectations of urban dwellers can be satisfied as society becomes more affluent. In the past, development has concentrated on improving and extending physical structures and amenities, such as housing and transportation. As the basic needs are gradually being fulfilled, the urge will be shifted to social issues, such as equality and the freedom of choice. To date, the emphasis has been on social equity. It is argued that freedom to choose also carries a social responsibility. However, it remains to be seen how much social responsibility the future generations will be willing to shoulder, especially when they have not had to undergo the hardship experienced by present generations. Urban problems in the future will centre on how to maximise the social significance of the city, in the face of an expanding economic base. Where, in the past, solutions of Singapore's urban problems have related to unity in diversity, in the future they will rely more on the ability of the city to find diversity in unity.

Notes

1. The Federation of Malaysia initially was made up of the following territories The Federation of Malaya, Sarawak, Sabah and Singapore.
2. For example, there were 67,000 applicants on the HDB's waiting list at the end of 1979, with 86 per cent of them wishing to purchase flats; see HDB (1980), p. 24.

References

Department of Statistics *Yearbook of Statistics Singapore 1979/80* (National Printers, Singapore, 1980)

Freedman, L. *Public Housing: The Politics of Poverty* (Holt, Rinehart and Winston, New York, 1969)

Gamer, R.R. *The Politics of Urban Development in Singapore* (Cornell University Press, Ithaca, 1972)

HDB (Housing Development Board) *Annual Report 1979/80* (Housing Development Board, Singapore, 1980)

Lee, S.A. 'The Economic System' in R. Hassan (ed.), *Singapore: Society in Transition* (Oxford University Press, Singapore, 1976), pp. 3–114

Lee, S.Y., Huang, H.C. and Yeo, G.K. 'Income Distribution of Singapore in 1966, 1973 and 1976' Paper Presented at the Second Southeast Asian Statistics Seminar (Singapore, 27–8 March 1978)

Lim, L.G. 'Singapore Case Study' in *Better Towns with Less Traffic* (OECD Conference, Paris, 1975), pp. 97–126

Lim, W.S.W. *Equity and Urban Environment in the Third World* (DP Consultant Service, Singapore, 1975)

Liu, T-K and Tan, S.A. 'Planning and Design' in Yeh, S.H.K. and Laquian, A.A. (eds.), *Housing Asia's Millions: Problems, Policies and Prospects for Low-cost Housing in Southeast Asia* (International Development Research Centre, 1979), pp. 127–64

McGee, T.G. *The Southeast Asian City* (Bell, London, 1967)

Ministry of Culture *Singapore Facts and Pictures 1979* (Information Division,

Ministry of Culture, Singapore, 1979)

Ong, T.C. 'A Nation for Car or People' *Journal of the Singapore Institute of Planners*, vol. 6 (1977), pp. 10–16.

Olszewski, K. 'The Principle of Flexibility as Applied to Structure of the Singapore Concept Plan' *Journal of the Singapore Institute of Planners*, vol. 2 (1972), pp. 5–17

Oshimas, H.T. 'Growth and Unemployment in Singapore' *Malayan Economic Review*, vol. 12, no. 2 (1967), pp. 32–58

Pang, E.F. and Seow, G. ' A Look in Singapore's Economy in the Eighties' *The Straits Times* (Singapore, 9 August 1979), pp. 2–4

Puthucheary, J.J. *Ownership and Control in the Malayan Economy* (Eastern University Press, Singapore, 1960)

Saw, S-H. *Population Control for Zero Growth in Singapore* (Oxford University Press, Singapore, 1980)

Singapore Improvement Trust *Master Plan: Report of Survey* (Government Printing Office, Singapore, 1955)

Smith, W. *et al. Singapore Mass Transit Study: Report in Brief* (National Printer, Singapore, 1974)

Tan, T.H. 'Socio-economic Characteristics of the Central Area Residents' *Planners* vol. 1, no. 4 (1972), pp. 7–14

Tan, T.M. 'Selected Aspects of Planning and Implementation in Singapore' Paper Presented at the Seminar on Planning for Large Southeast Asian Cities (Bangkok, 25 August 1979)

Teh, C.W. 'Public Housing' in Ooi, J.-B. and Chiang, H.D. (eds.), *Modern Singapore* (Singapore University Press, Singapore, 1969), pp. 171–80

Toh, R. (1977), 'Road Congestion Pricing: The Singapore Experience' *The Malayan Economic Review*, vol. 22 (1977), pp. 52–61

URA (Urban Redevelopment Authority) *Annual Report 1978/79* (Urban Redevelopment Authority, Singapore, 1979)

Vernon, R. *Sovereignty at Bay* (Longman, London, 1971)

Wang, L.H. 'Utilization of Land Space in Singapore' in Pereira, D.P. (ed.), *Focus on Environment: Implications for Singapore* (Select Books, Singapore, 1979), pp. 12–27

Watson, P.L. and Holland, E.P. 'Congestion Pricing: The Example of Singapore' *Ekistics*, vol. 42 (1976), pp. 14–18

—— 'Traffic Restraint in Singapore' *Traffic Engineering and Control*, vol. 19 (1978a), pp. 14–22

—— 'Relieving Traffic Congestion: The Singapore Areal License Scheme' Staff Working Paper 281 (World Bank, Washington DC, 1978b)

Yee, Joseph 'The Area Licensing Scheme in Singapore' Paper Presented at the Transpo-Asia 80 Asian Seminar (Singapore, 1980)

Yeh, S.H.K. and Laquian, A.A. (eds.) *Asia's Millions: Problems, Policies, and Prospects for Low-cost Housing in Southeast Asia* (International Development Research Centre, Ottawa, 1979)

Yeung, Y-M. *National Development Policy and Urban Transformation in Singapore* Research Paper 149 (Department of Geography, University of Chicago, 1972)

8 SHANGHAI

K.I. Fung and M. Freeberne

An era of modern city building began in China soon after the Chinese Communist Party came to power in 1949. Transformation of the economic role of cities became an integral part of the nation's development policy, under which existing 'consumer cities' were to be converted into 'producer cities', assuming a new role as growth centres of the nation's planned economic development. This chapter presents a case study of Shanghai, China's largest and most important industrial centre.

Pre-1949 Development of Shanghai

Between 1842 and the collapse of the Chinese Empire in 1911, many foreign settlements set up in the treaty ports underwent continuous expansion, but none was able to match the scale of spatial growth that occurred in Shanghai over a span of 85 years (1845-1930).

Initially, the Treaty of Nanjing (Nanking) on 29 August 1842, which led to the promulation of the Land Regulations of 1845 under the joint authority of the British and the Chinese, provided the legal basis for the British to found the first settlement in Shanghai. The site of this foreign enclave was located in the northern suburb of the Chinese walled city, and the entire settlement occupied an area of approximately 830 *mou* (56 hectares) (Figure 8.1). As the western boundary for the British settlement was undetermined in the 1845 Land Regulations, a further agreement was made between the two official representatives in 1846. Thereby the western limit was fixed along the Defence Creek, a southern tributary of the Suzhouhe; and the northern boundary was pushed northward to the southern bank of the Suzhouhe. These boundary changes subsequently enlarged the British territory to 2820 *mou* (190 hectares). A second foreign settlement appeared in the northern suburb of Shanghai in 1849. Through a successful negotiation of a separate Land Regulation with the Taotai (Intendant of Circuit and Superintendant of Customs), representative of the Chinese Imperial Court, the French established a settlement, called the French concession, between the British settlement and the Chinese city. It covered an area

250

Figure 8.1: Historical Development of Foreign Settlement and Concession in Shanghai

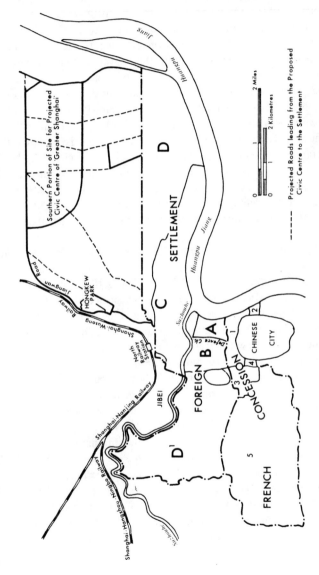

of 986 *mou* (66 hectares) (Jones, 1940). The Treaty of Huangsha signed between China and the United States at Canton in 1844 extended trade and residence rights in the treaty ports to American citizens. On 25 June, 1863, through an agreement between the American Consul-General and the Taotai, an American settlement was set up for the first time on Chinese soil. It was situated on the northern bank of the Suzhouhe extending along the Huangpu Jiang, to the east of the British settlement, but the exact territorial limits were not clearly determined in the agreement. On 21 September of the same year an agreement was made for amalgamation of the British and the American settlements, forming officially the international settlement. Its spatial extent, however, was not formally delimited until May 1893. The total area officially occupied by foreign settlements reached 12,630 *mou* (851 hectares), exceeding the size of the Chinese walled city by at least four times. Since the founding of these settlements the foreigners had been busy building roads, homes, sewage systems and warehouses, and the original marshland and cultivated fields outside the old Chinese city were transformed into thriving urban communities with alien characteristics.

The outbreak of the Taiping Rebellion in Guangxi province, in 1851, greatly stimulated developments within the treaty port of Shanghai and brought changes to the surroundings of the settlements. The devastating civil war that affected many provinces in south and east China sent a large number of refugees flocking towards the foreign-controlled territories in Shanghai for safety. The large number who sought refuge inside the settlements engendered a marked increase of Chinese population in the foreign communities. From a commercial point of view, this new development was not entirely unwelcome. Some foreign landowners found it an opportunity to make a quick and substantial profit by letting land or accommodation to the Chinese refugees.[1] When the Taiping Rebellion was crushed by the Imperial forces in 1864, the number of Chinese living in the international settlement and the French concession was believed to be over 100,000. The 1865 census registered a total of 90,587 Chinese as permanent residents. A reduction to 75,047 was recorded by the 1870 census. However, the census of 1876 showed a figure of 95,662, and marked the beginning of a continuous increase in the number of Chinese residents in the foreign settlements. Within the following six decades, the figure rapidly rose to 971,397 (Table 8.1).

Among those Chinese refugees who sought security in the settlement were wealthy entrepreneurs who brought with them their capital. This

Table 8.1: Chinese Population of Foreign Settlement, 1855–1930 (Shanghai Municipal Council Census Returns)

Year	Population
1855	20,000
1865	90,587
1870	75,047
1876	95,662
1880	107,812
1885	125,665
1890	168,129
1895	240,995
1900	345,276
1905	452,716
1910	488,005
1915	620,401
1920	759,839
1925	810,279
1930	971,396

Source: Shanghai Municipal Council Reports (1931)

influx of wealth created the first sudden activities in land sales and speculation. Meanwhile, many foreign banks and shipping companies established their branch office. The enormous amount of shipping and trade attracted from overseas to the treaty port necessitated the development of harbour facilities, wharves, docks and shipyards (Anon, 1935). Before the end of the nineteenth century Shanghai had emerged as one of the most important ports in the Orient, rivalling Yokohama and Singapore. The rapid increase of Chinese population in the foreign concessions, on the other hand, brought about an acute shortage of space for further development. The Shanghai municipal council (the governing body of the settlement dominated by the treaty powers) felt the urgent need for expansion into the suburbs. In 1898 amendment of the original Land Regulations and Byelaws was approved by the Chinese authorities. The following year witnessed enormous expansion of territory under the control of the treaty powers. An area of 11,377 *mou* (about 767 hectares) was added to the north of the international settlement, and 11,450 *mou* (about 772 hectares) to the west, making a total area of 33,503 *mou* (about 2259 hectares). After 1861 the French concession also underwent several phases of expansion. Between that

Table 8.2: Historical Development of Foreign Settlement and Concession in Shanghai

Foreign Settlement	Mou	Hectares
A. First delimitation of boundaries. Agreement dated 20 September 1846	830	56
B. Foreign settlement. Agreement dated 27 November 1848	2820	190
C. Area roughly defined as included in the 'American settlement' by agreement between the American Consul-General and the Intendant of Circuit, dated 25 June 1863 incorporated with the foreign settlement by agreement of 21 September 1863, and formally delimited May 1893	7856	530
D. Settlement extension, delimited 1899	11,377	767
D.[1] Settlement extension, delimited 1899	11,450	772
Total area of international settlement:	33,503	2259
French Concession		
1. Original concession as delimited by agreement between the French Consul and Taotai Lin, on 6 April 1849	986	66
2. Extension Proclamation dated 29 October 1861	138	9
3. Extension Proclamation dated 27 January 1900	909	62
4. Controlled by French prior to 1849, but officially added together with (3), and noted in proclamation dated 27 January 1900	116	8
5. Extension. Proclamation dated 20 July, 1914	13,001	877
Total area of French concession:	15,150	1022

Source: *Shanghai Municipal Council Reports* vol. 1, parts 1–3 (1931) (end piece)

year and 1900 the French municipality incorporated 1163 *mou* (about 78 hectares) lying to the east and northwest immediately outside the Chinese walled city. A major expansion toward the west took place in 1914. Incorporation of all the extension roads built by the French administration in the western suburb added 13,001 *mou* (877 hectares) to the concession (Figure 8.1 and Table 8.2).

At the beginning of the twentieth century the highly congested old Chinese city spilled out into the southern suburb, forming a densely populated and small industrial area, known as Nandao. A second

expansion of Chinese urban area occurred in Jibei, lying along the
Suzhouhe, and to the north of the international settlement. The third
Chinese urban district was Pudong, a relatively narrow belt of warehouses, wharves and factories that lined the right bank of the Huangpu
Jiang. In comparison, the total area of these urbanised areas administered by the Chinese municipal authorities was much smaller than that
of the international settlement and the French concession combined,
although the entire Chinese municipality, mainly rural and agricultural
in character, embraced an area of over 49,000 hectares. This Chinese
municipality came into existence in 1906. It mainly served the purpose
of restraining further expansion of the foreign settlements (Jones, 1940).

The 'external roads areas' at the Treaty Port

In the closing years of the Taiping Rebellion (1863–4), the foreign
powers in Shanghai also secured 'legal' rights in building roads and parks
outside the settlements. Two of these 'external roads areas' may be
identified: the western section extended for almost 10 km from the
western limit of the Settlement to Monument Road. The northern side
ran along Pearce Road and the southern bank of Suzhouhe, and the
southern boundary followed the full length of Hungrao Road. The
entire section covered an area of over 3090 hectares. In contrast, the
northern section was just over 115 hectares. It lay to the north of the
settlement, and the Shanghai-Wusong railway runs along its western
boundary (Figure 8.2). By 1925 there were already something
approaching 77,400 km of 'dirt' roads built outside the Settlement,
of which just over 69,200 km were in the western section, and the
remainder in the northern section. These road building activities by
the treaty powers within Chinese-controlled territory lying to the west
of the foreign communities set the stage for the suburban sprawl of
metropolitan Shanghai during the 1930s.

The upsurge in industrial development in Shanghai during the early
1900s further contributed to the relentless advance of the urban
frontier. Only a few decades earlier, the city had only a few modern
factories. Zeng Guofan and Li Hongzhang established the Jiangnan
arsenal at Hongkew in 1865; in 1886 several German merchants founded
the Chen Yu flour mill (Lieu, 1936); and the city's first modern cotton
mill was erected in 1889. The urban landscape in Shanghai began to
change drastically after the signing of the Treaty of Shimonoseki in
1896 between China and Japan. The Treaty granted all foreigners the

Figure 8.2: Extraterrestrial Expansion of Foreign Settlement in Shanghai, 1846-1914

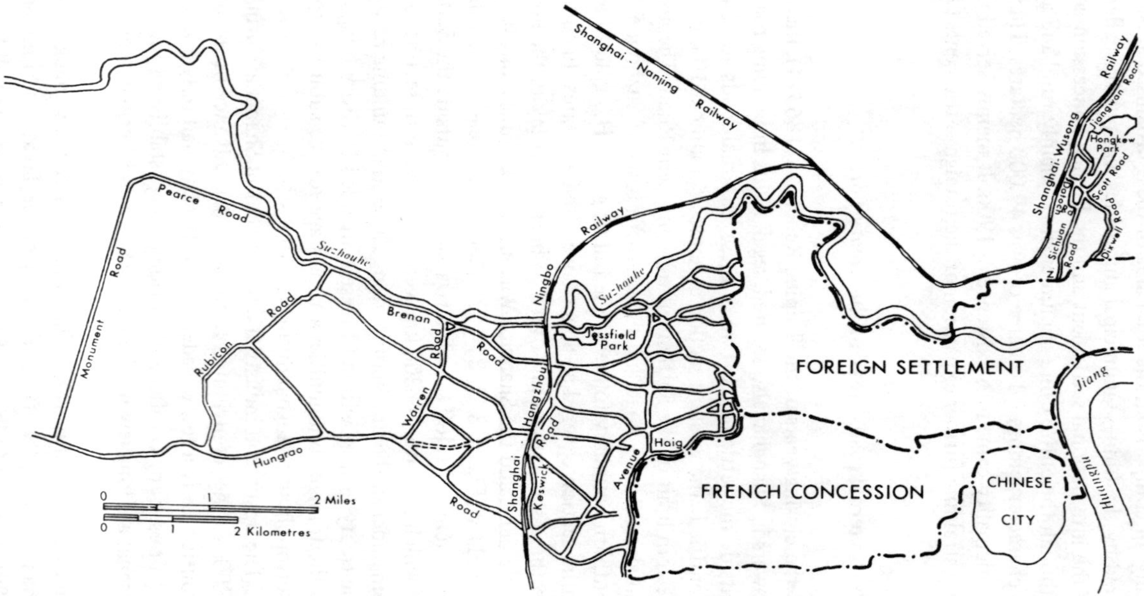

rights to establish factories in the treaty ports. Consequent upon this
new development, a substantial number of modern textile mills began
to appear in Shanghai. By the early 1930s numerous cotton spinning
and weaving mills concentrated in the central part of the settlement,
especially along the right bank of the Huangpu Jiang. Other major
concentrations of cotton mills, paper mills and flour mills were located
on both banks of the Suzhouhe, south of the Shanghai-Hangzhou-
Ningbo railway, and a large variety of light industries formed a linear
manufacturing belt in Pudong.

The city spread westward along Bubbling Well Road (a continuation
of Nanjing Road) west of the race course (originally established on the
outskirts) (Figure 8.3). This suburban road was a country drive before
1930. Subsequently, however, large department stores, recreation clubs
and halls, towering apartments, churches, and commercial buildings
arose on both sides. These developments continued to send out tentacles
in every direction, and they soon filled the entire area east of the legal
boundary for the settlement fixed by the 1899 Agreement (Moore,
1932). Keeping abreast with the continuous industrial growth and the
boom in building activity, the urban population increased rapidly.
In 1910 it reached one million (Potter, 1932). The metropolis became
highly congested, as its average population density grew to more than
three times that of London, five times that of New York, and slightly
higher than that of Tokyo. Within the next two decades Shanghai's
population further increased to three million. The overcrowded conditions in this teeming industrial city thus became even more serious
(Table 8.3). To avoid the ever-deteriorating urban environment within
the foreign-controlled territories, Europeans and wealthy Chinese
began to move out to the western section of the 'external roads areas'
(Chen Yanlin, 1933). The new development greatly stimulated the
construction activities in this western district. There is no surprise that,
out of a total of Tls^2 62,351,259 in building permits for 1931, the

**Table 8.3: Average Population Density in Shanghai, 1930-2 (persons/
km^2)**

	1930	1931	1932
Greater Shanghai municipality (Chinese-controlled territory)	3440.80	3711.80	3194.80
International settlement	44,595.93	45,364.20	47,557.26
French concession	42,544.72	44,619.57	46,825.04

Source: Shanghai Civic Association (1933).

Figure 8.3: Land Use in Shanghai, 1930

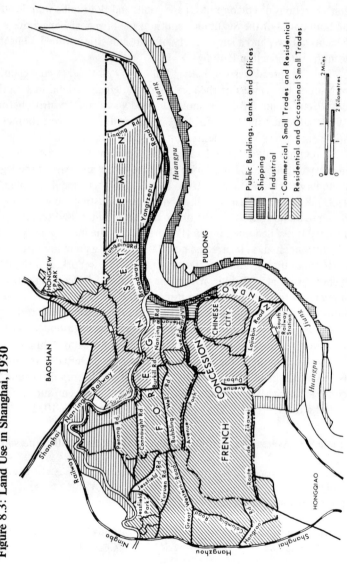

western suburb provided *Tls* 16,940,944. This represented more than twice the amount for the French concession and nearly half of that for the international settlement. By comparison with the 1925 figure, it was an increase of nearly seventeen times (Potter, 1932). The upsurge in building activities changed the urban-fringe landscape of the metropolis. In the middle of the 1920s the roads outside the settlement ran through the agricultural countryside, with here and there a Chinese village or a lonely foreign residence, but within several years the district became a pleasant residential suburb with beautiful homes and their spacious gardens occupying the entire lengths of many suburban roads (Anon, 1935). The good accessibility provided by these roads and cheaper land further encouraged new growths farther from the built-up areas of the treaty port. In the early part of the 1930s an irregular pattern of suburban growth appeared in the eastern section of the 'external roads areas', lying between the western limits of the settlement and the Shanghai-Hangzhou railway. Here recreational, institutional and educational and horticultural land uses were present;[3] and in 1931 as the *North China Herald* (11 August 1931) noted, many factories and shops appeared. The entire area, as a result, resembled the 'twilight zone' typical of many western cities in modern times. Nevertheless, the belt of chaotic development and mixed land use continued to expand apace. The fast rate of suburbanisation in this world city prompted the following comment: 'It is not too much to predict that in a few years' time a suburban Shanghai, very much like suburban London, will come into existence' (Anon, 1935b).

Development of North Suburban Shanghai

Indeed, while the city was sprawling actively westward, a new development, known as the Jiangwan civic-centre scheme, was instituted in the outskirts north of the international settlement, lying between the Shanghai-Wusong railway and the Huangpu Jiang (Figure 8.1). The creation of this urban area was a single phase of an ambitious and comprehensive plan, launched by the Chinese municipal authorities, to build a modern planned city of Shanghai. Upon completion of this first stage of the plan, the centre of the metropolis would be shifted from the international settlement to the Jiangwan civic centre, where vital administrative, economic and social activities of the entire city would then be concentrated. This future city centre would also be the first urban area built according to a preconceived plan in modern China.

The beginning of 1928 witnessed the unification of China, a short time after the northern expedition came to a successful conclusion. This allowed the Guomindang (the Nationalist Party) to inaugurate its national reconstruction programme, part of which included the redevelopment of land-use zoning for many of the existing cities. Some of these plans involved very elaborate planning, such as the garden-city scheme for Nanjing, capital of the Nationalist government; and the expansion of urban areas for Guangzhou, Kunming, Shenyang, Nanchang, Fushan and Zhuangjiakuo (Wu Shan, 1929). None of these, however, could surpass the comprehensive development plan drawn up by the committee on reconstruction for the 'special municipality of Greater Shanghai'.

The primary motive for implementing such an extensive urban-development project for the metropolis was fundamentally political in nature, strengthened by the growing national consciousness and aspirations which had prevailed since the founding of the Republic of China. Near the end of the Imperial era, many traditional Chinese cities were in an advanced state of decay, characterised by dark, narrow and winding streets, ill-odour, repulsive filth and squalid conditions. In strong contrast, the treaty ports and the industrial cities in Manchuria under foreign administration grew and emerged as centres of great economic importance. The existence of Shanghai and other treaty ports under foreign control had become an increasing grievance to the politically minded Chinese. There was a general demand on the part of the Nationalist government and other Chinese bodies to have foreign settlements handed over to the Chinese authorities. The time would also come when the Chinese could argue that their municipality was as good as the foreign settlements, and therefore the ultimate intention in creating a modern planned city next to the treaty port of Shanghai was no doubt to cajole the treaty powers to agree to incorporate the foreign settlements into Chinese-controlled territory (Green, 1934). In his speech on the objective of the development scheme for Greater Shanghai, Marshall Sun Chuan-fang (military governor of Jiangsu and Zhejiang provinces) stressed (*North China Herald*, 8 May 1926)

It is necessary to create an organization in Shanghai to unite all the administrative powers into one centre so that it might have the necessary authority to improve the municipal government, plan a new port, and settle diplomatic disputes, gradually converting the area outside the foreign settlements into a model city, the result of which should form the basis for our demand for the abolishing of foreign concessions.

The Greater Shanghai development programme was certainly the most comprehensive for one single urban settlement and its surrounding areas in the history of city planning and building in China. This urban and suburban planned development covered an area of almost 51,800 hectares. The entire scheme included provisions for flood prevention and harbour improvement, construction of ports on the southern bank of the Chang Jiang (Yangtze), railway connections, river crossings, arterial highways and a modern civic centre (Lillico, 1935). The preliminary plan proposed construction of a highway network to serve a large number of wharves along the Huangpu Jiang from Wusong to the village of Yingxianggang. Anticipating substantial increases in the volume of railway traffic, the planners proposed the construction of a branch line of the Shanghai-Nanjing railway from Chenyu to Wusong via Dachang Village, and of another branch line from Longhua to Chenyu, connecting the Shanghai-Nanjing railway and the Shanghai-Hangzhou-Ningbo railway. An industrial area was to be built in the northwestern suburb of the Jiangwan civic centre. Considerations of environmental protection formed the basis for the selection of this site; the prevailing winds would carry the smoke and dust from factories away to uninhabited areas. Other manufacturing districts were planned for Lunghua, Gaozhangmiao and Pudong. While most of the Greater Shanghai development scheme was still in the preliminary planning stage, the initial phase of the project involving the construction of the Jiangwan civic centre was well underway in 1929. The central part of this urban district was occupied by municipal offices, public building and facilities. The area to the north of the administrative nucleus was zoned for commercial use. Outside the business district were the residential zones. Approximately 69 hectares had been reserved for parks, open squares and boulevards. The first stage of the civic-centre project was started in 1929, when the *North China Herald* (7 December 1919) reported that over 7000 *mou* (over 3885 hectares) of suburban land located within the site for the proposed city centre were purchased by the Shanghai municipal planning commission. Following the land purchase, remarkable progress was made. In 1935, the Mayor's building, one of the most important buildings in the administrative complex, was completed, and the public library, the museum and the sports centre were in an advanced stage of construction. Other buildings completed early in 1937 included the city hall, which housed the bureaux of public works, social affairs, land administration, health and education, and other buildings for the bureaux of finance and public utilities (Boyden, 1937). Further progress was seriously handicapped, however, when Shanghai was seized by the Japanese army in August, 1937, and construction work at the civic centre came to a standstill during the Japanese occupation (Barnett, 1941). Construction work was not resumed at the end of the Sino-Japanese War in 1945, as a consequence of the ensuing outbreak of the civil war between the Nationalists and the Communists, which was fought over vast territories in China until September 1949.

Post-1949 Urban Renewal and Reconstruction in Shanghai

During the 1950s urban redevelopment work on a substantial scale was undertaken in many Chinese cities. Streets were widened and many slums cleared. Impressive progress was made in sanitation work and the installation of piped-water systems. In most cities the urban-transformation process entailed changes of existing land-use patterns.

During the course of Shanghai's development and expansion in the treaty-port era, the city was governed by three different administrations: the municipal councils of the international settlement and the French concession, and the government of Greater Shanghai. For almost a century the city grew of its own accord, without any coordinated planning by the three governing bodies. Much of this haphazard growth was evident from the buildings of different foreign architectural designs and the randomly spaced, narrow and winding streets. The metropolis, therefore, lacked the systematic physical layout of a grid-iron street pattern, typical of Chinese dynastic cities such as Beijing (Peking) and Xi'an. Only within the central business district occupying the 1843 British settlement were the streets laid out in an east-west and north-south pattern; for the rest of the city, including the external roads areas, all the roads ran in a predominantly east-west direction as the international settlement and the western section of the external roads areas spread mainly westward. After liberation, top priority was given to improving the urban-transportation network, including the straightening and widening of roads, the construction of north-south thoroughfares such as Xizang Road and Tianshan Road and the renovation and construction of bridges spanning the Suzhouhe. A higgledy-piggledy, confused land-use pattern had evolved from the unplanned growth of the city. Along both banks of the Huangpu Jiang, within the city's built-up areas, lay a belt of shipping establishments, factories, wharves, slums and warehouses. Small trade-cum-residential quarters extended well beyond Hongquiao Park in the north, and embraced practically the entire western part of the international settlement, and all of the French concession. Within the major industrial areas of Jibei, Nandao and Pudong, workshops and factories intermingled with high-density, dilapidated, flimsy and squalid dwellings (Figure 8.3). Only the central business district in the vicinity of the Bund showed a distinct concentration of large commercial enterprises and financial institutions. On 19 September 1951, the urban construction committee of Shanghai, the first urban-planning and construction authority in the People's Republic of China, was established. The urban-planning organ initiated study of the city's population characteristics and urban land-use patterns. The assembled data were to be used as the basis for the general planning and development of urban Shanghai. Meanwhile, as noted in *Xinwen Ribao*[4] (8 August, 1957), the immediate task of the committee involved the transformation of the existing intermixture of factories and dwellings into spatially distinct zones of industrial and residential land use. The 400 *mou* (about 27 hectares) race course built by the British during the treaty-port days was converted into a municipal central square, named the People's Square, and one of the city's largest recreational grounds, known as the People's Park. To improve the living environment, the committee began development of several municipal parks within the existing built-up areas and at the urban fringe. In the first seven years after liberation, public parks in Shanghai underwent very rapid increase, both in area and number. In 1949 the city had 14 parks occupying a total area of 988.2 *mou* (about 67 hectares).From 1868, when the first park was established, to 1949 the annual increase of park area was only 11.8 *mou* (less than one hectare), whereas between 1949 and 1957 park space increased to 2993.5 *mou* (about 200 hectares), representing an average annual increase of 250.7 *mou* (over 16 hectares). On a per capita basis, as noted in *Jihfang Ribao*[5] (11 August 1956), the area of public parks increased from 0.12 m^2 to nearly 0.33 m^2 during the period. Another major assignment of the planning authorities involved the removal of nearly 200 shack areas scattered within the old industrial districts of Caojiabin and Chujihui.

Spatial Developments in Shanghai, 1949–59

Two key policies relating to national industrial development issued by the central government exerted a far-reaching impact on the pace and

character of the spatial growth of Shanghai and its surroundings. The
first five-year plan, launched in 1953, placed special emphasis on
developing industries in the interior, in order to transform the traditional spatial imbalance of China's economy. Another policy, officially
adopted in August 1954, allocated all cities into one of three major
categories, in accordance with the degree of relevance to industrial and
urban development during the period of the first five-year plan, as
noted in *Renmin Ribao* (11 August 1954):

> In concrete terms, efforts must be concentrated in the development
> of new industrial cities where important industrial projects are to be
> located. Such cities previously had no industrial foundation. Now
> that large scale modern industries are being built, the construction
> of public utilities and facilities typical of modern cities must be
> undertaken to complement them. Cities in this category necessarily
> are the central focus in our urban development work. Next are the
> modern cities that have already acquired a certain industrial base.
> The present plan is to augment the existing factories and to build
> new factories in these cities. Cities in this category must be placed
> second in our nation's urban development scheme, and be redevel-
> oped and expanded in accordance with industrial growth. With
> regards to several large cities and most medium and small cities where
> industrial construction is minimal during the First Five Year Plan
> period (1953-1957), new projects are, basically speaking, not to be
> undertaken, even though such cities still possess many unjust con-
> ditions inherited from the old society and, in a number of ways,
> cannot satisfy the material and cultural needs of the people. In these
> instances, only maintenance and repair work can be allowed.

These policies led to remarkably different patterns of spatial growth
between cities in the three categories. Because of the construction of a
large proportion of new industrial projects at key-point cities (those
belonging to the first category in the classification), rapid territorial
expansion took place in all these new industrial bases. Large-scale
encroachment upon surrounding suburban areas of these cities by
municipal and industrial construction became a commonplace
phenomenon (Fung, 1974). As early as 1950, as reported in *Shaanxi
Ribao* (25 March, 1955), suburban villages as well as large tracts of
agricultural land outside the city of Xi'an in Shaanxi province were
expropriated for the immediate construction of industrial districts. In
the city of Zhengzhou in Henan province, another key-point city in the

interior, 9000 hectares of land outside the existing urban area were developed for industrial use (*XWRB*, 21 April 1953). Beijing, as the nation's capital and key-point city, received the lion's share of urban construction projects. From 1949 to 1957 the land-use patterns outside the city walls underwent very rapid changes. The city expanded virtually in all directions, particularly towards the west, northwest and east, along arterial transportation lines. Over 20,000 hectares of suburban land immediately outside the city walls was reserved for municipal construction purposes.

In contrast, the scale of expansion of built-up areas in Shanghai, a city allocated to the third category in the official classification of urban centres, was slow relative to that in key-point cities during the first half of the First Plan period. The urban-construction committee of Shanghai abandoned the Jiangwan civic-centre development scheme that had been proposed and partially completed by the Guomindang (Nationalist) regime before 1949. Instead, much effort was devoted to land-reform work in the suburban area. By the time the programme had been completed, in November 1951, about 184,000 *mou* (almost 12,500 hectares), or almost one-quarter of the total land area in suburban Shanghai, was confiscated or expropriated (*XWRB*, 8 December 1951). However, only a very small portion of this reserved land was actually put into non-agricultural use in the early 1950s. Two major urban developments were undertaken in suburban Shanghai which initiated the transformation of the agricultural landscape outside Shanghai's city limits. These projects included the relocation of the chemical industry from the urban area and the construction of housing estates for industrial workers at the urban fringes.

As a response to a central-government directive issued in 1950,[6] the Shanghai municipal authorities, as noted in *Wenhui Bao*[7] (29 October 1950), took immediate steps to move about 100 chemical plants and small workshops handling or producing inflammable materials from the densely settled industrial districts within the city to the less populous suburban areas. As a result of this relocation, a new centre for chemical works appeared at Taopu in the suburban district of Chenyu by 1954.

As in many other cities in China during 1952 and early 1953, a large number of workers' housing projects was erected in the urban fringe of Shanghai. Because of the availability of reserved land for municipal and industrial construction in suburban areas after the suburban land reform, and in anticipation of large-scale urban expansion, nearly all these new workers' living quarters were erected outside the city limits. Also, in order to alleviate the high-population-density problem and to improve the living environment of factory workers in the city, the urban construction committee selected sites in peripheral areas for the building project. This housing-development scheme, the largest ever undertaken in the history of Shanghai, consisted of 20,000 units of living quarters for workers, dispersed among nine separate sites (Figure 8.4). One of these housing projects, Caoyang Xin Cun (Caoyang new village), occupied an area of 94.6 hectares. The estate was designed to house a population of 26,241 persons. The dwellings were mainly two-storey structures of standard design, providing an average dwelling space of 4 m^2 per capita (Editorial, 1957).

Figure 8.4: Suburban Industrial Districts and New Workers' Villages in Shanghai

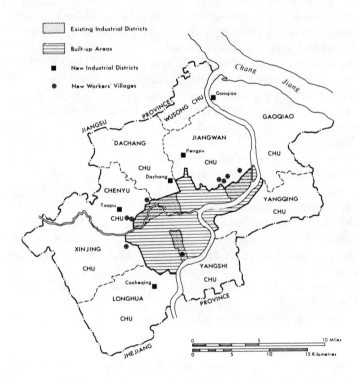

These housing estates comprised integrated community services such as dwellings for workers and their dependents, schools, day-care facilities, markets, clinics and public bath houses (*XWRB*, 29 October 1952). To eliminate long-distance travel by workers between their place of residence and the factories, all the new villages were located in close proximity to the existing industrial districts of Yangpu, Yulin, Putao, Jibei, Changning and Luwan situated within the city.

For example, Caoyand new village, located at Chenyu suburban district, is only about 1 km from the factory area in Putao. The Chinese city planners seemed to have followed the Soviet approach in the siting of these large housing projects for workers. Construction of workers' villages was the most extensive urban development project in post-1949 Shanghai, and contributed to the city's major spatial growth during the first half of the first five-year plan period.

New Phase of Development in Suburban Shanghai

For both economic and strategic reasons, the Chinese leadership intended to build up a modern and large heavy-industrial base in the sheltered interior regions, as stipulated in the first five-year plan. As a result, all the existing industrial cities along the coast were given low priority in development.

The closing years of the first plan period witnessed an abrupt revitalisation of Shanghai, however. The city's industrial production grew rapidly, and the structure of its manufacturing industries also underwent significant changes. The primary force behind these new developments was the modification of the nation's regional industrial policy early in 1956. The major reason for the policy change was to speed up both national economic growth and the construction of new industrial centres in the interior.

Since the spring of 1956, the upsurge in the level of investment in the heavy-industrial sector in Shanghai greatly stimulated the spatial development in the suburban areas of this metropolis. As noted earlier, during the early 1950s the city planners began to reorganise the confusing urban-land use, an intermixture of factories and dwellings, and to relocate chemical workshops and factories in the suburbs. From mid-1956 to the end of 1957, the department of industry in Shanghai invested 130 million *yuan* for the relocation project (*WHB*, 6 July 1958), which accelerated the process of urban land-use reorganisation and transformation of the city's suburban areas. In less than two years

a different spatial pattern of industrial land use emerged in metropolitan Shanghai. A total of four manufacturing centres – the industrial
districts of Caohejing, Dachang, Gaoqiao and Pengpu – were created in
the suburban areas within the period. Each of these industrial nodes
was an organised group of factories producing similar types of manu-
factured goods and those involved in different productive steps in a
single product. The Gaoqiao industrial district specialised in oil refining
and petrochemical production; the Caohejing industrial district in
precision scientific instruments; both the industrial districts of Pengpu
and Dachang in iron and steel manufacturing, and the Taopu industrial
district in chemicals and allied products. This method of functional
zoning was a rational approach in industrial land-use planning, commonly practised in other Chinese cities. With the exception of the
Gaoqiao industrial district, which was located to the northeast of
Shanghai municipality, at about seven miles from the city, all the other
suburban industrial nodes were established at the urban fringe. The
average distance between these manufacturing districts and the central
city is less than two miles. Apparently, the siting of these five suburban
industrial centres was based upon the following key principles of
industrial land-use planning: minimisation of industrial pollution,
coordination among manufacturing activities and rational selection of
physical sites in terms of availability of water, transportation facilities
and energy.

Accelerating Industrial Expansion and Planned Development in the Shanghai City Region

Towards the end of 1956 the state statistical bureau revealed the
industrial growth rates in coastal areas and inland regions. In the
provinces of Liaoning, Shandong, Hebei, Zhejiang, Jiangsu, Fujian and
Guangdong, and the three major cities of Beijing, Tianjin and Shanghai,
the total value of industrial production in the third quarter of the year
exceeded that of the first quarter by 15 per cent and was also 35 per
cent larger than in the same period in 1955. Between the first and the
third quarters of 1956, the coastal areas exceeded the interior in
industrial growth rate. The former recorded an increase of nine per
cent, whereas the latter achieved only 6.7 per cent (*XWRB*, 7 November
1956). The more rapid industrial growth in coastal areas in the second
half of 1956 strongly suggested that the revised regional-development
policy implemented in the spring of the same year was beginning to

make an impact. The success of this central-government policy strengthened the confidence of the Chinese leadership in raising the investment level for expanding the coastal industrial bases when the Great
Leap Forward was launched in 1958.[8]

Thus that year witnessed an enormous increase of capital input in
Shanghai's industrial sector. The total investment amounted to 973.6
million *yuan*, which was equivalent to 262 per cent of the total investment in 1957, or 71 per cent of the total investment in the entire first
plan period (*JFRB*, 7 June 1959). The high level of capital investment
was a decisive factor in the increase in the number of large industrial
enterprises in the city. Industrial development during 1953-7 mainly
involved the expansion of existing industrial plants and the amalgamation of small workshops to form large factories. In 1958 the
construction of new factories, particularly those in the heavy-industrial
sector, was given priority in the industrial-expansion programme of the
city. Altogether 43 new plants were built in Shanghai, an increase
second only to Beijing, where 66 new plants were added (Wu Yuan-li,
1963).

Pursuing the policy of decentralising industrial functions, the
municipal people's committee of Shanghai and the department of
industry erected these new factories in both the recently established
and existing suburban manufacturing zones. This contributed to the
rapid expansion and numerical increase of decentralised industrial
districts within the city region, which drastically changed the industrial
map of Shanghai. Since the first chemical-industrial district was established at Taopu in 1954, the total number of suburban manufacturing
centres increased to five by the end of 1957. By 1959 at least twelve
industrial districts existed in the city region. The new ones included
Minhang, Wusong, Pudong, Wujing, Xinjing, Changqiao, Zhoujiadao,
Anting, Songjiang and Wuguochang. With the exception of the Wusong
industrial district, all of these were located at a distance of about 30 km
from the central city.

The institution of a new spatial-planning unit in all the major cities
in China in 1958 facilitated the dispersal of industrial activities from
the central city to the suburban areas. Other important functions of
the city regions included the reorganisation and planning of agricultural
land use, with special emphasis on achieving self-sufficiency in vegetable
supply in the central city, population planning, the development and
utilisation of local transportation, and the mobilisation of manpower.
Each of these urban-centred administrative-cum-planning regions consisted of a large city and an extensive rural area under the direct

Figure 8.5: Boundary Changes of the Shanghai City Region

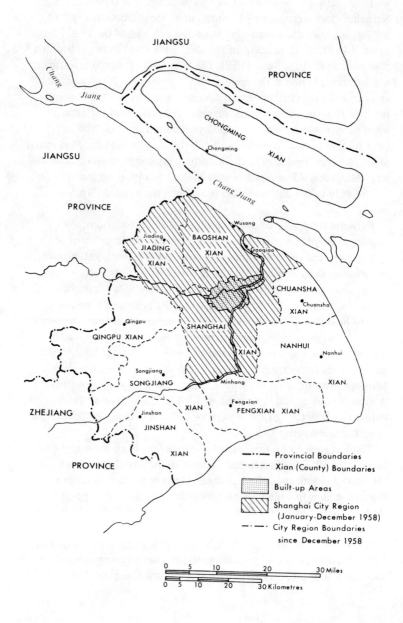

jurisdiction of the municipal government. On 17 January 1958, Shanghai incorporated the adjacent counties of Jiading, Boashan and Shanghai, forming an urban region with a total area of 86,300 hectares (*WHB*, 18 February 1958). Further expansion of the city region took place in December of the same year. The administrative boundaries were extended to include the surrounding counties of Chuansha, Nanhui, Fengxian, Jinshan, Songjiang, Qingpu and Chongming. The area of the entire unit reached 591,000 hectares (*JFRB*, 20 December 1958), and has not been changed since then (Figure 8.5).

The accelerated development of new manufacturing centres in suburban Shanghai is reflected by the unprecedented amount of sub-urban land designated for industrial use by the Shanghai municipal people's committee. In his speech at the second meeting of the third people's congress held in mid-1958, the mayor disclosed that over 36,800 *mou* of suburban land, equivalent to about 2460 hectares, had been approved for use for industrial construction. This surpassed the total amount of land used for industrial purposes during the entire first five-year plan period by over 50 per cent. It was also revealed that over 85 per cent of the land was used for industrial construction, transport-ation and warehouses in the industrial districts of Minhang, Wusong, Caoheqing, Zhoujidao and Taopu (*JFRB*, 6 June 1959). It should be noted that as these industrial nodes were scattered in the suburban area of the city region, despite the large-scale transformation of land from non-industrial to industrial and other urban uses, rapid expansion of the central city and subsequent encroachment upon market garden land of the suburban communes around the city fringes were avoided. Con-comitant with the building of new factories in the suburban areas, a large number of workers' houses was erected near the factory sites. During 1958 most of the 468 hectares of Shanghai's workers' residences were built in the suburban industrial districts. As reported by the *New China News Agency* (20 July 1959)[9] these housing estates possessed their own kindergartens, crèches, restaurants, shops, public libraries and recreational facilities. It may be claimed, therefore, that the year 1958 marked the beginning of the coordination of the dispersal of urban population and the decentralisation of industrial functions.

Satellite-town Development in Shanghai

Another significant aspect of urban decentralisation in metropolitan Shanghai during the Great Leap Forward should be noted. The actual and potential spatial growth and influx of peasants resulting from a substantial increase in state investment for industrial expansion in 1958 made it necessary to further disperse both residents and economic activities from the central city to the suburban areas. The adoption of a central policy to build small and medium-sized cities and to disperse population and industrial activities away from large cities, for economic and national security reasons, added impetus to the building of satellite communities in the city region.

In order to implement the policy of industrial decentralisation and population dispersal in Shanghai, the second meeting of the first people's congress of the Shanghai municipality was held between December 1957 and January 1958. A resolution concerning the construction of satellite towns in the city region was passed. Significantly, it was stressed at the meeting that these satellite settlements would not be allowed to develop into dormitory towns or health resorts (*WHB*, 18 February 1958), implying the creation of balanced and self-contained communities specifically designed for decentralising the city's population and industries.

When the city region of Shanghai was established in January 1958, one of the major objectives was to provide a wider range of sites for industrial district and satellite town development. The large territory of over 80,000 hectares enabled Shanghai's urban planners to locate future satellite industrial towns at an optimal distance from the central city. As conceived by the city planners of Shanghai, the optimal distance between the mother city and its satellites lies within a range of 20 to 70 km. This would certainly prevent the satellites from being subsequently absorbed, thereby aggravating the problem of rapid expansion of built-up areas of any large city, while retaining certain mutual advantages in industrial production and other functional relationships.

In February 1958, the municipal authorities of Shanghai initiated the drafting of the general development plan for the city's suburban areas and the survey of potential sites for satellite-town development. The development plan encompassed the siting of satellite towns and their industries, distribution and organisation of agricultural communes responsible for supplying subsidiary foods to the urban population of the parent city and the satellite towns, and detailed planning of transportation networks within the entire municipality. This regional plan also included the preliminary design of Shanghai's first satellite town, the industrial district of Minhang, and investigation of other potential sites for future satellite developments at Wuqing, Beiyangqiao,

Nanchang, Huangdao, Anting and elsewhere (Figure 8.6). Furthermore, it comprised planning for the integrated utilisation of major waterways for transportation purposes and farm irrigation, and for storage, shipping and marketing of fifteen selected types of industrial goods in the city (*WHB*, 10 January 1959).

As an integral part of the satellite-town development programme, an extensive road-construction project designed to improve linkage, and facilitate functional coordination, between Shanghai and its industrial

Figure 8.6: Proposed Satellite Towns of Shanghai, 1958

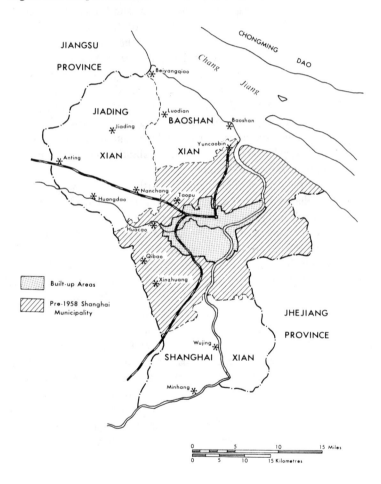

satellites was started early in 1958. By late 1959 a trunk-road system was completed, connecting Shanghai and Minhang, Wusong, Pengpu and Wujing. This improved road system was supplemented by the branch lines of the major railways in the region: the Shanghai-Hangzhou railway, the Shanghai-Wusong railway and the Shanghai-Nanjing railway. Further, a special railway for freight hauling, known as the Xinmin railway, was opened to traffic in the spring of 1959. This 13.7-km-long railway afforded a direct link between Xinqiao in Shanghai and Minhang, and played an important role in the industrial development of the satellite town (*XWRB*, 17 April 1959). To provide easy access to Minhang and the industrial districts of Wusong and Yuncaobin from various parts of the central city, construction of Zhongshan Road, originally proposed by the planning agency of the Greater Shanghai municipality before 1949, began at the end of 1959. This perimeter artery almost encircled the built-up area of the city, passing through the urban districts of Hongqiao, Jibei, Putao and Changning, and the suburban counties of Shanghai and Baoshan. Development of these land communication systems contributed to accelerating suburban agricultural production, in particular vegetables and other subsidiary foods, as well as achieving industrial decentralisation within the integrated administrative and planning unit.

The industrial district of Minhang, established in 1958, was selected by the Shanghai municipal bureau of urban planning and administration as the site for Shanghai's first satellite town. It was the administrative, cultural and economic centre of Shanghai *Xian* (county). The criteria for its selection were primarily the favourable geographical attributes of that particular site. The town of Minhang is spatially separated from Shanghai and is located at about 30 km south of the parent city, on the left bank of Huangpu Jiang. This river forms an essential component of Shanghai harbour, its navigation channel averaging 260 m in width. The river bed has been constantly dredged since liberation, providing a draught of over 8 m (Sun Jingzhi *et al.*, 1959). Freighters of up to 10,000 tons can reach Minhang on this major waterway and berth along the town's waterfront. The new satellite settlement is also connected with other industrial districts and communes within the region by a dense network of canals. These provide a cheap means of transportation for shipping the raw materials for, and finished products of, Minhang's industry. For land communication the satellite town is connected directly with Shanghai by a 32.5 km high-quality motor road built in 1958. The north-south-oriented transport artery branches off Zhongshan Road West in Shanghai, passing through the industrial district of Caoheqing and the towns of Meilong, Xinzhuang, Guqiao and Beiqiao before reaching Minhang. By means of this new Shanghai-Minhang highway, the travel time between Shanghai and its new satellite town is only about 25 minutes. The physical site of the town possesses another natural advantage: the terrain is flat, but it lies above the highest recorded flood level. Thus, no expensive engineering project for flood prevention was required. Other favourable factors include the availability of power and water supply, roads, urban infrastructure and public amenities in the suburban town (*Qian Sentie*, 1958).

The preliminary land-use plan of Minhang earmarked a total area of 1162.1 hectares of land located at the existing townsite for immediate development. This included 351 hectares for industrial use, 109 hectares for transportation and warehouse construction, 50.6 hectares for public-park development and 651.5 hectares for residential use, public buildings, open space, roads and public squares. As in other satellite communities, separate independent neighbourhoods were to be created, designed primarily to shorten the distance between residence and place of work. Each neighbourhood unit clustered around a factory or major commercial centre. Factories were sometimes surrounded by parks, which in turn were ringed by workers' housing projects. Scattered within the neighbourhood were schools, markets, clinics and shops. This urban design was not dissimilar to that in British new towns. Although most of the latter possessed similar types of basic public amenities and social services, some were provided with more ambitious developments for sports and recreation. For example, there was a fully equipped sports complex in both Harlow and Welwyn Garden City, comprising athletic tracks and an arena of international standard and other first-class sports facilities. Also, the town centre in many British new towns was artistically designed with reflecting pools, fountains, sculptures and mosaics.

To facilitate efficient industrial production, each of the satellite towns in the Shanghai city region accommodated related types of industry. In this respect, they shared the same characteristics of the industrial districts established during the first plan period.

Minhang, the first satellite town in the People's Republic of China, was designated a heavy industrial centre in the city region of Shanghai. According to data collected in the field, before 1949 Minhang had only three small workshops, manufacturing and repairing simple farm implements and repairing electrical machinery. The General Machinery Plant, the only industrial establishment at that time, occupied a floor space of 9417 m^2. In 1957 the amount of floor space for new industrial enterprises expanded to over 31 hectares. A number of large modern industrial plants, including heavy-machinery factories, metallurgical plants and Shanghai's largest integrated iron and steel works were under construction in 1958. In the following year, further industrial developments included the construction of an electrical-machinery plant, a turbine-manufacturing plant, a boiler factory, a heavy-lathe factory, a thermal power station and a modern waterworks (*JFRB*, 1 September 1959).

Concurrent with industrial construction, residential housing was built at a fast pace to accommodate an increasing number of factory workers and their families, who moved from Shanghai to the satellite town. In 1959 the Dongfeng (East Wind) new village at First Street and Hongqi (Red Flag) new village at Second Street were completed. These were two of the six large workers' housing projects with a total dwelling space of 100 hectares to be built in Minhang and other suburban industrial districts in 1959 (*XWRB*, 7 August 1959). Meanwhile, the construction of urban infrastructure and public amenities was also in progress, adding 13 principal buildings along First Street, the main street in Minhang. The major additions comprised general stores (and even a speciality shop for women's and children's goods), cinemas, barber shops, a public bath-house, a large market encompassing grocers, butchers and coal merchants and a general hospital with 300 beds. Upon completion, the main street of Minhang would rival the two east-west thoroughfares in the commercial heart of Shanghai – Nanjing Road and Huaihai Road. A description of Minhang evoked an image of the ideal garden city originally proposed by Ebenezer Howard, father of the British new towns (Zhang Xudang, 1960):

> On sunny days, the buildings lining the street give the place a gay and lively air: in shades of lemon, light grey and other bright colours, and each with its own distinctive style, they stand out in bold relief against the rows of newly planted trees and blue sky. First Street is 44 metres wide, twice the width of Nanking (Nanjing) Road. There are two malls close to the sidewalk and sauntering down the boulevard one feels as though (one) were walking in a park rather than along the town's busiest street. Here, shops are interspersed with apartment houses; it is a busy street but without the usual hustle and bustle characteristics of a shopping centre.

Suburban Satellites and Urban-population Redistribution

The establishment of the Shanghai city region in 1958 offered the
planners greater flexibility in decision-making in planning for subsidiary
food supply and for the decentralisation of industrial activities and
population from the congested central city. The building of 'secondary
centres' afforded more options for siting new industrial projects to be
installed in the municipality during the Great Leap Forward. Of utmost
importance, these satellites were designed as recipient points for urban
residents transferred from the parent city, and thus played a vital role
in the spatial redistribution of urban population within the city region.

Since its opening as one of the five treaty ports in 1842, Shanghai
rapidly developed into a primate city. By 1910 it had already become
China's most populous urban place in modern times, with a population
of 1,185,859 (Chang Sen-dou, 1968). The city's population continued
to climb in the following decades. It increased to 2.3 million in 1925,
and 3.7 million in 1936 (Chen, 1973). By 1947 it reached 4.4 million,
well over twice that of Tianjin, the second largest city, with a population of less than 2 million (Trewartha, 1951). At the time of the
Communist take-over, Shanghai's population had increased to 4.5
million.

The history of population control, in the form of organised emigration from Shanghai, began early in 1950, when an outbreak of
serious natural disasters in eastern China drove a large number of
refugees into the city. The military control commission implemented a
plan involving the mobilisation of over one million unemployed and
refugees to leave the city. Special offices of the provincial Communist
Party headquarters in Shandong, Anhui, Zhejiang and Jiangsu were
established, assisting the resettlement of returned refugees (*XWRB*,
14 February 1950).

Another method of reducing Shanghai's population has been to send
young intellectuals to frontier areas. The initial systematic mobilisation
of university graduates began in 1951. Rao Shaoshi, the local party
secretary, also secretary of the East China Bureau of the Central Committee and member of the Government Administrative Council,
launched the programme of 'unified allocation' of employment opportunity for university graduates and urged them to accept state assign-
ments at any location in China (*NCNA*, 26 July 1951). In 1952
Shanghai began to send secondary-school and primary-school graduates
to the industrial northeast. About 1000 secondary-school leavers were
sent to Shenyang; other destinations included Gansu, Qinghai and the

Xinjiang Uygur autonomous region in the remote northwest. The relentless efforts of the city administration were frustrated by the continuous inflow of peasants, however. According to the only modern national census, the population of Shanghai in 1953 was 6,204,417. Inevitably, further measures were taken to tighten control over population movement. The first people's congress in Shanghai launched a campaign to send ordinary citizens to the interior regions to participate in national industrial and agricultural production. Other emigration from the city was related to the industrialisation of inland areas. Throughout the first five-year plan period, Shanghai continued to draw on its large pool of skilled labour to assist in the development of other industrial centres in the nation. In June 1953, at the request of the Shanghai People's Government and the Shanghai Labour Union, 11,295 skilled metal workers participated in key-point projects in the interior, and 2098 factory workers left the city for the northeast, north China, and central-south China (*WHB*, 3 September 1954). From 1950 to the first quarter of 1956, Shanghai dispatched 210,000 workers and cadres, of whom 63,000 were skilled workers and about 5400 technicians. By January 1957 there were already at least 100,000 Shanghai residents in Xi'an and another 30,000 in Lanzhou (*XWRB*, 21 January 1957), both being important key-point cities in Shaanxi and Gansu, respectively. At the beginning of the national Great Leap movement, Xu Jian-guo, deputy mayor of Shanghai, informed the Third Meeting of the Second People's Concress that 1,080,000 had left the city in the previous seven years. Of these emigrants, 780,000 were returned to rural production; over 260,000 were sent to participate in economic construction; and about 30,000 took part in reclamation projects in other provinces. It may be argued that up to mid-1956 the municipal authorities had achieved some success in controlling population increase caused by immigration, as the rate of population growth in Shanghai was much lower than that in other key-point cities, as well as most of those not designated for active economic expansion. In fact, two-thirds of the increase from 1949 to mid-1956 was brought about by the high average annual rate of natural increase of 36.8 per thousand (Table 8.4) — almost twice that of the national average (Orleans, 1972).

The failure in accomplishing a better result in reducing the city's population was caused by problems relating to sending permanent residents out of the city. First of all, the municipal government found it increasingly difficult to mobilise industrial workers and construction labourers after late 1955. Factory administrative cadres were often reluctant to release engineers and skilled workers who responded to the

Table 8.4: Natural Increase Rate of Shanghai's Population, 1953-7

Year	Birth rate	Death rate	Natural increase rate
1953	40.4	9.9	30.5
1954	52.6	7.6	45.0
1955	41.4	8.1	35.3
1956	40.2	6.7	33.5
1957	45.7	5.9	39.8
Average			36.8

Source: Chandrasekhar (1960).

call of the central government to aid socialist construction in other parts of China — or so a secondary source alleged. (*China News Analysis*, 12 August 1955). Also the higher real wages in Shanghai might have presented another obstacle in the mobilisation of the city's workers to emigrate to other industrial centres. Some workers were unwilling to leave their job in the city, on account of the loss of actual income upon emigration. An editorial appeared in a local newspaper (*XWRB*, 14 August 1956), appealing for a reduction of workers' wages in Shanghai in order to facilitate the dispatch of industrial workers to support the construction of new industrial bases in the inland regions:

> If no adjustment is made to wages in Shanghai, there will be difficulties in distributing the labour force to support state construction. Wages in Shanghai should be reduced to a level of parity with those in other areas, and adjusted in accordance with the gradual unified rationalisation of wages in the nation.

Between June 1956 and October 1957 Shanghai's population underwent a sharp increase. It grew from 6.02 million to 7.2 million. According to the municipal record, about 60,000 of these secured temporary permits to stay in the city, about 300,000 were attributable to natural increase and 820,000 drifted into the city from the neighbouring provinces of Anhui, Jiangsu and Zhejiang as well as other areas. Previous influxes of peasants were partly motivated by the outbreaks of natural disasters in 1950, 1954/5 and early 1956 (Freeberne, 1962), and by the high tide of collectivisation in agriculture in 1955. The exceptionally large inflow that occurred between June 1956 and October 1957 must have been caused by the 1956 nation-wide upward adjustment of wages for industrial workers and other employees in cities (Table 8.5),

Table 8.5: Increase in Average Annual Wage of Workers and Other Employees, 1952-8 (Yuan).

	Average annual Wage	Wage relative to 1952 (1952 = 100)	Index numbers (preceding year = 100)
1952	446	100	—
1953	496	111.2	111.2
1954	519	116.4	104.6
1955	534	119.7	102.9
1956	610	136.8	*114.2*
1957	637	142.8	104.4
1958	656	147.1	103.0

Source: *Wei-da di shi-nian, Zhong-hua ren-min gong-he-guo jing-ji he wen-hua jian-she cheng-jiu di tong-ji (The Ten Great Years, Statistics on Economic and Cultural Achievements in the People's Republic of China)* (People's Publishing House, Beijing, 1959).

and the active industrial expansion in Shanghai. There was evidently a direct link between the urban economic expansion and the influx of peasants into cities. By way of comparison, early in 1958 the central government invested a substantial amount of capital for industrial construction in Guangzhou (a coastal city in southern China not designated for economic expansion during the first five-year plan period), thereby creating 100,000 jobs. In that year over one million peasants migrated into the city to search for employment opportunities.

Confronted by the problems of swelling population in the city, the civil administration employed several regulatory measures to curtail further increase. Among these the authorities included stricter household and job registration, stern rationing of staple commodities and vigorous promotion of birth control and family planning. At the third session of the second people's congress, the deputy mayor called for the population of the city to be limited to seven million. Since late 1957 and early 1958, besides returning peasant immigrants to the rural areas, the city began to 'send down' (*xiafang*)[10] administrative cadres and to return families of the military stationed in Shanghai to their native villages. A local press source (*XWRB*, 1 December 1958) reported the sending down of 140,000 administrative cadres to the city's suburban areas to take part in industrial production, basic construction and basic-level commercial work. Their destinations were most likely suburban industrial districts and the satellite town of Minhang, which were under intense development at that time. Evidently, the campaign continued throughout the period of the Great Leap. More cadres were sent out to suburban towns and communes. In the Spring of 1959, over 2400 became factory workers and construction labourers in satellite industrial communities. Most of these cadres were young and educated, but had no experience in manual labour and basic-level work. As part of the population-control measures, the city government provided subsidies to school graduates who settled down permanently in the suburban areas. When the Great Leap Forward began, new industrial developments of the metropolis were sited at small, functionally integrated and self-contained settlements in the city region. The decentralisation process often involved both factories and their workers, as most factories were responsible for housing their workforce. Construction of workers' villages at suburban locations played an important role in dispersing Shanghai's population. In August 1959 the Shanghai bureau of municipal construction and administration completed the Haibin new village a at Wusong, the Sidang new village at Yuncaobin, the Pengpu new village at Pengpu, the Shangjian new village at Zhaojiadao, and the Hongqi new village and the Dongfeng new village at Minhang. Each of these housing estates possessed a large variety of shops, urban infrastructure and public facilities. By the end of 1959 a total of 34 workers' villages had been completed.

Since the establishment of Minhang as a satellite town in 1958, more 'decentralised settlements' have been built in the city region. By the early 1960s six satellite communities had been completed, and five more were under construction (Snow, 1961). A team of British urban planners visiting Shanghai in 1974 reported that there were between 60 and 70 satellites in the suburban areas (Thompson, 1974). These small self-contained urban centres permitted the rationalisation of industrial location and served to absorb the surplus population in Shanghai. To take the example of Minhang, in 1949 the town was a small settlement with a population of only 6000, but in 1957 it increased to 33,000. Almost two decades later, as a result of planned dispersal of population from the central city, the number of inhabitants in the satellite town grew to over 70,000. Since the Cultural Revolution (1966-9) the population in urban Shanghai has been reduced by over 800,000 as the municipal authorities launched a new campaign to send youths to the suburban areas of the city region and other provinces. In 1976 out of the total population of 10.7 million in the special municipality, 5.23 million inhabited the central city, and most of the remaining 5.47 million the suburban industrial satellites. The reduction of population in the central city by nearly one million below the 1953 census figure of 6,204,417, and the reciprocal increase in the suburban areas, convincingly indicate the achievement of planned spatial redistribution of population with the city region of Shanghai.

With the inception of the 'Four Modernisations' after Mao's death in September 1976,[11] many existing major industrial complexes in China have been renovated or expanded, often by imported technology from Japan and the west. As part of the Sino-Japanese long-term (1978–85) trade agreement signed in Beijing on 16 February 1978, a modern integrated steel mill with a high degree of automation would be constructed in Shanghai by Nippon Steel. Deliberately avoiding the industrial concentration of existing industrial districts or satellite towns specialising in steel production, municipal authorities of the Shanghai city region have designated Boashan, a small town located on the southern bank of the Chang Jiang, as the site for this steel plant with its own power station, environmental-protection facilities and a loading and unloading wharf.[12] This giant steel works and the satellite town of Baoshan are presently under active construction. Completion of the project and the new town will further modify the map of the city region.

Summary and Conclusions

After Shanghai became a treaty port, the rates of its population growth and spatial expansion rivalled those of London and New York during the late nineteenth century. Western expansionism and semi-colonialism, as well as China's internal turmoils, constituted the major forces for the phenomenal growth of this world city. However, because of the absence of a single unified urban administrative and planning body in Shanghai during the treaty-port era, the resulting land-use patterns were in utter confusion. After the Guomindang (Nationalists) had secured political stabilisation in China in the 1920s, ambitious plans for developing the metropolis and its surrounding territory were launched, in order to compete with the treaty powers in their achievements in city building. This grand scheme was abandoned during the Sino-Japanese War. When the Chinese Communist Party came to power in 1949, the new leadership made a firm commitment to transform Shanghai into a truly prosperous people's city. Great emphasis was placed upon renewal of, and unified, planning for the Shanghai metropolitan area (including the Chinese city, the French concession and the foreign settlement) and the designated suburban territories in accordance with socialist concepts and principles in city and regional planning. During the early 1950s, mainly because of a state policy of suppressing capital investment in existing seaboard industrial cities, urban developments in Shanghai were limited to the construction of workers' housing projects outside the city limits and the reorganisation of the disorderly urban land-use patterns. Owing to the absence of large-scale industrial construction in this world city, its spatial growth was slow relative to that of Beijing, the national capital, and other major industrial centres that were designated for intense development during the first plan period. In addition, because of better urban-planning resources in the city, suburban development was orderly. The city's spatial form was compact, in contrast with the sprawling morphology of other industrial cities in China during that period. After mid-1956, the phenomenal rise of state capital input in coastal manufacturing centres greatly stimulated the expansion of industries in Shanghai. It also acted as a catalyst, accelerating the transformation of industrial land use in the city. The availability of suburban land at the disposal of Shanghai's urban planners facilitated the rational dispersal of manufacturing activities from the central city. By the end of 1957, industrial land use in the city's suburban areas had been organised into a multinodal pattern. The following year heralded the beginning of a new phase in the planning and development of this world city and its suburban areas; city planners began to design and build self-contained satellite industrial communities in the city region. These new suburban towns afforded more options for siting industrial projects which were to be installed in the municipality during the Great Leap Forward. They were also designed as recipient points for urban residents to be transferred from the congested parent city. In our view, it may be asserted that this new development is an accomplishment of the preliminary stage of socialist urban transformation of this largest foreign-created city in modern China. With regards to China's socialist approach in urban planning, in general, the move towards urban decentralisation after mid-1956 represents an emergence of a revolutionary concept of urbanism — part of a grand scheme to achieve the ideological goal of creating a classless society by breaking down the distinction between city and countryside, industry and agriculture, and mental and manual workers. Further, the implementation of the policy of arresting the growth of large cities by the building of small and medium-sized urban settlements takes the form of speeding up the process of rural industrialisation and farm mechanisation. The development of satellite towns in the city region of Shanghai, for example, will certainly aid the diffusion of technological and scientific innovations, and thus greatly accelerate the achievement of such an objective. It should be stressed that the Chinese approach in building small urban centres and containing the growth of large ones is in contrast to the urban policy of the Soviet Union, where the main criterion of successful development policy has been the size of urban and industrial expansion, so that the city is bound to maintain its dominance over the countryside (Khoreu and Khodzhayev, 1972). Without doubt, the accomplishment of large-scale urban transformation and the success in containing the spatial growth of large industrial centres in China, as exemplified by Shanghai, is a remarkable achievement in urban and regional planning. Such experiences should be studied closely by planners in both the developed and the developing countries.

In the present drive for modernisation in China, the relationship between the size of cities and national economic development has been often debated among urban planners. In a recent conference on China's urbanisation held in Beijing, two opposing views on the subject were presented (Anon, 1980). Some delegates favoured the continuing curtailment of growth of large population centres, so as to avoid the inherent problems of congestion, rapid deterioration of the urban environment induced by overconcentration of manufacturing activities and increasingly acute shortages of water and energy for domestic and industrial uses. Instead, the creation of small towns with an average population of 20,000 from each group of five people's communes was advocated; these small industrial settlements some 10,000 in number, would, it was argued, facilitate the spatial diffusion of economic benefits throughout rural China.

Another group of city planners contended that large cities played a relatively more important role in the current programme of modernisation, as a greater concentration of economic activities tended to yield higher efficiency and greater profit. At the same time, these planners also entertained the view that small towns based on commune-run industries will engender a more balanced regional economic development in China. Nevertheless, in order to achieve the goal of modernising China within the eight-year period (1978–85), the development of large cities should be given a higher priority. It is quite possible that the adoption of one of the above views will be influenced by the current thinking of China's economic planners. Future policies on city building that emerge from the above debates will certainly have an impact on the spatial patterns of industrial land use and settlement within the Shanghai city region.

Notes

1. The original Land Regulations of 1845 provided that the 'native inhabitants of the said quarters must not rent to each other nor may they again build houses there for the purpose of renting to Chinese merchants (Clause 15) (*Shanghai Municipal Council Reports*, 1931).

2. *Tls*: abbreviation for *'tael' (liang)*. One *tael* is equivalent to one Chinese ounce, i.e. 1/16 part of one *catty* (Arnold, 1920).

3. Land use in the eastern part of the 'external roads areas' (the western section) included the following: Jessfield Park, municipal schools, German school, country hospitals, German country club, Columbia country club, cathedral, Fu Tan university middle school, St John University, Guang Hua university, Hungrao Road nursery, sewage-treatment works, Hungrao golf links, Shanghai sanitorium, gun club, boy scout camps, St Mary recreation hall, McTyeire High School for Girls and cricket club.

4. Hereafter cited as *XWRB*.

5. Hereafter cited as *JFRB*.

6. In February 1950, a disastrous explosion occurred in Fuhua match factory, located in a densely inhabited section of Beijing, resulting in over 500 casualties, and the destruction of 2000 homes. The government administrative council immediately issued a directive instructing all municipal governments to remove from urban areas all factories involving raw materials of a noxious, poisonous or explosive nature, as well as warehouses storing similar types of materials. It was vehemently urged that such industries should be relocated in open spaces outside the cities; see *Nanfang Ribao (Southern Daily)*, Guangzhou (19 October 1950).

7. Hereafter cited as *WHB*.

8. The Great Leap Forward (*Da Yu Jin*) was a nationwide movement launched by Mao Zedong in 1958. The major objective was to speed up China's industrial development. Backyard furnaces were set up in rural areas to produce steel, using mainly scrap metals and indigenous methods. This ill-fated campaign was partially responsible for the national economic disaster in 1960, and subsequently abandoned.

9. Hereafter cited as *NCNA*.

10. *Xiafang* is a Chinese term meaning 'downward transfer' or 'sending down'. It first appeared in Chinese newspapers and official publications in early October 1957. *Xiafang* was a nationwide campaign initially designed to trim excess administrative personnel in government departments. Beginning in late 1957, thousands of cadres were sent from major cities to rural areas, as well as factories in smaller urban centres. It was believed that their participation in physical labour would toughen their revolutionary spirit as well as their body. The term acquired a diverse connotation during the Great Leap Forward (1958–60); the campaign included sending down of cadres, young intellectuals and urban residents to rural and suburban areas. During the 1960s it was often used interchangeably with *shang-shan xia xiang*, which literally meant going up the mountain and going down to the villages – another measure introduced by the government to disperse population from large urban centres.

11. The national drive for the 'Four Modernisations' was proposed by Mao Zedong in 1973. The programme aimed at achieving modernisation of China's industry, agriculture, science and technology, and national defence by the end of the century. The theme was reiterated by Hua Guofeng, the present chairman of the Chinese Communist Party and Premier, at the First Congress on Industry, held in May 1977. The ambitious plan was implemented by Deng Xiaoping, after his re-emergence in the same year.

12. The total cost of the steel plant is 1000 billion *yuan*. Its annual production

capacity is three million tons and its is scheduled to start production by the end of 1980. It will be the largest integrated steel plant in China *(Japan Economic Review*, 15 March 1978).

Bibliography

Anon 'Shanghai: Past, Present and Future' *The China Journal*, vol. 22, no. 5 (1935a), p. 215
— 'Two Views on China's Urbanization' *Beijing Review*, vol. 23, no. 11 (1980), pp. 6–7
Arnold, J. *Commercial Handbook of China*, vol. 2, Miscellaneous Series no. 84, (Department of Commerce, Bureau of Foreign and Domestic Commerce, Washington, 1920)
Barnett, R.R. *Economic Shanghai: Hostage to Politics 1937–1941* (Institute of Pacific Relations, New York, 1941)
Boyden, A. 'Changing Shanghai', *National Geographic Magazine*, vol. 72 (1937), p. 507
Chandrasekhar, S. *China's Population: Census and Vital Statistics*, 2nd edn. (Hong Kong University Press, Hong Kong, 1960)
Chang Sen-dou 'The Million City of Mainland China' *Pacific Viewpoint*, vol. 9, no. 2 (1980), p. 147
Chen, C.C. 'Urbanization in China' *Geographical Review* (January 1973), p. 67
Chen Yanlin *Shanghai dichan dachuan (Comprehensive Account of Real Estate and Property in Shanghai* (Shang-hai dichan yenjizuo, Shanghai, 1933)
Editorial 'Reduce the (Space Utilization) Standard for Buildings' *CSJS (Urban Construction)*, no. 6 (1957), p. 12
Freeberne, M. 'Natural Calamities in China 1949–61: An Examination of the Reports Originating from the Mainland' *Pacific Viewpoint*, vol. 3, no. 2 (1962), pp. 33–72
Fung, K.I. 'Land Use Transformation in Suburban China since 1949' in Lee, N. and Leung, C.K. (eds.), *China: Development and Challenge* (Centre of Asian Studies, Hong Kong, 1979), pp. 277–303
Green, O.M. 'The Future of Shanghai', *Asiatic Review*, vol. 30 (1934), p. 354
Jones, F.C. *Shanghai and Tientsin* (Oxford University Press, Oxford, 1940)
Khorev, B.S. and Khodzhayev, D.G. 'The Conception of a Unified System of Settlement and the Planned Regulation of City Growth in the USSR' *Soviet Geography*, no. 8 (1972), pp. 90–8
Lieu, D.K. *The Growth and Industrialization of Shanghai* (China Institute of Pacific Relations, Shanghai, 1936)
Lillico, S. 'The Civic Centre at Kiangwan' *China Journal*, vol. 22 (1935), p. 227
Moore, W.R. 'Cosmopolitan Shanghai: Key Seaport of China' *National Geographical Magazine*, vol. 62 (1932), p. 327
Murphey, R. *Shanghai: Key to Modern China* (Harvard University Press, Cambridge, Mass., 1953)
Orleans, L.A. *Every Fifth Child: The Population of China* (Eyre Methuen, London, 1972)
Potter, J.S. 'Shanghai's Spreading Acres' *China Journal*, vol. 16 (1932), p. 252
Qian Sentie (Shanghai Institute of Urban Planning and Design) 'The Planning Problems of Shanghai's Satellite Towns' *Jianchu Xuebao (Journal of Architecture)*, no. 8 (1958), p. 32
Shanghai Civic Association, *Statistics of Shanghai 1933* (Shanghai Civics Association, Shanghai, 1933)
Shanghai Municipal Council Reports, vol. 3 (North China Daily News and Herald

Ltd., Shanghai, 1931)

Shang Sidi *Shanghai dili jiamhua* (Introduction to the Geography of Shanghai) (Shanghai's People Publishing House, Shanghai, 1974)

Snow, E. *The Other Side of the River* (Random House, New York, 1961)

Sun Jingzhi *et al. Huadong dichu jingji dili (Economic Geography of East China Region)* (Science Publishing House, Beijing, 1959), p. 47

Thompson, R. 'Containing the City' *Architectural Design* (March 1974), p. 152

Trewartha, G. 'Chinese Cities: Numbers and Distribution', *Annal of the Association of American Geographers*, vol. 41, no. 4 (1951), p. 338

Wu Shan *et al.* (eds.) *Shi Zheng Chuan Shu (Handbook of Local Government)* (Daolu Yuekan Chubanshe, Shanghai, 1929)

Wu Yuan-lie 'Principal Industrial Cities in Communist China: Their Regional Distribution and Ranking' in Stuart Kirby, E. (ed.), *Contemporary China*, vol. 5, no. 1 (Hong Kong University Press, Hong Kong, 1963)

Zhang Xudang 'Minhang – Shanghai's First Satellite Town' *Beijing Review* (16 February 1960), p. 17

CONTRIBUTORS

Professor B. Arunachalam, Department of Geography, University of Bombay, India

Dr B. Ayeni, Department of Geography, University of Ibadan, Nigeria

Dr V.F. Costello, Department of Town and Country Planning, Bristol Polytechnic, England

Professor C.D. Deshpande, Department of Geography, University of Bombay, India

Dr A.M. Findlay, Department of Geography, University of Glasgow, Scotland

Dr M. Freeberne, School of Oriental and African Studies, London, England

Dr K.I. Fung, Department of Geography, University of Saskatchewan, Saskatoon, Canada

Dr A.G. Gilbert, Department of Geography, University College London, England

Dr R.I. Lawless, Centre of Middle Eastern and Islamic Studies, University of Durham, England

Dr M. Pacione, Department of Geography, University of Strathclyde, Glasgow, Scotland

Mr T.M. Tan, Department of Urban Planning, Singapore Polytechnic, Singapore

Dr L.H. Wang, Department of Geography, National University of Singapore, Singapore

Dr P.M. Ward, Department of Geography, University College London, England

INDEX

289